A. . . . . and Vector Scientific Computing

In this text, students of applied mathematics, science, and engineering are introduced to fundamental ways of thinking about the broad context of parallelism.
The authors begin by giving the reader a deeper understanding of the issues
through a general examination of timing, data dependencies, and communication. These ideas are implemented with respect to shared memory, parallel
and vector processing, and distributed memory cluster computing. Threads,
OpenMP, and MPI are covered, along with code examples in Fortran, C, and
Java.

   The principles of parallel computation are applied throughout as the authors
cover traditional topics in a first course in scientific computing. Building on
the fundamentals of floating point representation and numerical error, a thor-
ough treatment of numerical linear algebra and eigenvector/eigenvalue problems is provided. By studying how these algorithms parallelize, the reader is
able to explore parallelism inherent in other computations, such as Monte Carlo
methods.

Ronald W. Shonkwiler is a professor in the School of Mathematics at the Georgia
Institute of Technology. He has authored or coauthored more than 50 research
papers in areas of functional analysis, mathematical biology, image processing
algorithms, fractal geometry, neural networks, and Monte Carlo optimization
methods. His algorithm for monochrome image comparison is part of a U.S.
patent for fractal image compression. He has coauthored two other books, *An
Introduction to the Mathematics of Biology* and *The Handbook of Stochastic
Analysis and Applications*.

Lew Lefton is the Director of Information Technology for the School of Mathematics and the College of Sciences at the Georgia Institute of Technology,
where he has built and maintained several computing clusters that are used to
implement parallel computations. Prior to that, he was a tenured faculty member in the Department of Mathematics at the University of New Orleans. He
has authored or coauthored more than a dozen research papers in the areas
of nonlinear differential equations and numerical analysis. His academic in-
terests are in differential equations, applied mathematics, numerical analysis
(in particular, finite element methods), and scientific computing.

Cambridge Texts in Applied Mathematics

All titles listed below can be obtained from good booksellers or from Cambridge University Press.
For a complete series listing, visit http:publishing.cambridge.org/stm/mathematics/ctam

An Introduction to Parallel and Vector Scientific Computing

RONALD W. SHONKWILER
Georgia Institute of Technology

LEW LEFTON
Georgia Institute of Technology

CAMBRIDGE
UNIVERSITY PRESS

CAMBRIDGE UNIVERSITY PRESS
Cambridge, New York, Melbourne, Madrid, Cape Town, Singapore, São Paulo

Cambridge University Press
32 Avenue of the Americas, New York, NY 10013-2473, USA

www.cambridge.org
Information on this title: www.cambridge.org/9780521864787

First published 2006

Printed in the United States of America

A catalog record for this publication is available from the British Library.

Library of Congress Cataloging in Publication Data
Shonkwiler, Ronald W., 1942–
An introduction to parallel and vector scientific computing / by R. Shonkwiler and L. Lefton.
p.   cm. – (Cambridge texts in applied mathematics ; no. 41)
Includes bibliographical references and index.
ISBN-13:   978-0-521-86478-7
ISBN-10:   0-521-86478-X
ISBN-13:   978-0-521-68337-1   (pbk.)
ISBN-10:   0-521-68337-8   (pbk.)
1. Parallel processing (Electronic computers)   2. Vector processing (Computer science)
I. Lefton, L. (Lew), 1960–   II. Title.
III. Series: Cambridge texts in applied mathematics ; 41.
QA76.58.S545   2006
004.3′5–dc22   2006007798

ISBN-13:   978-0-521-86478-7   hardback
ISBN-10:   0-521-86478-X   hardback

ISBN-13:   978-0-521-68337-1   paperback
ISBN-10:   0-521-68337-8   paperback

Contents

Preface

Numerical computations are a fundamental tool for engineers and scientists. The current practice of science and engineering demands that nontrivial computations be performed with both great speed and great accuracy. More and more, one finds that scientific insight and technologial breakthroughs are preceded by intense computational efforts such as modeling and simulation. It is clear that computing is, and will continue to be, central to the further development of science and technology.

As market forces and technological breakthroughs lowered the cost of computational power by several orders of magintude, there was a natural migration from large-scale mainframes to powerful desktop workstations. Vector processing and parallelism became possible, and this parallelism gave rise to a new collection of algorithms. Parallel architectures matured, in part driven by the demand created by the algorithms. Large computational codes were modified to take advantage of these parallel supercomputers. Of course, the term *supercomputer* has referred, at various times, to radically different parallel architectures. This includes vector processors, various shared memory architectures, distributed memory clusters, and even computational grids. Although the landscape of scientific computing changes frequently, there is one constant; namely, that there will always be a demand in the research community for high-performance computing.

When computations are first introduced in beginning courses, they are often straightforward "vanilla" computations, which are well understood and easily done using standard techniques and/or commercial software packages on desktop computers. However, sooner or later, a working scientist or engineer will be faced with a problem that requires advanced techniques, more specialized software (perhaps coded from scratch), and/or more powerful hardware. This book is aimed at those individuals who are taking that step, from a novice to intermediate or even from intermediate to advanced user of tools that fall under the broad heading of scientific computation. The text and exercises have been shown, over many years of classroom testing, to provide students with a solid foundation, which can be used to work on modern scientific computing problems. This book can be used as a guide for training the next generation of computational scientists.

This manuscript grew from a collection of lecture notes and exercises for a senior-level course entitled "Vector and Parallel Scientific Computing." This course runs yearly at the Georgia Institute of Technology, and it is listed in both mathematics and computer science curricula. The students are a mix of math majors, computer scientists, all kinds of engineers (aerospace, mechanical, electrical, etc.), and all kinds of scientists (chemists, physicists, computational biologists, etc.). The students who used these notes came from widely varying backgrounds and varying levels of expertise with regard to mathematics and computer science.

Formally, the prerequisite for using this text is knowledge of basic linear algebra. We integrate many advanced matrix and linear algebra concepts into the text as the topics arise rather than offering them as a separate chapter. The material in Part II, Monte Carlo Methods, also assumes some familiarity with basic probability and statistics (e.g., mean, variance, t test, Markov chains).

The students should have some experience with computer programming. We do not teach nor emphasize a specific programming language. Instead, we illustrate algorithms through a pseudocode, which is very close to mathematics itself. For example, the mathematical expression $y = \sum_{i=1}^{n} x_i$ becomes

```
y=0;
loop i = 1 upto n
    y = y + xᵢ;
end loop
```

We provide many example programs in Fortran, C, and Java. We also have examples of code that uses MPI libraries. When this course was originally taught, it took several weeks for the students to get accounts and access to the Cray system available at that time. As a result, the material in the first two chapters provides no programming exercises. If one wishes to start programming right away, then he or she should begin with Chapter 3.

The purpose of the course is to provide an introduction to important topics of scientific computing including the central algorithms for numerical linear algebra such as linear system solving and eigenvalue calculation. Moreover, we introduce this material from the very beginning in the context of vector and parallel computation. We emphasize a recognition of the sources and propagation of numerical error and techniques for its control. Numerical error starts with the limitations inherent in the floating point representation of numbers leading to round-off error and continues with algorithmic sources of error.

The material has evolved over time along with the machines called super-computers. At present, shared memory parallel computation has standardized on the threads model, and vector computation has moved from the machine level to the chip level. Of course, vendors provide parallelizing compilers that primarily automatically parallelize loops that the programmer has requested, sometimes referred to as the DOACROSS model. This is a convenient model for engineers and scientists as it allows them to take advantage of parallel and vector machines while making minimal demands on their programming time. For the purpose of familiarily, we include a section on the basic concepts of distributed memory computation, including topological connectivity and communication issues.

In teaching the course, we employ a hands-on approach, requiring the students to write and execute programs on a regular basis. Over the years, our students have had time on a wide variety of supercomputers, first at National Centers, and more recently at campus centers or even on departmental machines. Of course, even personal computers today can be multiprocessor with a vector processing chipset, and many compiled codes implement threads at the operating system level.

We base our approach to parallel computation on its representation by means of a directed acyclic graph. This cuts to the essence of the computation and clearly shows its parallel structure. From the graph it is easy to explain and calculate the complexity, speedup, efficiency, communication requirements, and scheduling of the computation. And, of course, the graph shows how the computation can be coded in parallel.

The text begins with an introduction and some basic terminology in Chapter 1. Chapter 2 gives a high-level view of the theoretical underpinnings of parallelism. Here we discuss data dependencies and complexity, using directed acyclic graphs to more carefully demonstate a general way of thinking about parallelism. In Chapter 3, we have included a variety of machine implementations of parallelism. Although some of these architectures are not in widespread use any more (e.g., vector processors like the early Cray computers), there are still interesting and important ideas here. In fact, the Japanese Earth Simulator (the former world record holder for "fastest computer") makes heavy use of vector processing and pipelining. Chapter 3 includes an introduction to low-level implementations of parallelism by including material on barriers, mutexes, and threads. Of course, not every scientific computing application will require thread programming, but as mentioned earlier, these objects provide many useful ideas about parallelization that can be generalized to many different parallel codes.

We have even included a short introduction to quantum computing because this technology may one day be the future of parallel scientific computation.

In the second half of the book, we start with basic mathematical and computational background, presented as building blocks in Chapter 4. This includes material on floating point numbers, round-off error, and basic matrix arithmetic. We proceed to cover mathematical algorithms, which we have found are most frequently used in scientific computing. Naturally, this includes a large measure of numerical linear algebra. Chapters 5, 6, and 7 discuss direct methods for solving linear systems. We begin with classical Gaussian elimination and then move on to matrices with special structure and more advanced topics such as Cholesky decomposition and Givens' rotation. Iterative methods are covered in Chapter 8. We study Jacobi and Gauss-Seidel as well as relaxtion techniques. This chapter also includes a section on conjugate gradient methods. In Chapter 9, we examine eigenvalues and eigenvectors. This includes the power method and QR decomposition. We also cover the topics of Householder transformations and Hessenberg forms, since these can improve QR computations in practice.

Throughout all of Part II, our development of linear algebraic results relies heavily on the technique of partitioning matrices. This is introduced in Chapter 4 and continues through our presentation of Jordan form in Chapter 9.

The final section of the book is focused on Monte Carlo methods. We first develop classical quadrature techniques such as the Buffon Needle Problem in Chapter 10. We then advance in Chapter 11 to a presentation of Monte Carlo optimization, which touches on the ideas of simulated annealing, genetic algorithms, and iterated improvement with random restart.

Exercises are included at the end of every section. Some of these are meant to be done by hand, and some will require access to a computing environment that supports the necessary parallel architecture. This could be a vector machine, an SMP system supporting POSIX threads, a distributed memory cluster with MPI libraries and compilers, etc. We have attempted to isolate those exercises that require programming in a subsection of each exercise set. Exercises are followed by a number in parentheses, which is meant to be an indication of the level of difficulty.

Because scientific computing is often the result of significant research efforts by large distributed teams, it can be difficult to isolate meaningful self-contained exercises for a textbook such as this. We have found it very useful for students to work on and present a project as a substantial part of their course grade. A 10-minute oral presentation along with a written report (and/or a poster) is an excellent exercise for students at this level. One can ask them to submit a short project proposal in which they briefly describe the problem background, the mathematical problem that requires computation, and how this computation may parallelize. Students do well when given the opportunity to perform a deeper study of a problem of interest to them.

Acknowledgments

Ron Shonkwiler would like to thank his coauthor, Dr. Lew Lefton, for bringing thoughtfulness and a fresh outlook to this project and for his "way with words," and Lauren Cowles of Cambridge for her encouragement. Most of all, he would like to thank the many students who have taken the course on which this book is based. Their enthusiasm, creativity, energy, and industry have made teaching the course a challenge and a pleasure.

Lew Lefton would first and foremost like to express his deepest gratitude to his coauthor, Dr. Ron Shonkwiler. When they began collaborating on the project of getting the course notes into a book manuscript several years ago, Lefton naively thought it would be an interesting but straightforward project. He was half right; it has been very interesting. The notes have changed (improved!) signifcantly since that early draft and, having taught the course himself and gone through the process of publishing a book, he feels very fortunate to have had Ron, with his expertise and experience, as a guide. Lefton would also like to thank his wife, Dr. Enid Steinbart, and his daughters, Hannah, Monica, and Natalie, who put up with him spending more than his usual amount of "screen time" in front of the computer. He is truly grateful for their love and support.

PART I
Machines and Computation

1

Introduction – The Nature of High-Performance Computation

The need for speed. Since the beginning of the era of the modern digital computer in the early 1940s, computing power has increased at an exponential rate (see Fig. 1). Such an exponential growth is predicted by the well-known "Moore's Law," first advanced in 1965 by Gordon Moore of Intel, asserting that the number of transistors per inch on integrated circuits will double every 18 months. Clearly there has been a great need for ever more computation. This need continues today unabated. The calculations performed by those original computers were in the fields of ballistics, nuclear fission, and cryptography. And, today these fields, in the form of computational fluid dynamics, advanced simulation for nuclear testing, and cryptography, are among computing's Grand Challenges.

In 1991, the U.S. Congress passed the High Performance Computing Act, which authorized The Federal High Performance Computing and Communications (HPCC) Program. A class of problems developed in conjunction with the HPCC Program was designated "Grand Challenge Problems" by Dr. Ken Wilson of Cornell University. These problems were characterized as "fundamental problems in science and engineering that have broad economic or scientific impact and whose solution can be advanced by applying high performance computing techniques and resources." Since then various scientific and engineering committees and governmental agencies have added problems to the original list. As a result, today there are many Grand Challenge problems in engineering, mathematics, and all the fundamental sciences. The ambitious goals of recent Grand Challenge efforts strive to

- build more energy-efficient cars and airplanes,
- design better drugs,
- forecast weather and predict global climate change,
- improve environmental modeling,

3

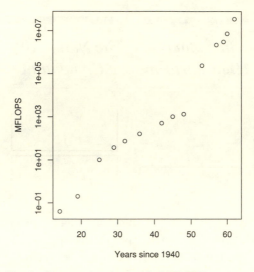

Fig. 1. Computational speed in MFLOPS vs. year.

- improve military systems,
- understand how galaxies are formed,
- understand the nature of new materials, and
- understand the structure of biological molecules.

The advent of high-speed computation has even given rise to computational subfields in some areas of science and engineering. Examples are computational biology, bioinfomatics, and robotics, just to name a few. Computational chemistry can boast that in 1998 the Noble Prize in chemistry was awarded to John Pope and shared with Walter Kohn for the development of computational methods in quantum chemistry.

And so it seems that the more computational power we have, the more use we make of it and the more we glimpse the possibilities of even greater computing power. The situation is like a Moore's Law for visionary computation.

1.1 Computing Hardware Has Undergone Vast Improvement

A major factor in the exponential improvement in computational power over the past several decades has been through advances in solid-state physics: faster switching circuits, better heat control, faster clock rates, faster memory. Along with advances in solid-state physics, there has also been an evolution in the architecture of the computer itself. Much of this revolution was spearheaded by Seymour Cray.

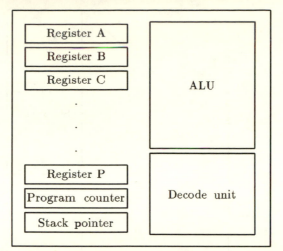

Fig. 2. Central processing unit.

Many ideas for parallel architectures have been tried, tested, and mostly discarded or rethought. However, something is learned with each new attempt, and the successes are incorporated into the next generation of designs. Ideas such as interleaved memory, cache memory, instruction look ahead, segmentation and multiple functional units, instruction piplining, data pipelining, multiprocessing, shared memory, distributed memory have found their way into the various catagories of parallel computers available today. Some of these can be incorporated into all computers, such as instruction look ahead. Others define the type of computer; thus, vector computers are data pipelined machines.

The von Neumann Computer

For our purposes here, a computer consists of a central processing unit or *CPU*, memory for information storage, a path or *bus* over which data flow and a synchronization mechanism in the form of a *clock*. The CPU itself consists of several internal registers – a kind of high-speed memory, a program counter (PC), a stack pointer (SP), a decode unit (DU), and an arithmetic and logic unit (ALU) (see Fig. 2). A program consists of one or more contiguous memory locations, that is, chunks of memory, containing a *code segment* including subroutines, a *data segment* for the variables and parameters of the problem, a *stack segment*, and possibly additional memory allocated to the program at run time (see Fig. 3).

The various hardware elements are synchronized by the clock whose frequency f characterizes the speed at which instructions are executed. The

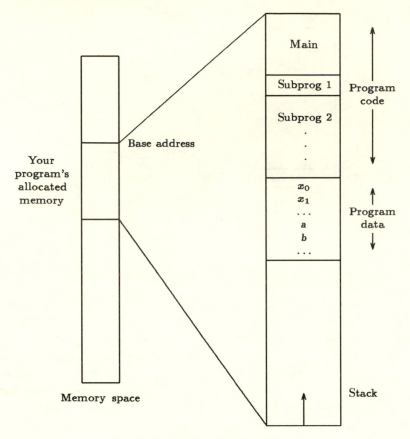

Fig. 3. Organization of main memory.

frequency is the number of cycles of the clock per second measured in megaHertz (mHz), 1 mHz $= 10^6$ Hz or gigaHertz, (gHz), 1 gHz $= 10^9$ Hz. The time t for one clock cycle is the reciprocal of the frequency

$$t = \frac{1}{f}.$$

Thus a 2-ns clock cycle corresponds to a frequency of 500 mHz since 1 ns $= 10^{-9}$ s and

$$f = \frac{1}{2 \times 10^{-9}} = 0.5 \times 10^9 = 500 \times 10^6.$$

If one instruction is completed per clock cycle, then the instruction rate, *IPS*, is the same as the frequency. The instruction rate is often given in millions of instructions per second or *MIPS*; hence, *MIPS* equals megaHertz for such a computer.

The original computer architecture, named after John von Neumann, who was the first to envision "stored programming" whereby the computer could change its own course of action, reads instructions one at a time sequentially and acts upon data items in the same way. To gain some idea of how a von Neumann computer works, we examine a step-by-step walk-through of the computation $c = a + b$.

Operation of a von Neumann Computer: $c = a + b$ Walk-Through

On successive clock cycles:

Step 1. Get next instruction
Step 2. Decode: fetch a
Step 3. Fetch a to internal register
Step 4. Get next instruction
Step 5. Decode: fetch b
Step 6. Fetch b to internal register
Step 7. Get next instruction
Step 8. Decode: add a and b (result c to internal register)
Step 9. Do the addition in the ALU (see below)
Step 10. Get next instruction
Step 11. Decode: store c (in main memory)
Step 12. Move c from internal register to main memory

In this example two *floating point numbers* are added. A floating point number is a number that is stored in the computer in mantissa and exponent form (see Section 4.1); integer numbers are stored directly, that is, with all mantissa and no exponent. Often in scientific computation the results materialize after a certain number of *floating point operations* occur, that is, additions, subtractions, multiplications, or divisions. Hence computers can be rated according to how many floating point operations per second, or FLOPS, they can perform. Usually it is a very large number and hence measured in mega-FLOPS, written MFLOPS, or giga-FLOPS written GFLOPS, or tera-FLOPS (TFLOPS). Of course, 1 MFLOPS $= 10^6$ FLOPS, 1 GFLOPS $= 10^3$ MFLOPS $= 10^9$ FLOPS, and 1 TFLOPS $= 10^{12}$ FLOPS.

The addition done at step 9 in the above walk-through consists of several steps itself. For this illustration, assume 0.9817×10^3 is to be added to 0.4151×10^2.

Step 1. Unpack operands: 9817 | 3   4151 | 2
Step 2. Exponent compare: 3 vs. 2

Step 3. Mantissa align: 9817 | 3   0415 | 3
Step 4. Mantissa addition: 10232 | 3
Step 5. Normalization (carry) check: $\boxed{1}$ 0232 | 3
Step 6. Mantissa shift: 1023 | 3
Step 7. Exponent adjust: 1023 | 4
Step 8. Repack result: 0.1023×10^4

So if the clock speed is doubled, then each computer instruction takes place in one half the time and execution speed is doubled. But physical laws limit the improvement that will be possible this way. Furthermore, as the physical limits are approached, improvements will become very costly. Fortunately there is another possibility for speeding up computations, parallelizing them.

Parallel Computing Hardware – Flynn's Classification

An early attempt to classify parallel computation made by Flynn is somewhat imprecise today but is nevertheless widely used.

	Single-data stream	Multiple-data streams
Single instruction	von Neumann	SIMD
Multiple instructions		MIMD

As we saw above, the original computer architecture, the von Neumann computer, reads instructions one at a time sequentially and acts upon data in the same way; thus, they are single instruction, single data, or SISD machines.

An early idea for parallelization, especially for scientific and engineering programming, has been the vector computer. Here it is often the case that the same instruction is performed on many data items as if these data were a single unit, a mathematical vector. For example, the scalar multiplication of a vector multiplies each component by the same number. Thus a single instruction is carried out on multiple data so these are SIMD machines. In these machines the parallelism is very structured and fine-grained (see Section 1.3).

Another term for this kind of computation is *data parallelism*. The parallelism stems from the data while the program itself is entirely serial. Mapping each instruction of the program to its target data is done by the compiler. Vector compilers automatically parallelize vector operations, provided the calculation is *vectorizable*, that is, can be correctly done in parallel (see Section 3.6).

Modern languages incorporate special instructions to help the compiler with the data partitioning. For example, the following statements in High Performance Fortran (HPF)

```
real x(1000)
!HPF$ PROCESSORS p(10)
!HPF$ DISTRIBUTE x(BLOCK) ONTO p
```

invokes 10 processors and instructs the 1,000 elements of x to be distributed with $1,000/10 = 100$ contiguous elements going to each.

Another approach to SIMD/data partitioned computing, massively parallel SIMD, is exemplified by the now extinct Connection Machine. Here instructions are broadcast (electronically) to thousands of processors each of which is working on its own data.

True, flexible, parallel computation comes about with multiple independent processors executing, possibly different, instructions at the same time on different data, that is, multiple instruction multiple data or MIMD computers. This class is further categorized according to how the memory is configured with respect to the processors, centralized, and shared or distributed according to some topology.

We consider each of these in more detail below.

1.2 SIMD–Vector Computers

In the von Neumann model, much of the computer hardware is idle while other parts of the machine are working. Thus the Decode Unit is idle while the ALU is calculating an addition for example. The idea here is to keep all the hardware of the computer working all the time. This is parallelism at the hardware level.

Operation of a Vector Computer – Assembly-Line Processing

First the computer's hardware is modularized or *segmented* into functional units that perform well-defined specialized tasks (see, for example, the Cray architecture diagram Fig. 16). The vector pipes are likewise segmented. Figure 4 shows the segments for the Cray add pipe.

It is desirable that the individual units be as independent as possible. This idea is similar to the modularization of an assembly plant into stations each of which performs a very specific single task. Like a factory, the various detailed steps of processing done to the code and data of a program are formalized, and specialized hardware is designed to perform each such step at the same time as

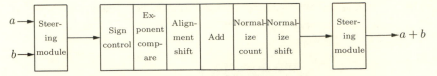

Fig. 4. A block diagram of the Cray add unit.

all the other steps. Then the data or code is processed step by step by moving from segment to segment; this is *pipelining*.

In our model of a computer, some of the main units are the fetch and store unit, the decode unit, and the arithmetic and logic unit. This makes it possible, for example, for the instructions of the program to be fetched before their turn in the execution sequence and held in special registers. This is called *caching*, allowing for advance decoding. In this way, operands can be prefetched so as to be available at the moment needed. Among the tasks of the decode unit is to precalculate the possible branches of conditional statements so that no matter which branch is taken, the right machine instruction is waiting in the instruction cache.

The innovation that gives a vector computer its name is the application of this principle to floating point numerical calculations. The result is an assembly line processing of much of the program's calculations. The assembly line in this case is called a *vector pipe*.

Assembly line processing is effective especially for the floating point operations of a program. Consider the sum of two vectors $\mathbf{x} + \mathbf{y}$ of length 200. To produce the first sum, $x_1 + y_1$, several machine cycles are required as we saw above. By analogy, the first item to roll off an assembly line takes the full time required for assembling one item. But immediately behind it is the second item and behind that the third and so on. In the same way, the second and subsequent sums $x_i + y_i$, $i = 2, \ldots, 200$, are produced one per clock cycle. In the next section we derive some equations governing such vector computations.

Example. Calculate $y_i = x_i + x_i^2$ for $i = 1, 2, \ldots, 100$

```
loop i = 1...100
      y_i = x_i*(1+x_i)    or?    y_i = x_i + x_i * x_i
end loop
```

Not all operations on mathematical vectors can be done via the vector pipes. We regard a *vector operation* as one which can. Mathematically it is an operation on the components of a vector which also results in a vector. For example, vector addition $\mathbf{x} + \mathbf{y}$ as above. In components this is $z_i = x_i + y_i$, $i = 1, \ldots, n$, and would be coded as a loop with index i running from 1 to n. Multiplying two

Table 1. *Vector timing data**

Type of arithmetic operation	Time in ns for n operations
Vector add/multiply/boolean	$1000 + 10n$
Vector division	$1600 + 70n$
Saxpy (cf. pp 14)	$1600 + 10n$
Scalar operation**	$100n$
Inner product	$2000 + 20n$
Square roots	$500n$

* For a mid-80's memory-to-memory vector computer.
** Except division, assume division is 7 times longer.

vectors componentwise and scalar multiplication, that is, the multiplication of the components of a vector by a constant, are other examples of a vector operation.

By contrast, the inner or dot product of two vectors is not a vector operation in this regard, because the requirement of summing the resulting componentwise products cannot be done using the vector pipes. (At least not directly, see the exercises for pseudo-vectorizing such an operaton.)

Hockney's Formulas

Let t_n be the time to calculate a vector operation on vectors of length of n. If s is the number of clock cycles to prepare the pipe and fetch the operands and l is the number of cycles to fill up the pipe, then $(s + l)\tau$ is the time for the first result to emerge from the pipe where τ is the time for a clock cycle. Thereafter, another result is produced per clock cycle, hence

$$t_n = (s + l + (n - 1))\tau,$$

see Table 1.

The *startup time* is $(s + l - 1)\tau$ in seconds. And the *operation rate*, r, is defined as the number of operations per unit time so

$$r = \frac{n}{t_n}.$$

Theoretical peak performance, r_∞, is one per clock cycle or

$$r_\infty = \frac{1}{\tau}.$$

Thus we can write

$$r = \frac{r_\infty}{1 + \frac{s+l-1}{n}}.$$

This relationship is shown in Fig. 5.

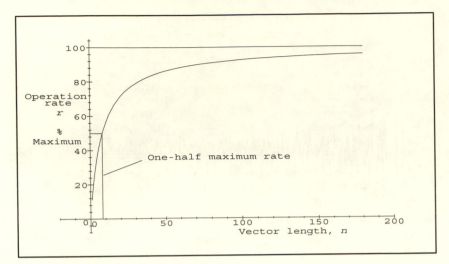

Fig. 5. Operation rate vs. vector length.

Hockney's $n_{1/2}$ value is defined as the vector length for achieving one-half peak performance, that is,

$$\frac{1}{2\tau} = \frac{n_{1/2}}{(s + l - 1 + n_{1/2})\tau}.$$

This gives

$$n_{1/2} = s + l - 1$$

or equal to the startup time. Using $n_{1/2}$, the operation rate can now be written

$$r = \frac{r_\infty}{1 + \frac{n_{1/2}}{n}}.$$

Hockney's *break-even point* is defined as the vector length for which the scalar calculation takes the same time as the vector calculation. Letting $r_{\infty,v}$ denote the peak performance in vector mode and $r_{\infty,s}$ the same in scalar mode, we have

$$\text{vector time for } n = \text{scalar time for } n$$

$$\frac{s + l - 1 + n_b}{r_{\infty,v}} = \frac{n_b}{r_{\infty,s}}.$$

Solving this for n_b gives

$$n_b = \frac{n_{1/2}}{\frac{r_{\infty,v}}{r_{\infty,s}} - 1}.$$

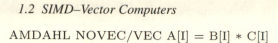

AMDAHL NOVEC/VEC A[I] = B[I] * C[I]

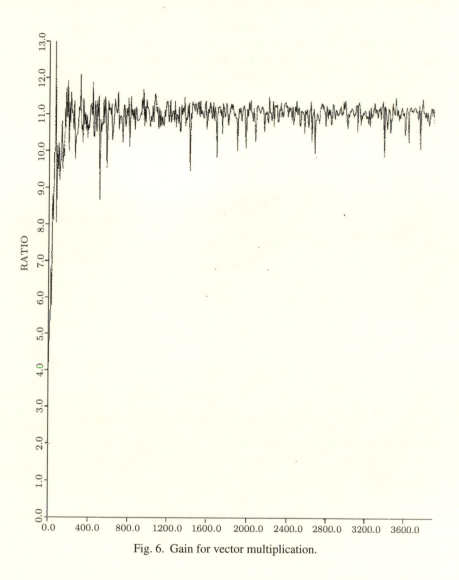

Fig. 6. Gain for vector multiplication.

This calculation is not exactly correct for a register machine such as the Cray since, by having to shuttle data between the vector registers and the vector pipes, there results a bottleneck at the vector registers. Of course, $r_{\infty,v} > r_{\infty,s}$ (or else there is no need for a vector computer). At one time that ratio was about 4 for Cray machines and n_b was about 8.

A vector operation such as

$$\mathbf{c} = \mathbf{a} + \alpha * \mathbf{b} \quad c_i = a_i + \alpha b_i, \quad i = 1, \ldots, n,$$

in which two different vector pipes are used, the add pipe and the logic pipe in this example, is called a *saxpy* (standing for scalar alpha x plus y). Such an operation *chains* which means the result of the multiply operation, αb_i, is fed directly into the add pipe along with a_i. In this way the preparation time for the add operation is saved (the preparation time for the a_i takes place during the multiply operation). Consequently, the time for the first result, c_1, is $(s + 2\ell)\tau$ and the time for the entire vector of length n is

$$t_n = (s + 2\ell - 1)\tau + n\tau. \tag{1}$$

This effect is clearly shown in Table 1.

The *gain*, G_n, or equivalent number of CPUs, is defined as the speedup of the vector calculation for a vector length of n. It is comparable to an effective number of parallel processors,

$$G_n = \frac{\text{scalar time for } n}{\text{vector time for } n}$$

$$= \frac{n/r_{\infty,s}}{(s + l - 1 + n)/r_{\infty,v}}$$

$$= \frac{r_{\infty,v}}{r_{\infty,s}} \frac{n}{n_{1/2} + n}.$$

Typical gains for Cray machines are on the order of 11. Note that break-even occurs when $G_n = 1$ (see Fig. 6).

1.3 MIMD – True, Coarse-Grain Parallel Computers

A descriptive explanation of the concepts of parallel computation such as grain size, task dependencies, and data partitioning can be made by an analogy with a service shop.

The "Jiffy-Lube" Model

An auto service company advertises a "12-point check" done in 15 minutes. The check consists of changing the oil and filter, a lubrication, interior vacuum, battery check, windshield wiper check, brake fluid check, tire pressure check, and so on. When an auto pulls into the bay, 6 attendants, say, do these tasks in parallel and, in the process, demonstrate the basic ideas of parallel programming.

In *coarse-grain parallelism*, major tasks of the problem are done in parallel. In the Jiffy-Lube model, the vacuuming and the electrolyte and brake fluid checks can be done while the oil is being changed.

In *fine-grain parallelism* subtasks, usually work requiring similar processing such as done in loops, are done in parallel. In the Jiffy-Lube model, checking the tire pressure could be delegated one tire per attendant.

Data or task dependencies arise when certain tasks can be started only after certain other tasks are completed and their results made available. In the coarse-grained Jiffy-Lube model, the oil cannot be refilled until the oil filter has been changed constituting a task dependency. On the other hand, since the car is not raised on a hoist, the vacuuming is independent of the other tasks. In the fine-grained model, suppose a tire leaks beyond repair and five attendants are assigned to tighten the lug nuts as the new tire is mounted. Since lug nut tightening must proceed in the order $1 - 3 - 5 - 2 - 4 - 1 - \cdots$ (as recommended by auto manufacturers), this subtask has fine-grained data dependency. The lug nuts cannot be tightened in an arbitrary order.

We list some other terms which arise in either coarse-grained computation or fine-grained computation:

Data partitioning: multiple but essentially identical processes each working on a portion of the data to be processed;

Function partitioning: multiple processes performing quite different tasks;

Prescheduled loops: loop index distribution to multiple processors fixed by the programmer in source code, or by the compiler at compile time;

Statically scheduled loops: loop index distribution fixed at run time (it can depend, for example, on the number of processors);

Dynamically scheduled loops: loop index distribution determined by the processes themselves, when a processor becomes available, it takes the next index to work on.

Prescheduled and statically scheduled loops can be organized in two differents ways: block scheduling and stride scheduling. In *block scheduling*, each process receives a contiguous block of indices to work on. The following pseudocode illustrates the idea. In this example, $id = 0, 1, \ldots, nprocs - 1$ identifies each process for `nprocs` number of processors. N is the number of loop iterations to be done and i is loop index.

Block Scheduling

```
// get block size, last block could be smaller
  Bsize = N/nprocs;
  if( N ≠ nprocs*Bsize )
```

```
      Bsize = Bsize+1;
   if( id ≠ 0 ) {
     Bstart = (id-1)*Bsize;
     Bend = id*Bsize - 1
   }
   else { // want proc 0 to do last block
     Bstart = (nprocs-1)*Bsize;
     Bend = N-1
   }
// following in parallel, each processor using its Bstart
//and Bend
   loop i=Bstart,..., Bend
      ⋮
```

Block scheduling is often used when there is data dependency in the loop between consecutive indices. Block scheduling reduces this issue to block boundaries.

In *stride scheduling*, each process skips over a fixed number of indices between each index it executes. Stride scheduling is easier to implement as the following pseudocode shows.

Stride Scheduling

```
      loop i=id, id+nprocs, id+2*nprocs, ..., N
         ⋮
```

1.4 Classification of Distributed Memory Computers

This section is intended to acquaint the reader only with the salient concepts and issues of distributed computation. Our treatment is only a brief introduction to the field. The interested reader is directed to [1] for an in-depth treatment.

Bus contention is a limiting factor in shared memory parallel computation. With more and more data having to flow over the bus, delays set in; the bus saturates. Beyond that, providing for large amounts of shared memory entails design constraints from heat dissipation to conductor congestion to the size of the computer itself. This last is a consequence of the finite speed of electrical signals.

The alternative is distributed memory computation. In this scheme, each processor has its own private memory not directly accessible to the other processors. If some processor requires access to data assigned to another processor, it must be communicated by way of data links. The exact pattern of these links defines the topology of the network. Some successful topologies are ring, mesh, hypercube, and LAN (local area network).

Packets and Data Types

Data communication is usually in the form of *packets* which are assemblages of data having limited size and transmitted as a unit. Besides the data to be moved, packets can contain other information as well such as addressing and error correction information. If the amount of data to be transmitted at any one time exceeds the packet length, then the data are divided into several packets.

Some interprocessor communication consists of a transmission from one processor to another. The problem of sending, from one processor, a different packet to every other node is called a *single-node scatter*. The dual problem in which a different packet is received at a given node from every other node is a *single-node gather*.

If a processor must make the same transmission to all processors on the network, this activity is called a *single-node broadcast*. A *multinode broadcast* is when every processor makes a single-node broadcast at the same time.

A *single-node accumulation* is when all processors transmit data to a single node and at links along the way, the data are combined. For example, in forming a matrix–vector multiply using one processor per component, the result on processor i is the sum $y_i = a_{i1}x_1 + a_{i2}x_2 + \cdots + a_{in}x_n$, which is formed from the products $a_{ij}x_j$ obtained on processor j, $j = 1, \ldots, n$; these products are accumulated by the nodes along the path to processor i. A *multinode accumulation* is a single-node accumulation at each node simultaneously.

Communication Links and Delays

We assume that communication links are bidirectional and that if several channels are incident to a processor, then all channels can be in use simultaneously.

The time required for communication can be attributed to four effects: (a) *communication processing time* – the time to prepare the data for communication, (b) *queuing time* – packets must wait in a queue for their turn at transmission until the link becomes free, (c) *transmission time* – the time needed to transmit all the bits of the data, and (d) *propagation time* – the time needed for a bit to make its way from sender to its final receiver.

The four components of the delay are larger or smaller depending on the topology of the network and on the technology of the transmission. Propagation time is large if there are many links between the sender and the receiver. Queuing time is large for a LAN but very small for a direct link. Communication processing time is a calculation done on the host processor and is relatively constant. For most existing systems, communication delay is much larger than the time required to execute a basic numerical operation such as a floating point operation. A useful parameter for a given network is the cost of the communication of a packet of data in terms of an equivalent number of floating point operations with respect to time.

Network Topologies

A network can be described as a graph; the vertices are the *nodes* or processors of the network while the arcs are the communication links. The *diameter* of the network is the maximum number of links between any two nodes. The (*arc*) *connectivity* is the minumum number of links that must be removed to disconnect the network.

Ring

Let the nodes of a ring be labeled $1, 2, \ldots, p$, and then the arcs are $(1, 2), (2, 3), \ldots, (p - 1, p)$, and $(p, 1)$. The number of links incident at any node is 2. The diameter of the network is $(p - 1)/2$ and the connectivity is 2. Since both links at every node can be in use simultaneously and in both directions, the time for a multinode broadcast is also $(p - 1)/2$.

Mesh

The mesh topology is popular because for many problems it mimics the geometry of physical space. In a d-dimensional mesh, the nodes are conceptually arrayed on the points of a d-dimensional space having integer coordinates. Each node has a label $(i_1, i_2, \ldots, i_d)$, where $i_k \in \{1, 2, \ldots, n_k\}$. Here n_k is the extent in the kth dimension. The number of processors p is the product $p = n_1 n_2 \ldots n_d$. If the extents are equal, $n_1 = n_2 = \cdots = n_d = n$, then $p = n^d$. The links of the mesh are from each node to its nearest neighbors. Thus a node in the interior of the mesh has $2d$ links; for example, the node $(2, 3, 4)$ of a 3-dimensional mesh communicates with the 6 nodes $(1, 3, 4)$, $(3, 3, 4)$, $(2, 2, 4)$, $(2, 4, 4)$, $(2, 3, 3)$, and $(2, 3, 5)$. In general, the node $(i_1, i_2, \ldots, i_d)$ has a link with $(j_1, j_2, \ldots, j_d)$ if the sum $\sum_{k=1}^{d} |i_k - j_k| = 1$.

The diameter of the mesh is $\sum_{k=1}^{d}(n_k - 1)$. By removing the d links to node $(1, 1, \ldots, 1)$, the network is disconnected so the connectivity is d. The maximum time for a single node broadcast is from node $(1, 1, \ldots, 1)$ to $(n_1, n_2, \ldots, n_d)$ or $\sum_{k=1}^{d}(n_k - 1)$. If the extents are equal or approximately equal, then $n \approx p^{1/d}$; hence, in terms of p the single node broadcast time is on the order of $dp^{1/d}$. This is also the time for a multinode broadcast.

Hypercube

A d-dimensional hypercube is a d-dimensional mesh with extent 2 in every direction. For the hypercube, we use base 0 indexing so the coordinates in each dimension are either 0 or 1. As in the case of the mesh, nodes of a hypercube may be labeled $(i_1, i_2, \ldots, i_d)$, where now each i_k is either 0 or 1. Here again two nodes are directly linked if and only if their labels differ in exactly one coordinate. The *Hamming distance* between two nodes equals the number of places at which their labels differ. In terms of this distance, two nodes are linked if and only if their Hamming distance is 1.

Since there are exactly two indices in each dimension, there are $p = 2^d$ number of nodes in a d-dimensional hypercube. Each node has incident d communication links; hence, the connectivity is also d. The diameter is d as well; in terms of the number of processors this is $\log_2 p$. In fact, the Hamming distance between two nodes equals their communication distance. Moreover, a packet can be routed over links in any manner by which the Hamming distance is reduced by 1 each step.

Hypercubes may be constructed recursively. A 1-dimensional hypercube is the linked pair 0 and 1. Having constructed a $d - 1$-dimensional hypercube, denote it by A; make a copy and denote that B. For each node $(i_1, \ldots, i_{d-1})$ of A, make a link to the same node of B. Finally append a leading 0 to the labels of A and a leading 1 to the labels of B.

The time for a single-node broadcast on a hypercube is d. To figure the time for a multinode broadcast, note that each node must receive a packet from $2^d - 1$ other nodes. But each node has only d links incident on it. Therefore the minimal time is $(2^d - 1)/d$; this time is also achievable.

LAN

The LAN model is that of processors connected to a single cable that serves as a bus. Packets are addressed and a processor broadcasts it along the cable to all other nodes. But only the node to which the packet is addressed retains it. To communicate, a node must wait for access to the cable. As more nodes are attached to the cable and more packets must be exchanged, the network may be driven to saturation.

Our assumptions about bidirectional and simultaneous communication do not hold for a LAN. A single-node broadcast is the mode of all transmission. A multinode broadcast is not possible except as a sequence of single-node broadcasts. Since each node is one link from every other node, a single-node accumulation must be made on the destination node. Likewise, a multinode accumulation is solved as a sequence of single-node accumulations.

From the point of view of any given node, the network need not be strictly local; it can exchange packets with similar networks so long as there is a bridge or even a series of bridges to the other network. In this way, the Internet can be co-opted into a gigantic parallel computer suitable for certain tasks that require only minimal communication. One such task is the breaking of certain types of crytographic information exchange. There are many other distributed projects organized at `www.distributed.net`.

1.5 Amdahl's Law and Profiling

Let W be the amount of work to be done for a particular job as a function of time, and let r be the rate at which it can be done by one processor. Then the time required for one processor to do the job is T_1, given by

$$T_1 = \frac{W}{r}.$$

Now suppose that f fraction of the computation, by time, must be done serially and the remaining $1 - f$ fraction can be done perfectly parallelized by p processors (see Fig. 7). Then the time, T_p, for the parallel computation is given by

$$T_p = \frac{fW}{r} + \frac{(1-f)W}{pr}.$$

Of course, if the entire calculation can be parallelized, that is, $f = 0$, then all the work will be done in p fraction of the time. We say the *speedup SU* is p,

$$SU = \frac{T_1}{T_p} = p.$$

This is known as *linear speedup*. But as it is, the speedup works out to be

$$SU = \frac{T_1}{T_p} = \frac{W/r}{(W/r)\left(f + \frac{(1-f)}{p}\right)}$$
$$= \frac{p}{f(p-1) + 1},$$

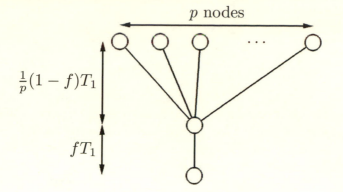

Fig. 7. $1 - f$ fraction in parallel, f fraction in serial.

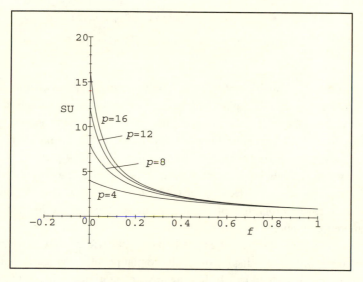

Fig. 8. Amdahl speedup as a function of f.

(see Figs. 8 and 9). This relationship is known as *Amdahl's Law*. This is a hyperbola with vertical asymptote at $f = -1/(p - 1)$ and horizontal asymptote at $SU = 0$. Now $0 \le f \le 1$ and at $f = 0$ $SU = p$ as we have seen, on the other hand, at $f = 1$ all the work is done serially and so $SU = 1$. Now consider how the speedup behaves as a function of p, as $p \to \infty$, the vertical asymptote closely approximates the vertical axis. This steepness near $f = 0$ means that the speedup falls off rapidly if there is only a tiny fraction of the code which must be run in serial mode.

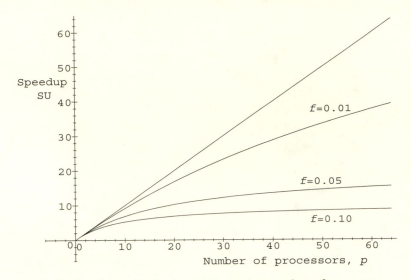

Fig. 9. Speedup vs. fraction in serial for various numbers of processors.

At first the consequences of Amdahl's Law seem bleak, at least as far as speedup is concerned. But it should be kept in mind that the fraction f is by time and not by code. As a matter of fact, most scientific programs spend the majority of their execution time in a few loops within the program. Thus if these loops parallelize (or vectorize), then Amdahl's Law predicts that the efficiency will be high. Hence the programmer should become aware of these computationally intensive sections of code and ensure that they parallelize. There are software *profiling* tools for finding these places in the code. We will have more to say about this below.

Of course, it is to be expected that certain subtasks will go slowly; for example, input and output, the display of results so that people can interact with the computer. This time should not be held against an algorithm. What is important is that the parts of the program that can be parallelized are parallelized to the fullest extent possible.

In addition to subparts of a program having to run serially, there are other limitations on the speed of computation. Heavy matrix manipulation programs come up against limited memory bandwidth very quickly. If all 30 CPUs of a UE6000 computer average one main memory reference every 90 bus cycles (quite possible), then there is a reference every third bus cycle. A request/reply occupies the bus for about 6 cycles. That is already twice what the bus can handle, and this ignores bus contention and possible I/O activity.

Execution Profilers

One type of profiler produces a histogram style report as to where the program is spending its time. The profiler works by dividing the executable, more or less evenly, into several "buckets," for example using 4 byte granularity. As the program is executing, it is suspended periodically, and the count for the bucket in which execution is taking place at that moment is incremented. Hence the profile report will show high counts where the program spends more time and low counts where it spends less time. From such a report it is easy to see which parts of the code deserve the greatest optimization effort.

Another type of profiler counts the number of times subprograms (subroutines, functions, methods, etc.) of the program are entered. This report shows which subprograms are heavily used and therefore deserve optimization effort. As we will see, in most scientific computation basic linear algebra subprograms (BLAS) are a case in point (see Chapter 4). And for that very fact, a great deal of effort is spent on achieving the greatest speed of these routines.

Using a profiler is a 2-step operation. This is necessary in order that the overhead of the operation be kept to a minimum so as to minimally disturb execution time. First the program runs normally at which time the various profiling data are recorded. Afterward, special display and interpretation tools are used to access and display the information.

The typical procedure for invoking a profiler is exemplified by the gcc compiler as follows:

```
cc -pg prog.c <any libraries> -o prog.out
```

then execute `prog.out` to get gmon.out; inspect `gmon.out` with

```
gprof prog.out.
```

Exercises

1. (5) Research a Grand Challenge problem and write a short essay about it. Be sure to explain the nature of the problem, the benefit in its solution, obstacles to its solution, the proposed solution approach, and the types of numerical algorithms that will be used.

2. (4) Following the thoughts of Seymour Cray many years ago, assume a modification to the von Neumann computer in which the fetch unit, the decode unit and ALU operate independently and simultaneously, for example, the fetch unit can move data between main memory and internal registers (assigned to the ALU) or cache memory (assigned to the decode

unit) simultaneously with the operation of the other units. Perform the addition $a + b = c$ showing what each unit could do at each time step. How many time steps are needed for the operation?

3. (3) A. In each of the following, given the clock speed in mHz, find the cycle time (in nanoseconds): (a) 2, (b) 16, (c) 50, (d) 100, (e) 150, (f) 200, (g) 300. B. For each of the following, find the clock speed (in mHz) given the cycle time: (a) 8.5 ns, (b) 6 ns, (c) 20 ns, (d) 200 ns. C. Assuming all else the same, how much faster is a Pentium processor running at 2 gHz than an 8080 processor at 2 mHz regarding clock speed alone?

4. (3) The speed of an electronic signal in a wire is about 2/3 the speed of light in a vacuum (186,000 miles/s or 299,792,458 m/s). If the clock speed of a CPU is 2.4 gHz, how far does an electronic signal travel in one clock cycle? How far for a bus speed of 266 mHz?

5. (4) Consider three ways of computing $x_i^2 + x_i^3, i = 1, \dots, 10{,}000$, namely

$$y_i = x_i * x_i + x_i * x_i * x_i$$
$$y_i = x_i * (x_i + x_i * x_i)$$
$$y_i = x_i * x_i * (1 + x_i).$$

Calculate the time for each using the Vector Timing Data Table (p. 11). Be sure to take chaining (saxpy operations) into consideration.

6. (2) Using the Vector Timing Data Table (p. 11), what is the MFLOP rate for a vector add operation as a function of vector length N?

7. (3) The matrix–vector product $y = Ax$, where A is upper triangular, $a_{ij} = 0$, $j < i$, $i = 1, \dots, n$, and x is the vector of 1s, is to be done on a vector computer. Use the Vector Timing Data Table (p. 11) to figure the MFLOP rate for the entire operation. (Since x is the vector of 1's, this product amounts to forming the sum of vectors of decreasing length.)

8. (6) Use the Vector Timing Data Table (p. 11) to calculate (a) $n_{1/2}$, (b) n_B, and (c) gain G with respect to the machine having those characteristics (see Eq. (1)).

9. (4) (a) To compute the sum $\sum_{i=1}^{n} a_i$, for $n = 2^r$, vector computers use the following *pseudovectorization* method; divide the list in half making the first half into a vector and the last half into another vector, do a vector add. This gives a list half as long which is the sum of two elements each. Now repeat this process. Assume the process continues until, in the last step, the two "vectors" added are each of length 1 and each consists of the sum

of one half the terms. (In actuality, the pseudo-vectorization software is written to abandon the vector computational mode when the vector length break-even point is reached.) Find the time required and MFLOPs for this pseudo-vectorization. (b) Suppose the vector startup must be paid only once, since after that, the arguments are in the vector registers. Now what is the time? (c) Using your answer to part (b), time the inner product of $2n$ length vectors, and compare with the Vector Timing Data Table (p. 11).

10. (3) Given the data of Table 1 for a vector operation and a saxpy operation, find s and l.

11. (6) Show how to do an $n \times n$ matrix vector multiply $y = Ax$ on a ring, a 2-dimensional mesh and a hypercube, each of appropriate size. Specify how the matrix and vector components are to be distributed initially among the nodes and how the data is to be communicated. The resultant vector y must have its components distributed among the processors in the same way that x does.

12. (6) Show how to do an $n \times n$ matrix–matrix multiply $C = AB$ on a ring, a 2-dimensional mesh and a hypercube, each of appropriate size. Specify how the matrix components are to be distributed initially among the nodes and how the data is to be communicated. The resultant matrix C must have its components distributed among the processors in the same way as A and B do.

13. (5) (a) Show that every cycle in a hypercube has an even number of nodes. (b) Show that a ring with an even number of nodes $p \geq 4$ can be mapped into a hypercube of some dimension and that if p is odd then it cannot be mapped into a hypercube of any dimension.

14. (3) Under the assumption for Amdahl's Law, find what fraction of a program must be in parallel to maintain an efficiency of 75% for the number of processors p equal to (a) 4, (b) 8, (c) 16. (*Efficiency* is defined as the speedup divided by the number of processors.)

15. (2) Although LU decomposition will be discussed in at length in Chapter 5, no knowledge of it is needed for this exercise. In LU decomposition of a square matrix A, pivoting must be done in serial mode. Assuming pivoting amounts to 5% of the work of the calculation and the rest perfectly parallelizes, find the speedup using (a) 2, (b) 4, (c) 8, (d) 16, (e) 32, and (f) 64 processors.

16. (3) Suppose that $1/k$th of the processing of an algorithm must be done serially. Show that the maximal speedup achievable for the algorithm by parallel processing is k.

Programming Exercises

(4) Write an MPI program (see Section 3.5) to determine the time required to send a transmission between two nodes. What is this time in terms of a floating point operation? (See the Appendix for the program mpiSendAround, which sends a packet around a ring of p processors.)

2

Theoretical Considerations – Complexity

2.1 Directed Acyclic Graph Representation

Just as a graph is an effective way to understand a function, a directed acyclic graph is an effective way to understand a parallel computation. Such a graph shows when each calculation is done, which others can be done at the same time, what prior calculations are needed for it and into what subsequent calculations it feeds.

Starting from a directed acyclic graph and given a set of processors, then a schedule can be worked out. A schedule assigns each calculation to a specific processor to be done at a specified time.

From a schdule, the total time for a computation follows and, from this, we get the difficulty or complexity of the computation.

A Directed Acyclic Graph Defines a Computation

A computation can be accurately depicted by means of a directed acyclic graph (DAG), $G = (N, A)$, consisting of a set of vertices N and a set of directed arcs A. In such a portrayal the vertices, or nodes, of the graph represent subtasks to be performed on the data, while the directed arcs indicate the flow of data from one subtask to the next. In particular, a directed arc $(i, j) \in A$ from node i to j indicates that calculation j requires the result of calculation i.

The input data is shown at the top of the graph. We take the flow of data from the top to the bottom of the graph (or, less often, from left to right). This also becomes the flow of time; it follows that the graph can have no cycles. With this convention, we may omit the direction indicators on the arcs. An arc from i to j is said to be *incident* at j and i is a *predecessor* node for j. A *positive path* is a sequence of nodes $i_0, \ldots, i_K$ such that i_{k-1} is a predecessor of i_k for $k = 1, \ldots, K$. The operation performed at node i is dependent on all its predecessors and, by extension, on all operations on every positive path to i.

27

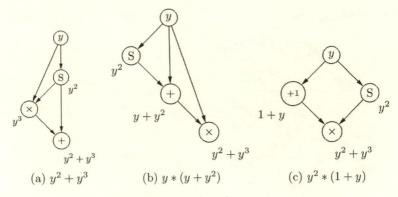

Fig. 10. (a,b,c) calculating $y^2 + y^3$ in three different ways.

In Fig. 10 we give three DAGs for the computation of $y^2 + y^3$. Inside each node we show the operation performed, an S indicates squaring the node's input.

The DAG for a computation shows the order in which the calculations occur step by step and the data dependencies of the computation. But the graph can contain execution and communication time information as well. Along with each node, we associate the execution time for that node. In the case of identical processors, this time is independent of the processor, which will be executing that task, called *symmetric multiprocessing*. If the processors work at different rates, then the nodal information must reflect these differences. In this case, scheduling the computation becomes more complicated.

In another example we show the DAG for *nested polynomial evaluation* due to Newton. Let $p(x) = a_n x^n + a_{n-1} x^{n-1} + \cdots + a_1 x + a_0$ be a given polynomial and suppose we want its value for $x = c$. Notice that by factoring x (or c) as much as possible leads to the equivalent form

$$p(c) = (\ldots(((a_n * c + a_{n-1}) * c + a_{n-2}) * c + a_{n-3}) * c + \cdots) * c + a_0.$$

This calculation can be written in a table form and is known as *synthetic division*

	a_n	a_{n-1}	a_{n-2}	$\cdots$	a_0	$\mid c$
$+$		$b_n * c$	$b_{n-1} * c$	$\cdots$	$b_1 * c$	
	a_n	$b_n * c + a_{n-1}$	$b_{n-1} * c + a_{n-2}$	$\cdots$	$b_1 * c + a_0 = p(c)$	
	b_n	b_{n-1}	b_{n-2}	$\cdots$	b_0	

With notation as in the table, one can show directly that

$$p(x) = \left(b_n x^{n-1} + b_{n-1} x^{n-2} + \cdots + b_1\right)(x - c) + b_0$$

so $b_0 = p(c)$. If $p(c) = 0$ then $b_n x^{n-1} + b_{n-1} x^{n-2} + \cdots + b_1$ is the quotient polynomial.

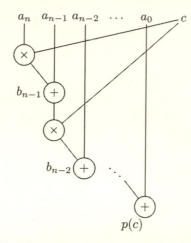

Fig. 11. DAG representation nested multiplication.

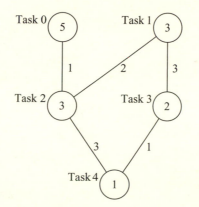

Fig. 12. DAG representation of the 5-task problem.

The DAG for this calculation is shown in Fig. 11. This is apparently a very serial algorithm, but we will see later on, in the exercises, how the calculation can be parallelized.

Communication time may be indicated as weights assigned to the arcs of the graph. As in the case with execution times, communication delays can differ depending on the processor, which eventually carries out the task. For example, if this is the same as the processor which performs the predecessor task, then the communication time is 0. In practice, processors signal their completion of a task and wait at synchronization points of the algorithm.

In Fig. 12 we show a DAG for a 5-task problem with nodal times and communcation delays. See Table 2 to glimpse the combinatorial difficulty in scheduling parallel computations.

Table 2. *Five-task 3 processor scheduling problem*

The problem of scheduling processes on a symmetric multiprocessing computer is an example of combinatorial optimization. In general, this problem is NP-complete. Here is an example of such a problem in which 5 tasks are to be executed using 3 processors. The dependencies and communication times are given in Fig. 12. A solution can be coded in two different ways: PAT shows which processor is assigned to task 0, 1, ..., 4; TAP shows which tasks are assigned to processor 0 | processor 1 | processor 2.

Index	PAT	TAP	Valuation	Index	PAT	TAP	Valuation
0	0,0,0,0,0	0,1,2,3,4,|,|	14	21	0,1,2,0,0	0,3,4,|,1,|,2	13
1	0,0,0,0,1	0,1,2,3,|,4,|	16	22	1,0,0,0,2	1,2,3,|,0,|,4	13
2	0,0,0,1,0	0,1,2,4,|,3,|	15	23	1,0,0,2,0	1,2,4,|,0,|,3	10
3	0,0,1,0,0	0,1,3,4,|,2,|	17	24	1,0,2,0,0	1,3,4,|,0,|,2	13
4	0,1,0,0,0	0,2,3,4,|,1,|	11	25	1,2,0,0,0	2,3,4,|,0,|,1	11
5	1,0,0,0,0	1,2,3,4,|,0,|	10	26	0,0,2,2,1	0,1,|,4,|,2,3	18
6	0,0,0,1,1	0,1,2,|,3,4,|	15	27	0,0,2,1,2	0,1,|,3,|,2,4	17
7	0,0,1,0,1	0,1,3,|,2,4,|	14	28	0,0,1,2,2	0,1,|,2,|,3,4	17
8	0,0,1,1,0	0,1,4,|,2,3,|	16	29	0,2,0,2,1	0,2,|,4,|,1,3	12
9	0,1,0,0,1	0,2,3,|,1,4,|	13	30	0,2,0,1,2	0,2,|,3,|,1,4	13
10	0,1,0,1,0	0,2,4,|,1,3,|	9	31	0,1,0,2,2	0,2,|,1,|,3,4	12
11	0,1,1,0,0	0,3,4,|,1,2,|	13	32	0,2,2,0,1	0,3,|,4,|,1,2	13
12	1,0,0,0,1	1,2,3,|,0,4,|	13	33	0,2,1,0,2	0,3,|,2,|,1,4	14
13	1,0,0,1,0	1,2,4,|,0,3,|	10	34	0,1,2,0,2	0,3,|,1,|,2,4	12
14	1,0,1,0,0	1,3,4,|,0,2,|	12	35	0,2,2,1,0	0,4,|,3,|,1,2	13
15	1,1,0,0,0	2,3,4,|,0,1,|	16	36	0,2,1,2,0	0,4,|,2,|,1,3	13
16	0,0,0,1,2	0,1,2,|,3,|,4	16	37	0,1,2,2,0	0,4,|,1,|,2,3	14
17	0,0,1,0,2	0,1,3,|,2,|,4	17	38	1,0,0,2,2	1,2,|,0,|,3,4	13
18	0,0,1,2,0	0,1,4,|,2,|,3	18	39	1,0,2,0,2	1,3,|,0,|,2,4	10
19	0,1,0,0,2	0,2,3,|,1,|,4	13	40	1,0,2,2,0	1,4,|,0,|,2,3	14
20	0,1,0,2,0	0,2,4,|,1,|,3	12				

Event schedule diagram for solution 8: PAT = 0,0,1,1,0; total time = 16
    time: 1 2 3 4 5 6 7 8 9 0 1 2 3 4 5 6 7 8

P_0	receive:	$-$ $-$
P_0	task:	_1_ ___0___ $\underline{4}$
P_0	send:	___ $-$
P_1	receive:	___ $-$
P_1	task:	_3_ __2__
P_1	send:	$-$ ___

For the most part, the nodal operations of a DAG are very basic, such as arithmetical operations, comparisons, etc. In this case we assign one unit of time to each of them and show on the same horizontal level, all those calculations that can be done at the same time. *Diagram time*, or just time, in such a graph is synonymous with the number of horizontal steps from the top. Time in the usual sense is referred to as *clock time* or *wall time* (in reference to the clock on the wall) to distinguish it from diagram time.

A Schedule

Let a pool of processors, p in number, and a directed acyclic graph (N, A) having nodes $i = 1, 2, \ldots, |N|$, for a parallel computation be given. For i not an input node, let P_i be the processor assigned to do the calculation at node i. Also let t_i be the time the node i calculation is completed ($t_i = 0$ for input nodes). Then a *schedule* S is a list $[i, (P_i, t_i)]$, $i = 1, \ldots, |N|$ subject to the constraints:

(a) a processor can do only one node at a time,
(b) if $(i, j) \in A$, then $t_j > t_i$, i.e. node j can be done only after node i.

The *time*, t_S, for a schedule S is the maximum, $\max_{1 \leq i \leq |N|} t_i$. The *time*, T_p, for a calculation using p processors is the minimum time over all schedules using p processors and all DAGs for the computation. The *complexity* of the computation, T_∞, is the minimum of T_p over all $p \geq 1$.

Obviously the bigger a problem, the more time required for its execution. What is important in complexity is how fast the time grows as the problem gets bigger. Often the *size of a problem* is determined by a single integer parameter n. For example, in root finding the degree of the polynomial quantifies the size of the problem; in solving a linear system it would be the number of unknowns. When the size of the problem grows according to a parameter n, then T_∞ will be a function of n.

The notation $T_\infty = O(g(n))$ means for some constant $c > 0$, $T_\infty \leq cg(n)$. More generally, for any function $f(n)$,

$$f(n) = O(g(n)) \quad \text{if} \quad |f(n)| \leq cg(n)$$

for some $c > 0$. We say that as n gets big, $f(n)$ has *order (of magnitude)* at most $g(n)$. The notation $f(n) = \Theta(g(n))$ means that for positive constants c_1 and c_2, $c_1 g(n) \leq |f(n)| \leq c_2 g(n)$. This means $f(n)$ has order at least $g(n)$ and at most $g(n)$ as well, so it has order $g(n)$.

For example, $T_\infty = O(1)$ means that the complexity is essentially constant as a function of size. Or, in another case, $T_\infty = O(\log n)$ means $T_\infty \leq c \log n$ for some $c > 0$. Unless otherwise stated, when discussing execution complexity, $\log n$ means the logarithm to the base 2, that is, $k = 2^{\log k}$. In another example use of the notation, if $f(n) = O(4n^3 + n^2)$, we can simply write $f(n) = O(n^3)$.

On some occasions it is desirable to emphasize the coefficient of the order. For example, one approach to a problem might require time on the order of $n^2/3$

and another, the order of $4n^2/3$. This means that asymptotically as $n \to \infty$ the constant c in the first case can be taken as $1/3$ and in the second case as $4/3$. Evidently the second calculation requires about 4 times the amount of work as the first.

Banking Processors

Once a DAG has been constructed for an algorithm, as we have seen above, it must be scheduled. But it may well be that there are insufficiently many processors to execute all the nodes at some given level. In this case the DAG can still be implemented with the given set of processors provided they take turns serving as virtual processors, this is called *banking processors*.

For example, the first level of DAG for summing the components of a vector of length 64 requires 32 processors (see Fig. 14). But suppose only 8 processors are available. In that case, real processor number 0 might play the role of virtual processors 0, 8, 16, and 24 on successive time steps. Continuing, real processor number p, $p = 1, \ldots, 7$, computes the node assigned to virtual processor v, where $v = p \mod N$ and $N = 8$ here.

Of course, this would be reflected in the schedule for the eight processors.

Speedup and Efficiency

The *speedup* $SU(p)$ of a parallelized calculation using p processors is defined as the time required for the calculation using one processor divided by the time required using p processors,

$$SU(p) = \frac{T_1}{T_p},$$

where T_1 and T_p are defined above.

As it is often used causally, it is not always clear to what time T_1 refers. It could refer to that of a standard benchmark algorithm, or maybe to the time for the best possible algorithm for the calculation (which may not yet be known) or maybe even a serial adaptation of the parallel algorithm. Hence it is important to be explicit about its meaning.

After speedup, another important consideration is the fraction of time the processors assigned to a computation are kept busy. This is called the *efficiency* of the parallelization using p processors and is defined by

$$Ef(p) = \frac{SU(p)}{p}.$$

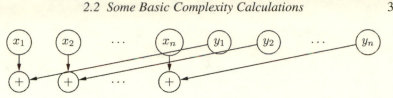

Fig. 13. DAG for vector addition.

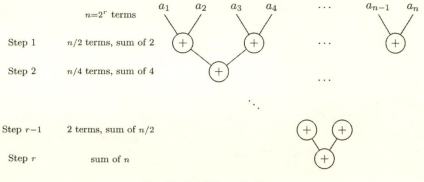

Fig. 14. DAG for reduction.

Efficiency measures the average time the p processors are working. If the speedup is *linear* meaning equal to p, then the efficiency will be 100%.

2.2 Some Basic Complexity Calculations

Vector Operation

As our first example, consider a vector operation such as the component by component addition of two vectors of size n. Given n processors, this can be done in one time step as follows: assign processor i to add the components $x_i + y_i$ in parallel with the other processors (see Fig. 13). So $T_\infty = 1$. Obviously $T_1 = n$ and so $SU_n = n$ and $EF_n = n/n = 1$.

Reduction

It is often necessary to derive a scalar value from a vector, one which depends on all the components of the vector. Any such operation is called a *reduction* or *fan-in*. The most common example is summing the components of a vector. Other examples are forming the minimum or maximum of the components.

Consider the task of summing the n components of a vector, $\sum_{i=1}^{n} a_i$. If n is a power of 2, $n = 2^r$ for some $r = 1, 2, \ldots$, then we could proceed as in Fig. 14.

The following is pseudocode for the case $n = 2^r$,

```
loop k = 1...r
    n ← n/2
    in parallel
        loop i = 1...n
            xᵢ ← xᵢ + xᵢ₊ₙ
        end loop
    synchronize
end loop
```

Evidently the time using one processor is $T_1 = n - 1$ since there are $n - 1$ indicated additions. As diagrammed, using $n/2$ processors the time is $r = \log n$. Additional processors do not improve the time so we have $T_\infty = T_{n/2} = \log n$. It follows that $SU(n/2) = \frac{n-1}{\log n}$. Since the full complement of processors is needed only for one step we expect the efficiency to be poor. Indeed we have $Ef(n/2) = \frac{2(n-1)}{n \log n} \approx \frac{2}{\log n}$, which tends to 0 in the limit, $Ef \to 0$ as $n \to \infty$.

If n is not an exact power of 2, for example $2^k < n < 2^{k+1}$, then simply add 0s to the sequence until n plus the number of added 0s is the next higher power of 2. This adds at most 1 to the time, that is to say, $r = \lceil \log n \rceil$, where the ceiling function, $\lceil \cdot \rceil$, is the smallest integer equal to or greater than (i.e., to the right of) $\log n$ on the real line. Hence the complexity is exactly written as $T_\infty = \lceil \log n \rceil$.

In reality, the 0s need not be added of course. For example, in summing $n = 5$ numbers, during the first time step the additions $a_1' = a_1 + a_2$ and $a_2' = a_3 + a_4$ take place; a_5 is not involved yet. Next in step 2, $a_1'' = a_1' + a_2'$, and finally in the third step, $sum = a_1'' + a_5$. Hence 3 steps are required, one more than the two required in summing four addends.

Recursive Doubling

Given a finite sequence of numbers, $a_1, a_2, \ldots, a_n$, compute the sequence of all partial sums (or all partial products),

$$s_1 = a_1$$
$$s_2 = a_1 + a_2$$
$$\vdots$$
$$s_n = a_1 + a_2 + \cdots + a_n.$$

This problem occurs, for example, in calculating a cumulative distribution function (cdf) from a discrete probability density function (pdf).

At first one might guess this will take more time than a simple reduction since n sums need to be formed. But in fact, the single processor time is the same, equal to $T_1 = n - 1$, and so is the parallel time. However more processors are needed in the parallel algorithm. The time for a single processor is obtained from the following algorithm:

```
s₁ ← a₁
loop k = 2...n
    sₖ ← sₖ₋₁ + aₖ
end loop
```

For the parallel algorithm, we proceed in steps. Again, assume that n is a power of 2.

Step 1

$$
\begin{matrix}
a_1 & & s_{11} \\
a_2 & a_1 & s_{12} \\
a_3 & a_2 & s_{23} \\
a_4 & + & a_3 & = & s_{34} \\
a_5 & a_4 & s_{45} \\
\vdots & \vdots & \vdots \\
a_{2^r} & a_{2^r-1} & s_{2^r-1,2^r}
\end{matrix}
\quad .
$$

Note that s_{ij} is the sum of a's from subscript i to and including subscript j. On each subsequent step, the column added in is begun twice as far down as the step before and, correspondingly, the number of correct sums doubles. Thus for step 2 we have

Step 2

$$
\begin{matrix}
s_{11} & & s_{11} \\
s_{12} & & s_{12} \\
s_{23} & s_{11} & s_{13} \\
s_{34} & + & s_{12} & = & s_{14} \\
s_{45} & s_{23} & s_{25} \\
\vdots & \vdots & \vdots \\
s_{2^r-1,2^r} & s_{2^r-3,2^r-2} & s_{2^r-3,2^r}
\end{matrix}
\quad .
$$

And continue for $r = \log 2$ iterations.

If n is not a power of 2, as above we proceed as if the complement to the next power of 2 is filled out with 0s. This adds 1 to the time.

We have the following results. Using 1 processor, $T_1 = n - 1$ and, using $p = n - 1$ processors, $T_\infty = T_{n-1} = r = \lceil \log n \rceil$. The speedup is $SU(n-1) = \frac{n-1}{\lceil \log n \rceil}$, and the efficiency is $Ef = \frac{1}{\lceil \log n \rceil}$. So the efficiency is better but still as $n \to \infty$, $Ef \to 0$.

Powers – Russian Peasant Algorithm

For a number a and a positive integer n, we want to compute all of its powers up to a^n. This is like the partial sums problem above, for products instead of sums, except that all terms of the sequence are the same, being equal to a. Appropriately, a simpler algorithm does the job. The algorithm described below is called the "Russian Peasant Algorithm" because it is similar to a multiplication technique of the same name. The technique relies on base 2 operations (doubling and halving).

Of course, using logarithms the problem can be solved in one (or constant) time with $n - 1$ processors since $a^k = e^{k \ln a}$. However, our intended application of this result is the computation of the powers of a matrix; thus, we are interested in a direct solution.

In the case of one processor, recursively compute $a^k = a * a^{k-1}$ for $k = 2, \ldots, n$; this requires $T_1 = n - 1$ units of time. In the parallel case, a solution is given in Fig. 15 for $n = 2^r$ a power of 2. As usual, if n is not a power of 2, then the time increases by 1.

We record the following results. Using 1 processor, $T_1 = n - 1$ and, using $p = n/2$ processors (in the last step), $T_\infty = T_{n/2} = r = \lceil \log n \rceil$. The speedup is $SU(n/2) = \frac{n-1}{\lceil \log n \rceil}$, and the efficiency is $Ef = \frac{2(n-1)}{n \lceil \log n \rceil}$.

Matrix Powers

For a given square matrix A of size $m \times m$, we want to calculate its powers A^2 through A^n. Again, if n is a power of 2, we proceed as in Fig. 15. However, now the multiplication at each node is a matrix–matrix product by square matrices of size $m \times m$.

In Section 4.3 we will consider matrix–matrix products in detail and examine various computational possibilities for the calculation. However, the complexity issue of the calculation is straightforward because each term of the resultant matrix is just the dot product of m-dimensional vectors. That is each element c_{ij} of the resultant matrix is the dot product of the ith row of the first factor with the jth column of the second. For each such calculation, use m processors to

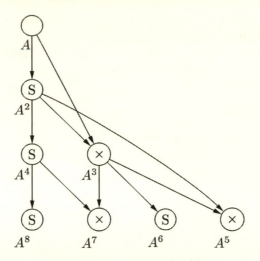

Fig. 15. Russian peasant algorithm.

do all the scalar multiplications in one time step, and then half of them, $m/2$, to
do the reduction sum of the resultant products. Thus we see that each c_{ij} takes
$1 + \lceil \log m \rceil$ time and uses m processors.

Since there are m^2 such dot products to compute for the matrix–matrix product, by using m^3 processors they can all be done in time $1 + \log m$. Hence, from
above, the entire calculation takes $\lceil \log n \rceil (1 + \lceil \log m \rceil)$ time and uses $p = \frac{n}{2} m^3$
processors.

The single processor time for this calculation takes $m + (m - 1)$ time for
each dot product, there are m^2 to do for each matrix–matrix product, and, as
above, $n - 1$ matrix products must be done. Hence $T_1 = (n - 1)m^2(2m - 1)$.
Therefore, the speedup is

$$SU(nm^3/2) = \frac{(n - 1)(2m - 1)m^2}{\lceil \log n \rceil (1 + \lceil \log m \rceil)} \approx 2nm^3/(\log n \ \log m).$$

The efficiency is

$$Ef \approx \frac{4nm^3}{nm^3 \ \log n \ \log m}.$$

2.3 Data Dependencies

A loop can be executed in parallel when the results are independent of the order
in which the iterations are done. A data dependency occurs when a variable is set
in one iteration of the loop and read in another. We categorize several types of

dependencies: contention, induction variable, forward dependency, backward dependency, and run-time break.

With regard to the pseudocode below, the variable "id" is unique for each process and takes on the values $0, 1, \ldots,$ nprocs $- 1$ up to the number of processes less 1.

Contention

A variable is both read and written in the same loop. A correct result occurs only if access to the variable is synchronized.

```
/* access to the variable sum must be synchronized */

    sum ← 0;
    loop i = 1...n
        sum ← sum + aᵢ;
    end loop
```

Suppose that this loop were carried out by two processes with the value of $n = 2$; thus, at the end of the loop we want sum $= a_1 + a_2$. Both might access sum when its value is 0, each then adds its component of the vector a; the final result will be either a_1 or a_2, depending on which process wrote last.

Induction Variable

An induction variable is one that is defined in terms of itself such as i in the next example. The input is a list of floating point values $p_1, p_2, \ldots, p_n$ with $n = 2k$. The objective is to form two arrays of ordered pairs $x_1 = p_1, y_1 = p_2,$ $x_2 = p_3, y_2 = p_4, \ldots, x_k = p_{n-1}, y_k = p_n$.

```
/* the variable i is both read and written in the loop */
    i ← 0;
    loop k = 1...n
        i ← i + 1;
        xₖ ← pᵢ;
        i ← i + 1;
        yₖ ← pᵢ;
    end loop
```

If the loop is executed with index $k = 2$ before $k = 1$, then $x_2 = p_1$ instead of the intended $x_1 = p_1$.

Forward Dependency

As an example, suppose it is desired to shift an entire array of values each to one index lower, $x_i \leftarrow x_{i+1}, i = 1, \ldots, n$. (Assume that the original x_1 is to be discarded.)

```
loop i = 1...n
    xᵢ ← xᵢ₊₁;
end loop
```

Here x_1 is intended to be set to the original value of x_2, but if loop index $i = 2$ is the first one to execute, then x_2 will be changed beforehand. In fact, if the loop were executed in reverse order, then all values will be set to x_{n+1}.

All the variables x_i for $i = 2, \ldots, n$ are both written to and read in the loop. In the correct execution order, each is read *before* it is written hence a *forward dependency*. A forward dependency such as this can be overcome by utilizing a temporary array to hold the original values. For example,

```
in parallel
loop i = 2...n + 1
    tempᵢ ← xᵢ;
end loop
synchronize
in parallel
loop i = 1...n
    xᵢ ← tempᵢ₊₁;
end loop
```

Of course, the new code fragment is now twice the work so speedup is halved.

Another solution is to *block schedule* the loop. Suppose n is even, $n = 2k$, and two processes are to do the work. The first handles indices $1, \ldots, k$ and the second handles $k + 1, \ldots, 2k$. Now only the original value x_{k+1} has to be saved (for symmetry x_{n+1} can be too).

```
in parallel
if ( id == 0 ) {
    Bstart ← 1;
    Bend ← k - 1;
    temp ← xₖ₊₁;
}
else {
    Bstart ← k + 1;
    Bend ← n - 1;
```

```
    temp ← x_{n+1};
}
synchronize //x_k+1 must be saved before proceeding
in parallel
loop i = Bstart...Bend
    x_i ← x_{i+1};
end loop
x_{Bend+1} ← temp;
```

Of course, in this code fragment it is assumed that *id*, *i*, *Bstart*, *Bend*, and *temp* are private variables. It is further assumed to be synchronized so that the *temp* variables are written before the loop executes.

Backward or Recursion Dependency

Here, as in mathematical recursion, a variable at one index is defined in terms of itself at smaller indices. For example, the partial sums problem has a recursion dependency

```
    s_1 ← a_1;
    loop i = 2...n
        s_i ← s_{i-1} + a_i;
    end loop
```

This example fails the Cray "ABC" test (see Section 3.6).

Several examples of recursion are given in the problems at the end of this chapter.

Another recursion example in a slightly different form is the following:

```
    loop i
        if (x_i == 0) x_i ← f(x_{i-1});
        else x_i ← g(x_i);
    end loop
```

Run-Time Break

A run-time break occurs, for example, when a sequence of data is being processed and is supposed to stop the first time a flag occurs. This can happen in a code to add the terms of a positive sequence until encountering the first term less than 10^{-16} say.

2.4 Programming Aids

An important programming aid is a *debugger*. There are very good debuggers available for understanding the execution of parallel (and nonparallel) code. For the GNU family of compilers, try gdb. An excellent graphical front-end for gdb and other text level debuggers is ddd. On Solaris platforms dbx is a good choice.

In addition, there are profiling utilities that we mentioned in the last chapter.

Exercises

1. (3) Let c_i denote cities whose map coordinates, (x_i, y_i) $i = 0, 1, \ldots, n$, are given. Let $t = (c_0, c_1, \ldots, c_n, c_0)$ be a "tour" of the cities which starts in city c_0, proceeds to c_1, then c_2 and so on back to c_0. Can the calculation of the length of the tour be done in parallel? Make a DAG of this calculation.

2. (4) Carefully write pseudocode for calculating all powers of x up to $n = 2^r$ by the Russian Peasant algorithm. Pay attention to the loop indices.

3. (3) Carefully write pseudocode for performing a fan-in, a sum say, of $n = 2^r$ numbers. Pay attention to the loop indices.

4. (6) Carefully write pseudocode for calculating all the partial sums of a list of $n = 2^r$ numbers. Pay attention to the loop indices.

5. (3) Given a sequence $a_1, a_2, \ldots, a_n$, show how to calculate all partial products $p_1 = a_1$, $p_2 = a_1 a_2, \ldots, p_n = a_1 a_2 \ldots a_n$, in $O(\log n)$ time.

6. (3) Show that the calculation of all the matrix products $A^2, A^3, \ldots, A^n$, can be done in $O(\log m \cdot \log n)$ time where A is an $m \times m$ matrix. How many processors are required? (It is not necessary to write pseudocode to answer this question.)

7. (5) Investigate a modified fan-in algorithm in which p processors divide the n summands into blocks of size n/p. Each processor adds the terms of its block serially. Then processing switches to the usual fan-in algorithm. For a fan-in of $n = 2^r$ elements, and, with r a power of 2 dividing n, plot *SU*, *Ef*, and the product *SU*Ef* as functions of r for (a) $p = r$, and (b) $p = 2^r / r$. (This is a theoretical plot, although feel free to code it and get results if you like.)

8. (4) Show that the evaluation of an nth degree polynomial can be done in $O(\log n)$ time. How many processors are required?

9. (5) (a) Show that the complexity, T_∞, for squaring an $n \times n$ matrix A is $O(\log n)$ time using n^3 processors. (b) What is T_{n^2}? (c) What is T_n? (Hint: All rows and columns can be done in parallel, the operation for a row and column is basically a dot product.)

10. (4) For the vector linear recurrence

$$x(t+1) = A(t)x(t) + u(t),$$

where $A(t)$ is a given $m \times m$ matrix and $u(t)$ a given m-dimensional vector for all $t = 0, 1, \ldots, n-1$, obtain an $O(\log m \cdot \log n)$ time parallel algorithm for computing the m-dimensional vector $x(n)$. Assume that $x(0)$ is also given.

11. (3) Make a DAG of the three code segments in the subsection headed "Forward Dependency."

12. (8) Let $p(x) = a_0 + a_1 x + a_2 x^2 + \cdots + a_n x^n$ be a polynomial of degree $n = r2^r$ for some positive integer r. Analyze the complexity and the number of processors needed in the following method for evaluating it. First, write p in the form

$$p(x) = a_0 + q_1(x) + x^r q_2(x) + x^{2r} q_3(x) + \cdots + x^{(s-1)r} q_s(x)$$

where $s = 2^r$ and

$$q_i(x) = a_k x + \cdots + a_{k+r-1} x^r, \quad k = (i-1)r + 1.$$

Now perform the following steps:

a. compute $x^2, \ldots, x^r$;
b. compute $q_1(x), \ldots, q_s(x)$;
c. compute $x^r, x^{2r}, \ldots, x^{(s-1)r}$;
d. multiply $x^r q_2(x), x^{2r} q_3(x), \ldots, x^{(s-1)r} q_s(x)$;
e. add $a_0 + q_1(x) + x^r q_2(x) + \cdots + x^{(s-1)r} q_s(x)$.

13. (5) Let A be an $n \times n$ upper triangular matrix such that $a_{ii} \neq 0$ for $1 \leq i \leq n$, and let b be an n-dimensional vector. The *Back Substitution* method to solve the linear system $Ax = b$ begins with determining x_n by solving the scalar equation $a_{nn} x_n = b_n$. Then x_{n-1} is determined by solving $a_{n-1,n-1} x_{n-1} + a_{n-1,n} x_n = b_{n-1}$ and so on. See p. 132. Let G be the DAG for back substitution. (a) Determine an optimal schedule for G using $p = n - 1$ processors. What is the speedup? (b) Can the calculation be done faster with $p > n$? (c) What about with $p = n$?

14. (5) Write a pseudocode for a shared memory computer to perform a back substitution as described above, using p processors where p evenly divides n.

15. (6) A first-order linear recurrence has the form

$$y_1 = b_1$$
$$y_i = a_i y_{i-1} + b_i, \quad 2 \leq i \leq n$$

(a) Show that a first-order linear recurrence can be computed in $O(\log n)$ time using how many processors? (b) Show that polynomial evaluation by nested multiplication is a first-order linear recurrence. (c) Show that Back Substitution is a (vector) first-order linear recurrence. (That is, y_i and b_i are vectors and a_i is a matrix). Find the complexity if a_i is an $m \times m$ matrix.

16. (4) For the scalar difference equation

$$x(t + 1) = a(t)x(t) + b(t)x(t - 1), \quad t = 0, 1, 2, \ldots, n - 1$$

consider the problem of computing $x(n)$. The inputs are $x(-1)$, $x(0)$, $a(0), \ldots, a(n - 1)$, $b(0), \ldots, b(n - 1)$. Assuming as many processors as needed, find an algorithm that takes $O(\log n)$ time. Hint: Write the difference equation in vector form and reduce the problem to the multiplication of n 2×2 matrices.

Construct and analyze a DAG for the following six problems. That is, find the optimal time T_∞, find the optimal speedup SU, and find the best efficiency *for this speedup*.

17. (4) Computing a 3×3 by 3×1 matrix product (matrix–vector product). Generalize to an $n \times n$ matrix by n vector product.

18. (3) Computing the dot product of two n vectors.

19. (4) Computing a 3×3 matrix by 3×3 matrix product. Generalize the result to $n \times n$ matrices.

20. (5) Squaring a symmetric $n \times n$ matrix.

21. (3) Calculating all the powers $x^2, x^3, \ldots, x^n$, of x.

22. (7) (a) Evaluating a polynomial directly. (b) Evaluating a polynomial by nested multiplication (synthetic division).

23. (3) Consider the following parallel extension of the bisection method for root finding. On beginning, $b > a$ and $f(a) * f(b) < 0$. With p equal to the number of processes, the interval $[a, b]$ is uniformly divided into $p + 1$ subintervals, $d = (b - a)/(p + 1)$, $x_1 = a + d$, $x_2 = a + 2d$, $\ldots$, $x_p = a + pd$. The kth process evaluates $f(x_k)$; then the first change in sign is detected, that is, the smallest k such that $f(x_k) * f(x_{k+1}) < 0$; a and b are updated, $a \leftarrow x_k$, $b \leftarrow x_{k+1}$; and the process repeats. Show what parts of this algorithm can run in parallel and what parts run serially. How must the parallel processes be synchronized?

3

Machine Implementations

High-performance computation was first realized in the form of SIMD parallelism with the introduction of the Cray and Cyber computers. At first these were single processor machines, but starting with the Cray XMP series, multiprocessor vector processors gained the further advantages of MIMD parallelism. Today, vector processing can be incorporated into the architecture of the CPU chip itself as is the case with the old AltiVec processor used in the MacIntosh.

The UNIX operating system introduced a design for shared memory MIMD parallel programming. The components of the system included multitasking, time slicing, semaphores, and the fork function. If the computer itself had only one CPU, then parallel execution was only apparent, called *concurrent* execution, nevertheless the C programming language allowed the creation of parallel code. Later multiprocessor machines came on line, and these parallel codes executed in true parallel.

Although these tools continue to be supported by operating systems today, the fork model to parallel programming proved too "expensive" in terms of startup time, memory usage, context switching, and overhead. Threads arose in the search for a better soluton, and resulted in a software revolution. The threads model neatly solves most of the low-level hardware and software implementation issues, leaving the programmer free to concentrate on the the essential logical or synchronization issues of a parallel program design. Today, all popular operating systems support thread style concurrent/parallel processing.

In this chapter we will explore vector and parallel programming in the context of scientific and engineering numerical applications. The threads model and indeed parallel programming in general is most easily implemented on the shared memory multiprocessor architecture.

However, distributed memory systems are more readily available and cheaper to build, indeed many exist without additional cost as local area networks (LANs). With the advent of MPI (message passing interface) and other high-quality distributed memory parallel compilation/execution systems, there is every advantage to be gained by making use of these systems. MPI is widely available with both free and vendor supplied implementations. Our introduction in this chapter shows how easy MPI is to use and why it is fast becoming a standard.

3.1 Early Underpinnings of Parallelization – Multiple Processes

Early computers could execute only one program at a time, starting from punch cards dropped into a reader and ending with punch cards representing the output. It was quickly realized that this computational model wasted too many valuable CPU cycles. Thus was born the concept of multitasking, time-slicing, and the computer process. A *process* consists of an execution stream, resources such as a stack and file descriptors, and address space. A process executes for a short period of time, a time slice, and then the *CPU state* is saved, that is the values of its internal registers including the PC and stack pointer, and some other process executes (see Fig. 2, p. 5). This is called a *context switch*. Later the process will be brought back to execution picking up exactly where it was stopped as if nothing had happened. In this way, the CPU can do useful work on a second process while some slow event is occurring, such as I/O, on the first one. And of course, many user jobs are performed seemingly simultaneously.

The Fork Operation

In the process model, a parallel computation is initiated by means of the `fork()` system call. When the fork instruction is encountered in the execution of a program, the operating system makes an exact duplicate of the program in a new address space creating a new process called the *child*. (Nowadays, the copy is made by the technique of *copy-on-write* meaning the copy is made only if some memory must be modified.) The original process is the *parent*. Now both processes execute *concurrently*, meaning, on a uniprocessor computer each executes during its time slice which is arbitrarily interleaved with those of the other executing processes on the system. On a multiprocessor computer, as many processes execute simultaneously as there are processors. Thus the parent and the child run in true parallel in this case.

The child process is a duplicate of the parent in that the execution stream, the global and static data, the local data (automatic data), the stack, and the internal state of the CPU are duplicated. (Memory addresses are appropriately modified in order that the child process runs in its new address space.) However there is one difference between the two, the return value of the `fork()` function itself. This permits the two processes to follow independent courses from then on. The child's return value is 0 while the parent's return value is the process identification number (pid) of the child, this is always positive.

Parallel programming would not get far without the ability to transmit data and messages between processes. On a multiprocessor computer the simplest solution to this problem is shared memory. Not only does shared memory obviate the need to transmit updates to data sets as processing proceeds – since changes are written directly and seen immediately by the other processes, but also it obviates the need for keeping multiple copies of the same, possibly large, data sets at all. Shared memory is another exception to the exact duplication rule of the fork() function.

As an example of parallelization by the fork model, consider the following simple program, in pseudocode, for adding the values of x_1, x_2, x_3, and x_4.

```
/* Program using two processes for adding x₁,x₂,x₃,x₄ */
shared data :
  x₁,x₂,x₃,x₄, child's_sum, parent's_sum
unshared data :
  id, i, nprocs, sum
program begin
  nprocs ← 2;
  read_values_of(x₁,x₂,x₃,x₄);
  sum ← 0;
  id = fork();
  if ( id == 0 ) i ← 1;  else  i ← 2;

  loop  while  i < = 4
    sum ← sum + xᵢ;
    i ← i + nprocs;
  end  loop
  if ( id == 0 )
    child's_sum ← sum;
    exit();
  end  if
  else  parent's_sum ← sum;
  print  child's_sum + parent's_sum;
program end
```

The program starts by initializing nprocs to 2, sum to 0 and the *x* values as desired in a subroutine perhaps. Then it forks. The operating system creates a second, nearly identical, copy of the program, namely the child. Actually this is easy for the operating system to do since one of its basic tasks is to load and begin the execution of programs. The child process in our example has its own separate copy of id, i, nprocs, and sum. The last three have the same values as the parent, namely nprocs is 2, sum is 0, and i is the same also although the latter's value has not been set by the program up to now. However the value of id is different between the parent and the child; the child's value is 0 while the parent's is nonzero. Of course, the variable id must never be in shared memory. The shared data has also not been duplicated. Both parent and child can read or modify it. It would be undesirable to duplicate a large amount of data in a fork operation. Furthermore, the two processes can communicate through the shared memory. Near the end of this program, the child will communicate its sum to the parent process through shared memory.

The work of the program has been divided up in advance by the programmer and fixed in the code, the child will add the odd terms, the parent the even ones. This is said to be *static scheduling*.

One consequence of the operation as described above is that the programmer cannot anticipate the relative rates of execution of the two processes. It may well happen in our example that the child process is held up to a greater extent than the parent with the result that the latter arrives at the print statement before the child has written its sum to shared memory. Hence the reported value for the sum in this program is unreliable. This is an example of a *race condition* since the correct result depends on which process wins the race to the update statement.

Before discussing synchronization mechanisms, we note at this point that the fork operation is a relatively time-consuming one. Space must be found in memory, and the entire program must be read from memory and transferred to the other place with all addresses modified – this could require disk access – a stack created and initialized and so on.

Barriers

A *barrier* is a means for achieving sychronization at designated places in the source code. Associated with a barrier is a specific number of processes, for example, N. Every process arriving at the barrier must wait until all N reach that point, then they are all released. When all processes have arrived at and been released from the barrier, it is automatically reinitialized and can be used again.

This is just the sort of synchronization device to solve the *race condition* above. Consider a modification of the program above by the addition of a barrier named, say, A.

```
/* Program using two processes for adding x₁,x₂,x₃,x₄ */
shared   data :
  x₁,x₂,x₃,x₄, child's_sum, parent's_sum

unshared  data :
  id, i, nprocs, sum

program begin
  nprocs ← 2;

  initialize_barrier(A,nprocs);

  read_values_of(x₁,x₂,x₃,x₄);
  sum ← 0;
  id = fork ();
  if ( id == 0 ) i ← 1;  else  i ← 2;
  loop  while  i <= 4
    sum ← sum + xᵢ;
    i ← i + nprocs;
  end  loop
  if ( id == 0 )
    child's_sum ← sum;
  else  parent's_sum ← sum;

  barrier(A);
  if ( id == 0 ) exit();

  print  child's_sum + parent's_sum;
program end
```

Now the first process to arrive at the barrier waits until the second arrives. Therefore, when the print statement is reached, both processes have written their computed values into shared memory.

Actually barriers were not implemented per se in early operating systems; instead, they could be effected by a more general synchronization mechanism known as a *semaphore* (see [2, 3]).

Mutexes

Situations arise in parallel computation in which data must be modified by only one process at a time. In our example, suppose the x's are computed by a function g, that is $x_i = g(i)$, but the time required for the computation very much depends on i. In this case we want to *dynamically schedule* the calculation of x_i so that any process ready to do work takes the next index.

To implement dynamic scheduling, we need a *shared index si* and a way to synchronize access to it – only one process at a time must be allowed to change its value. This is the purpose of a *mutex*, to make small sections of code *mut*ually *ex*clusive.

Here is the modification to our previous example. We assume the function $g(i)$ is implemented externally.

```
/* Using a mutex to implement dynamic scheduling */

shared  data:
  si, x₁,x₂,x₃,x₄, child's_sum, parent's_sum
  LOCK: lok

unshared  data:
  id, i, nprocs, sum

program begin
  nprocs ← 2;
  si ← 0;
  initialize_barrier(A,nprocs);
  sum ← 0;
  id = fork ();
  loop
    mutex_lock(lok);
      i ← si;
      si ← si + 1;
    mutex_unlock(lok);
    if ( i > 4 ) break loop;
    sum ← sum + g(i);
  end  loop
  if ( id == 0 )
    child's_sum ← sum;
  else  parent's_sum ← sum;
  barrier(A);
  if ( id == 0 ) exit();
  print  child's_sum + parent's_sum;
program end
```

The first process to enter the loop grabs the lock. In the locked code, a process gets the next index and corresponding bit of work to do. Next the shared index is incremented and, very importantly, the process unlocks the lock. A mutex is implemented by means of a memory cell that can be tested and set in one indivisible atomic operation.

The work of the loop will be done when the shared index, and hence also the local index, exceeds 4 in this example. Until then, depending on how fast a process can do a given piece of work, it returns to the top of the loop and gets another index to work on.

Without the synchronization enforced by the mutex, it could happen that one process gets a value of si but before incrementing and writing it back, its timeslice is up; this is called *preemption*. Then another process accesses si and so gets the same value. With mutual exclusion however, and assuming the shared index is not modified anywhere else in the program, it is guaranteed that all indices will be done once and only once.

What happens to a process that attempts to acquire a locked mutex? For processes there are two solutions with complimentary benefits, the *busy wait* and the *sleep wait*. In the busy wait solution, during its timeslice, a waiting process repeatedly tries to acquire the lock in a tight programming loop; that is, it *spins*. The drawback of this is that until the lock frees up, these spin cycles waste computer time. The advantage is simplicity and low overhead.

In the alternative, sleep wait, the process is placed on a sleep queue until the lock becomes available. This solution requires the operating system to provide some mechanism for determining the availability of the lock and a means for selecting which process to wake up if there is more than one waiting. The disadvantage of this method is that it could take more computer time to put the process to sleep and wake it up than spinning. And it requires more programming and more memory to implement.

Solutions to this problem are vendor specific.

3.2 Threads Programming

While the fork operation can form the basis of a method for parallel execution, it has the drawback of being "expensive" in that it takes considerable time and kernel resources to set up and maintain the separate processes. Threads provide an alternative model. A *thread* is a line or flow of control through a program. In the threads model, there is no code duplication. Furthermore, threads provide an elegant solution to the problem of shared memory versus unshared memory.

To grasp how threads work, return to the von Neumann programming model and consider what happens when a subroutine executes. Processing begins by creating, on the stack, all the variables local to the routine. Processing then continues in the subroutine until a return statement is encountered (or an implicit return at the end of the subroutine). The local variables disappear upon exit and any return value is passed back via a CPU register.

Now consider the possibility of parallelizing such a subroutine by merely providing a separate program counter and private stack for each line of execution! Such a thread inherits the CPU state with its program counter pointing to the subroutine and its stack pointer pointing to its private stack area. When the thread begins executing, it is in that subroutine and any local variables are created on its own stack. Therefore the unshared data between different threads are the local variables of the subroutine while all other program data are shared. No code duplication is required since all such sibling threads use the same physical code of the subroutine.

There remains the problem of scheduling CPU time for a thread in order for it to execute. Threads are not mapped onto processes. Processes do not share address space, but it is often advantageous to allow multiple threads to work within the address space of a process to cooperate in completing the work of the process. These are referred to as *sibling threads*. Furthermore, a process consumes more in the way of operating system resources than what is needed for a thread. As a result, a thread is executed by what is known as a *light weight process* (LWP).

There are three models for scheduling threads onto LWPs: many to one, one to one, or many to many [4]. In the many-to-one model, a program can create a large number of threads if needed but program execution goes no faster on a multiproccessor computer since only one thread at a time is on an LWP. In the one-to-one model, there can be only a limited number of threads for the same reason as there can be only a limited number of processes – limited kernel resources. However, the many-to-many has neither restriction, its drawback being the difficulty in its implementation, which is largely a solved problem.

In the many-to-many model, the operating system maintains a pool of LWPs for the purpose of executing threads. Usually there are many more threads than LWPs so threads take turns or *multiplex* among themselves for the use of an LWP [3]. This context switching among threads is performed by the thread library and not by the kernel.

The following discussion about threads is generic. The ideas presented are universal among computer vendors even though various application programming interfaces (APIs) can differ significantly [4].

Mutexes, Barriers, and Condition Variables

Thread mutexes work exactly like those discussed in the previous section for processes. To use a mutex, a thread first trys its lock. If the lock is open, the thread gains access to the protected section of code while simultaneously closing the lock. Only one thread can execute in the locked section of code at a time. Upon leaving this guarded region, the thread must unlock the mutex. If the mutex is already locked when a thread tries for it, then the thread *sleeps* until the mutex becomes unlocked.

Mutexes are used to protect access to data, to ensure that data are consistent. The section of code in which this occurs is called a *critical section*. Since other threads which require access to a locked critical section must wait, critical sections should be kept as short as possible as that can significantly affect the performance of the program.

Although a mutex is intended to protect data, in reality it protects a critical section of code. If the same data is accessed at several places in the program, then the same mutex must be used at each place.

As discussed above, a barrier-type synchronization provides a rendezvous point for all threads coooperating in the barrier. But, for the most part, the similarity to process style barriers ends there. Instead threads adopt the *thread join* solution for this functionality. Essentially, thread join is a one-time barrier. Since threads are cheap and quick to create and exit, a thread that must not contiune until several other threads complete other task, waits to "join" with them, one by one. When two threads join, one of them goes away, that is, *exits*. After the designated siblings have all joined, the one remaining thread is allowed to continue.

If the true barrier functionality is needed, it is possible is to write one's own barrier using condition variables (discussed below) (see [5]).

To illustrate these ideas, we revisit the dynamically scheduled vector sum program, this time using 3 worker threads to sum 10 terms. By the nature of threads, the parallel work must be done in subroutines.

```
/* Program to add x₁, x₂,..., x₁₀ */
    global data
        float: sum, x[1...10];
        integer: n=10, nthreads=3, si=1; //initialize
            shared index to 1
        mutex: lokA, lokB; //to protect the shared index
            and the global sum

    program begin

        thread_t workerId[3]; //create 3 worker id's of
            type thread_t
/*-- create nthreads threads and send them to work --*/
        loop  i=1..nthreads
            thread_create(&workerId[i],work(),NULL);
                // no args for work()
```

```
        end loop
        loop  i=1..nthreads
            thread_join(workerId[i]);
        end loop
        print ("global sum is ",sum);
    program end
/*****/
    work()
    begin
        integer: i, myid;
        float: mysum=0;
        myid = thread_self();


        loop
        {
            mutex_lock(lokA);
                i ← si; si ← si + 1;
            mutex_unlock(lokA);
            if( i > n ) break;
            mysum ← mysum + x_i;
            if(myid == 1) //thread 1 quits after one term
            {
                mutex_lock(lokB);
                    sum ← sum + mysum;
                mutex_unlock(lokB);
                    thr_exit();
            }
        end loop
/*-- begin  locked code --*/
            mutex_lock(lokB);
                sum ← sum + mysum;
            mutex_unlock(lokB);
        end
```

In this threaded program the unshared data is the data local to the subroutine work, namely the looping index i, the identity variable myid, and the thread's component of the sum, mysum. In particular, the vector to be summed is in global, and therefore, shared memory, and does not have to be duplicated (*n* might be very big).

The program begins with the main thread creating `nthreads` number of worker threads and setting them to work in the subroutine `work`. The call `thread_create` is handled by the thread library, which creates each thread and establishes an identity for it. This identity, a unique small integer, is accessible via the call `thread_self`.

After creating the threads, the main thread waits for them to complete their work by "joining" with each of them. The order of joining does not matter, the main thread will not advance beyond the loop until all threads have joined in. Hence this section of code acts like a barrier.

In the subroutine `work`, each thread obtains an index `i` to work on from the global variable `si` in the critcal section protected by `lokA`.

After adding the designated term to its local sum, all threads but one return to the top of the loop to seek another index. (The one exiting early is done for purely demonstration purposes.) When all the work is done, each of these remaining threads exits the loop and adds its local sum into the global sum. For this, exclusive access to the shared variable `sum` is needed; hence, this step must be done in the *mutex* `lokB`.

To demonstrate `thread_exit`, one of the threads exits after summing just one term. This call is the opposite effect of `thread_create`; it terminates a thread. A thread may call exit on another thread or on itself. Moreover, when a thread reaches the end of its initial subroutine, `work` in the example, then an *implicit call to exit* is made for the thread. This is exactly the fate of the other threads when they reached the end of `work`.

Of course, the early exiting thread must also combine its local sum with the global sum. Even though it is exiting early, there is no guarantee that its attempt to access the shared `sum` will be safe. Hence that must be done in a critical section. Notice that the same mutex, `lokB`, must be used to protect the global sum.

Finally, back in the main program, it is safe for the main thread to print the global sum only after all worker threads have exited. The thread join loop ensures this. It does not matter in which order the `thread_exit` by an exiting thread and the `thread_join()` by the joining thread occurs.

The main thread is special in only one way; when it reaches the end of `main`, it implicitly calls exit for the process (as well as itself). This will exit not only the main thread but also all threads associated with the process.

Otherwise the main thread is the same as its siblings. For example, it could call `thread_exit` on itself after creating the sibling threads thereby preventing the implicit process exit since it would never reach the end of `main`. In this case, some other sibling thread would have to print the combined sum before reaching the end of `work`.

Condition Variables

A *condition variable* is a device for notifying an interested thread of an event or condition having occurred. This makes it possible for a thread to suspend its activity until the condition has been satisfied. It is implemented as a structure incorporating a mutex together with a variable or variables that constitute the condition.

When a thread succeeds in acquiring the mutex, it tests whether the condition has been satisfied; it will have exclusive access to the condition at this time. If so, the thread continues with its execution and releases the mutex when appropriate. On the other hand, if the condition has not been completely satisfied, then the mutex is released automatically and the thread is put to sleep to wait on the condition becoming true. When some other thread changes one of the condition variables, it sends a signal, which wakes up some sleeping thread. This thread then automatically reacquires the mutex and, very importantly, reevaluates the condition. Just as before, if the condition evaluates to true then the thread continues, otherwise it is put back to sleep.

We will encounter condition variables again when taking up Java threads.

Because creating a thread is very fast and cheap, many threads can be created. In the example below we implement the Russian Peasant Algorithm, using one thread per multiplication. Hence the implemention of the computation closely follows its DAG diagram.

An implementation of the Russian Peasant Algorithm

```
/* Program to calculate the powers of x */
/* The power xⁿ will be stored in yₙ */
      global data
         float: x, y[1...32];

      program begin
      integer: k, i, n;
         y₁ ← x;
         n ← 1;
         loop  k=1...5  // 5 = log(32)
/*-- create one thread for  each product --*/
            loop  i=1...n
               thread_create(mult(),n);  // pass the value
                                          //of n to mult()
            end loop
            while ( thread_join() == 0 );  // barrier
            n ← 2*n;
```

```
        end loop
    program end
/*****/
    mult(integer: n)
    begin
    integer: i;
        i = thread_self();   // who am I
        y_{i+n} ← y_i*y_n;
    end
```

Deadlock

Deadlock is a situation where one or more threads are unable to continue execution because they are waiting on acquiring a mutex which, due to programming logic, will never happen.

The simplest case is when a thread, executing in a locked section of code, attempts to reacquire the mutex. This will be impossible because the mutex is locked and hence the thread will be unable to proceed. But for that reason the thread will be unable to release the lock as well.

Of course, this case is easy enough to avoid.

A more subtle case occurs when a thread needs to acquire two mutexes, say A and B, to complete its work. One thread grabs the lock to A but before it can get B, some other thread gets B. Then the first will not be able to get B and the second will not be able to get A. So the two are deadlocked and nothing short of exit will aleviate their mutual problem.

This second situation can be avoided by making threads acquire the two locks in a specific order, A first, and then B.

3.3 Java Threads

Threads are built into the Java programming language. The object-oriented structure of the language dovetails naturally with threads making their use comfortable and convenient. Quite simply, an instantiated[1] object can be run in its own thread. For synchronization, Java uses mutexes, condition variables, and thread join.

In addition, there has been an effort to formulate a basic scientific computational package in the Java programming language. One of these is "Colt," see http://hoschek.home.cern.ch/hoschek/colt/.

---

[1] In object-oriented programming, instantiated means to create an instance of.

Two Styles of Threaded Programming

One way to execute an object as a thread is to extend or subclass the Thread class. Alternatively one can implement the Runnable interface. These two methods are illustrated in the following matrix multiply programs, $y = Ax$.

Matrix A and vector x are created in `main` and passed to the instantiated objects. One object is created to calculate each row. The result is written into the appropriate component of the statically allocated resultant vector y, namely the component corresponding to the object's id. In the Java language, a thread created and assigned to an object begins executing in the object's `run()` method. Finally, as for threads generally, Java supports thread `join()` as a barrier synchronization device. This forces the main thread to wait until all threads have completed their calculation before printing the result (of one component).

Technique by extending the thread class

```java
import java.io.*;

public class
matMultSubclass extends Thread
{
    public static final int N = 400;
    public static double[] y = new double[N];
    private int id;
    private double[][] A;
    private double[] x;

    public
    matMultSubclass(int myid, double[][] A, double[] x)
    {
        id = myid;   this.A = A;   this.x = x;
    }
    public void
    run()
    {
        for (int j=0;   j<x.length;   ++j)
            y[id] += A[id][j]*x[j];
    }
    public static void
    main(String args[])
    {
        double[][] A = new double[N][N];
```

```
      double[] x = new double[N];
      Thread[] mMS = new matMultSubclass[N];   //one thread
         //per row initialize the data
      for ( int i=0;  i<N;  ++i )
      {
         x[i] = 1;
         for ( int j=0;  j<N;  ++j )
            A[i][j] = 1;
      }
         //instantiate the row calculators
      for ( int i=0;  i<N;  ++i )
      {
         mMS[i] = new matMultSubclass(i,A,x);
         mMS[i].start();
      }
         //wait for  them to finish
      try {
         for ( int i=0;  i<N;  ++i ) mMS[i].join();
      }
      catch(InterruptedException e) {}
      System.out.println("y[0]= " +y[0]);
   }
}
```

Technique by implementing the Runnable interface

```
import java.io.*;

public class
matMultRunnable implements Runnable
{
    public static final int N = 400;
    public static double[] y = new double[N];
    private int id;
    private double[][] A;
    private double[] x;

    public
    matMultRunnable(int myid, double[][] A, double[] x)
    {
        id = myid;  this.A = A;  this.x = x;
    }
    public void
```

```
run()
{
   for ( int j=0;  j<x.length;  ++j )
      y[id] += A[id][j]*x[j];
}
public static void
main(String args[])
{
   double[][] A = new double[N][N];
   double[] x = new double[N];
   Runnable[] mMS = new matMultRunnable[N];
      //one thread per row
   Thread[] th = new Thread[N];

      //initialize the data
   for ( int i=0;  i<N;  ++i )
   {
      x[i] = 1;
      for ( int j=0;  j<N;  ++j )
         a[i][j] = 1;
   }
      //instantiate the row calculators
   for ( int i=0;  i<N;  ++i )
   {
      mMS[i] = new matMultRunnable(i,A,x);
      th[i] = new Thread(mMS[i]);
      th[i].start();
   }
      //wait for  them to finish
   try {
      for ( int i=0;  i<N;  ++i ) th[i].join();
   }
   catch(InterruptedException e) {}

   System.out.println("y[0]= " +y[0]);
}
}
```

Every Object Has a Mutex

In Java, every object has an associated mutex, which can be used, for example, to protect its fields. In addition, every class has a mutex associated with it as well. Invoking the mutex of an object is as simple as marking one or more of its

methods as synchronized. If more than one method is so marked, then they
are all protected by the same mutex. It is also possible to name the object whose
mutex is to be used as an argument to sychronized().

In the next example we implement dynamic scheduling to add the elements
of an array using a mutex to protect the static shared index si.

Dynamic Scheduling in Java

```
import java.io.*;

class dynamSched implements Runnable
{
    private static int si=0;
    private static int N=1000000;
    private static int[] x;

//sss===
    public void
    run()
    {
        int i=0;
        int mysum=0;

        for (;;)
        {
            synchronized(this)
            {
                i = si++; //short for i = si; si = si + 1
            }
            if ( i>=N ) break;
            mysum += x[i]; //short for mysum = mysum +x[i]
        }
        System.out.println(Thread.currentThread().getName()+
            " gets mysum= "+mysum);
    }
//mmm===
    public static void
    main(String[] args)
    {
        x = new int[N];
        for ( int i=0;  i<N;  ++i ) x[i] = 1;
```

```
Runnable ds = new dynamSched();
Thread[] th = new Thread[3];
for( int i=0; i<3; ++i )
{
    th[i] = new Thread(ds,""+i); //all work in the
    //same object name of the thread is i
    {
    th[0].start();
    th[1].start();
    th[2].start();
  }
}
```

Condition Variables Are Keyed to `wait()` and `notify()`

Condition variables are protected by a mutex and so are introduced by the `synchronized()` keyword. The condition should always be checked in a loop, for example, a `while()` loop, with a call to `wait()` should the condition be unmet. This causes the thread to be put to sleep and simultaneously release the mutex. Meanwhile, upon updating the condition, a second thread must call `notify()` to wake up a thread waiting on the condition; calling `notifyAll()` wakes all threads waiting on the condition. The first thread now reevaluates the condition and proceeds if it evaluates to true.

In the following we modify `dynamSched` above to have the main thread print out the partial sums of the three worker threads one by one. Thus we have set up a classic producer/consumer situation with three producers, the sibling threads, and one consumer, the main thread. As each thread acquires the class mutex, it adds its partial sum to the global sum, updates the head count, reverses the open condition, and notifies all threads waiting on the class mutex. Since we must be sure to wake the consumer thread, which alone will find its condition satisfied, we use `notifyAll()`.

Upon waking, the main thread prints the current value of the global sum, reverses open, notifies a producer thread, and loops if the head count is yet to account for all sibling threads.

Dynamic Scheduling with a Condition Variable to Combine Sums

```
import java.io.*;

class dynamSched2 implements Runnable
{
    private static int si=0;   //shared index
```

```
    private static int N=1000000;
    private static int[] x;
    private static int sum = 0;
    private static int nThreads = 3;
    private static int headCount = 0;
    private static boolean open = true; //condition variable
//sss===
    public void
    run()
    {
        int i=0;
        int mysum=0;
        for (;;)
        {
            synchronized(this)
            {
                i = si++;
            }
            if ( i>=N ) break;
            mysum += x[i];
        }
        try {
        synchronized( dynamSched2.class)
        {
            while ( !open ) dynamSched2.class.wait();
            sum += mysum;  ++headCount;
            open = false;
            dynamSched2.class.notifyAll(); //notify() could
deadlock
        }
        } catch( InterruptedException e ) {}
    }
//mmm===
    public static void
    main(String[] args)
    {
        x = new int[N];
        for ( int i=0;  i<N;  ++i ) x[i] = 1;

        Runnable ds = new dynamSched2();
        Thread[] th = new Thread[nThreads];
```

```
for ( int i=0;  i<nThreads;  ++i )
{
    th[i] = new Thread(ds,"" +i); //all use the same
                                  //code
}
th[0].start();
th[1].start();
th[2].start();
try {
    do }
        synchronized( dynamSched2.class)
        {
            while ( open ) dynamSched2.class.wait();
            System.out.println("sum is now " +sum);
            open = true;
            dynamSched2.class.notify();
        }
    } while ( headCount < nThreads);
} catch( InterruptedException e ) {}
System.out.println("combined sum= " +sum);
    }
}
```

3.4 SGI Threads and OpenMP

Many scientific computations do not require coarse grain parallelism. These programs do the bulk of their work in loops and only need to parallelize these loops in order to achieve effective parallelization. This fact fits well with many who would write scientific and engineering programs since it greatly simplifies their task.

As a consequence, compiler writers have created the "DOACROSS" style of parallel programming, or even, in many cases, automatic parallelization (or vectorization).

Silicon Graphics computers (as well as other major vendors) support the OpenMP application programming interface (API) for multiprocessing directives. The complete manual for this is available at www.openMP.org. We give here an overview of its use. Adding "-mp" to the compile command causes the embedded directives to be read; otherwise, they appear as comments is the source code.

From the OpenMP man page. "The OpenMP API supports multiplatform shared-memory parallel programming in C/C++ and Fortran on all architectures, including Unix platforms and Windows NT platforms. Jointly defined by a group of major computer hardware and software vendors, OpenMP is a portable, scalable model that gives shared-memory parallel programmers a simple and flexible interface for developing parallel applications for platforms ranging from the desktop to the supercomputer.

"The OpenMP directives, library routines, and environment variables will allow you to create and manage parallel programs while ensuring portability. The directives extend the sequential programming model with single-program multiple data (SPMD) constructs, work-sharing constructs, synchronization constructs, and provide support for the sharing and privatization of data. The library routines and environment variables provide the functionality to control the run-time execution environment."

SGI also supports automatic parallelization via the automatic parallelizing option or apo (compile with -apo, this also invokes -mp).

DOACROSS Style Parallelization

In this model, program execution begins in the master thread and proceeds serially until a multiprocessing compiler directive is encountered. Good candidates for multiprocessing are the major or time-consuming loops of the program. At this point the objective is to create a collection of sibling or team threads to execute the loop in parallel. After the loop is completed, the threads are `joined` and execution continues serially until the next designated parallel section.

Although the innermost loop of a nested set of loops is the main target for vectorization on vector machines, in using threads it is preferrable to try and parallelize outermost loops. Vectorization is a much finer-grain parallelization in that it acts on arithmetic operations themselves. By contrast, parallelizing the outermost loop of a nested set saves the thread creation and destruction overhead which would occur on each iteration of the outer loop if the parallel section were inside.

To invoke OpenMP in Fortran, precede the block to be parallelized with

```
C$OMP PARALLEL [clause]
```

and end it with

```
C$OMP END PARALLEL
```

in C or C++ use

```
#pragma [clause] {...}
```

with the block occurring between the opening brace and closing brace.

Arguments: the "clause" in these examples, as noted above are used to specify the shared variables versus local (or thread specific) variables, reduction (or fan-in) variables, and other parameters, see below.

In the next example we form the matrix product $y = Ax$ parallelizing the computation by rows.

In Fortran

```
c
c-- compile with f77/f90 -mp matMult.f
c
c23456789
      program matMult()
      parameter(n=400)
      real a(n,n), y(n), x(n)
      integer i,j
c------ initialize the data
      do i=1,n,1
         x(i) = 1.0
         do j=1,n,1
            a(i,j) = 1.0
         end  do
      end  do
c$omp parallel shared(a,y,x) private(i,j)
         do i=1,n
            y(i) = 0.0
            do j=1,n
               y(i) = y(i) + a(i,j)*x(j)
            end do
         end do
c$omp end  parallel

      write(*,*)'y(1) is ',y(1)
      stop
      end
```

In C/C++

```
#include  <stdio.h>
#define  N 400

double a[N*N], y[N], x[N];
```

```
void main (void)
{
    int i,j;
    int n=N;   //to get N past the pragmas

      /* initialize arrays */
    for( i=0;   i<N*N;   ++i ) a[i] = 1;
    for( i=0;   i<N;   ++i ) x[i] = 1;

      /* do rows in parallel */
#pragma parallel shared(a,y,x) byvalue(n) local(i,j)
#pragma pfor iterate(i=0;n;1) // by ones
{
      for( i=0;   i<n;   ++i) {
          y[i] = 0;
          for( j=0;   j<n;   ++j)
              y[i] += a[i*n+j]*x[j];
      } //end loop
} //end parallel section
    printf("y[0] = %1f\n" ,y[0]);
}
```

The meaning of these and other directives are

- shared()   names: the variables that are to be shared among the threads;
- private() (Fortran) or local() (C/C++)   names: the variables that are specific or different for each thread;
- byvalue() (C/C++)   variables that are used by value rather than by reference, such a variable cannot be modified in the parallel section;
- critical (Fortran/C/C++):   a section of code that will be executed by a single thread at a time, a mutex locked section;
- reduction()   names: a scalar variable which is the result of some operation (e.g. + or *) on the components of a vector, i.e. a fan-in variable;
- parallel do (Fortran) or pfor iterate(;;) (C/C++)   calls for the parallel execution of a loop;
- barrier (Fortran) or synchronize (C/C++)   a barrier, threads wait at this point until all arrive, then all proceed; and
- numthreads(min,max)   if only one argument is given, this tells the compiler the (suggested) number of threads to use (this value should not exceed the available number of processors, cf. IRIS PowerC User's Guide, Chapter 5, p. 6), if an argument is given for min, then the section is not executed in parallel unless that many threads are available.

3.5 MPI

Among parallel programming methods, the easiest is vector, then shared memory with parallel directives such as OpenMP, then shared memory threads and finally the most difficult is distributed memory.

Distributed memory programming has all the usual issues such as global data versus local data, race conditions, synchronization, and dead lock, and it has in addition the necessity of managing the movement of data among the processing elements.

Fortunately MPI is available. It was written with a great deal of thought by a committee of people with a great deal of experience in parallel programming. MPI goes a long way to make distributed computation accessible to busy scientists and engineers.

Why distributed memory computation? For two reasons, first there are limits to what is possible with shared memory computation. As the number of processors increases, the bus becomes busier until it saturates; the same for cross-bar switched systems. In addition to that, a simple back of the envelope calculation shows that the speed of an electronic signal in a wire limits the distance a processor can be from the data and the diameter of the physical memory itself. This places a severe limitation on the number of processors possible (see Peter S. Pacheco, Parallel Programming with MPI, Morgan Kaufmann Publishers, San Francisco, 1997, p. 3).

The other reason is that distributed computing resources exist. Many organizations have dozens of computers wired together, for instance, on a ethernet cable. Most of them are grossly underutilized. Therefore, so much the better to be able to use them.

Note that MPI is sufficiently rich and that to discuss it all takes a book or two (Using MPI, Portable Parallel Programming with the Message Passing Interface, by William Gropp/Ewing Lusk/Anthony Skjellum and Using MPI-2, Advanced Features of the Message Passing Interface, by William Gropp/Ewing Lusk/Rajeev Thakur, published by the MIT Press, Cambridge, Mass). It is not our intention to be a book on MPI. However, we do want to provide enough of an introduction that the reader will be able to construct, visualize, debug, and execute useful scientific programs, using the language.

Introduction to Message Passing

Distributed memory parallel computation is fundamentally still an implementation of a directed acyclic graph and, as such, is subject to all the usual issues of parallel computation. As in shared memory parallel, issues such as reduction, synchronization, and data dependence must also be solved here. Further paradigms such as the master–slave model also apply here. In addition to the usual issues, what is new here is the need for transmitting data attached to one processor, usually recently computed, to one or more other processors. Thus this discussion of MPI will focus on the communication facilities of MPI.

Before beginning, it should be mentioned that MPI is implemented as a library, which can be called from standard computing languages such as Fortran, C, C++, and Java.

To introduce MPI, we will use it to solve the problem of calculating the product of a large number of matrices, N in number, each matrix P_n, $n = 1, \ldots, N$, being distinct. This problem arises in studying the transitions between possible solutions of a discrete optimization problem (see Section 11.1).

To enhance clarity and to focus on MPI, we will outline only the structure of the program. These segments of the program will be indicated by matching angle brackets $<$ and $>$. However we will provide exact syntax in Fortran and C for MPI statements, Fortran specific code is indicated by an "f" following the line number and C by a "c." Following the program, we will discuss the MPI statements. For the complete program, see the listing at the end of this section.

Matrix Product program structure

(! introduces comments in Fortran, // introduces comments in C)

```
 1   <begin program matrixMultiply>
 2   <preliminaries, e.g. variable declarations, library
     inclusions, etc.>
 3
4f   !start parallel (Fortran)
5f   call MPI_INIT(ierr)
6f   call MPI_COMM_RANK(MPI_COMM_WORLD, myRank, ierr)
7f   call MPI_COMM_SIZE(MPI_COMM_WORLD, nProcs, ierr)
8f
4c   //start parallel (C)
5c   MPI_Init(&argc,&argv);
6c   ierr = MPI_Comm_rank(MPI_COMM_WORLD, &myRank);
7c   ierr = MPI_Comm_size(MPI_COMM_WORLD, &nProcs);
8c
 9   <each processor computes r = log(nProcs), log base 2>
10   <master (proc 0) reads value of N from the console>
11
12f  !broadcast N to all processors (Fortran)
13f  call MPI_BCAST(N,1,MPI_INTEGER,0,MPI_COMM_WORLD,ierr)
```

```
14f
12c  //broadcast N to all processors (C)
13c  ierr = MPI_Bcast(&N,1,MPI_INTEGER,0,MPI_COMM_WORLD);
14c
 15  <each processor computes its block of indices to
     process>
 16  <each processor computes the product of its block>
 17
18f  ! fan-in the products via binary tree (Fortran)
19f  ! "odd" procs send their results to the next lower
     "even" proc
20f  ! "even" procs multiply the received matrix with its
     own
21f    h = 1
22f    do 10 k = 2, r
23f      if( mod(myRank,2*h) .eq. 0 ) then
24f      call MPI_RECV(recvdMat, Q*Q, MPI_DOUBLE_PRECISION, &
25f      myRank+h, 9, MPI_COMM_WORLD, status, ierr)
26f      call matProduct(myMat,recvdMat)
27f      else if( mod(myRank,2*h ) .eq. h ) then
28f      call MPI_SEND(myMat, Q*Q, MPI_DOUBLE_PRECISION, &
29f      myRank-h, 9, MPI_COMM_WORLD, ierr)
30f      GOTO 20
31f      endif
32f    h = h*2
33f 10 continue
34f
18c  // fan-in the products via binary tree (C)
19c  // "odd" procs send their results to the next lower
     // "even" proc
20c  // "even" procs multiply the received matrix with its own
21c  for( h=1, k=2; k<=r; ++k)
22c  {
23c    //send/receive to calculating node
24c    if( myRank %(2*h) == 0 )
25c    {
26c      //receive data from proc_{myrank+h}, tag is 9
27c      ierr = MPI_Recv(recvdMat, Q*Q, MPI_DOUBLE,
28c        myRank+h, 9, MPI_COMM_WORLD, &status);
29c      //multiply with myMat
```

```
30c     matProduct(myMat,recvdMat);
31c     }
32c     else if( myRank %(2*h) == h )
33c     {
34c       ierr = MPI_Send(myMat, Q*Q, MPI_DOUBLE,
35c         myRank-h, 9, MPI_COMM_WORLD);
36c       break; //now this process can vanish
37c     }
38c     h *= 2;
39c  }
40c
 41  <master prints result>
 42
43f  ! end parallel (Fortran)
44f    20 call MPI_FINALIZE(ierr)
45f
43c  // end parallel (C)
44c  ierr = MPI_Finalize();
45c
 46  <subprograms: calcMatrixElements, matProduct,
     figureBlocks>
 47  <end program>
```

Compiling the program is essentially done in the usual way but with the provision for loading MPI libraries. Since this can vary from site to site, systems administrators often provide scripts for both compilation and execution. For example, compiling in Fortran might be

```
mpif77 <program> <math libraries, etc.>
```

and in C might be

```
mpicc <program> <math libraries, etc.>
```

Running the program might be

```
mpirun -np #procs <absolute path to the executable>
```

or

```
mpiexec -n #procs <absolute path to the executable>.
```

Table 3. *MPI function prototypes*

MPI function	Argument types
(Fortran)	
MPI_INIT(ierror)	integer ierror
MPI_COMM_SIZE(comm, size, ierror)	integer comm, size, ierror
MPI_COMM_RANK(comm, rank, ierror)	integer comm, rank, ierror
MPI_BCAST(buffer, count, datatype, root, comm, ierror)	<type> buffer(*), integer count, datatype, root, comm, ierror
MPI_SEND(buffer, count, datatype, dest, tag, comm, ierror)	<type> buffer(*), integer count, datatype, dest, tag, comm, ierror
MPI_RECV(buffer, count, datatype, source, tag, comm, statue, ierror)	<type> buffer(*), integer count, datatype, source, tag, comm, ierror, status(MPI_STATUS_SIZE)
MPI_FINALIZE(ierror)	integer ierror

(C)
int MPI_Init(int *argc, char **argv)
int MPI_Comm_size(MPI_Comm comm, int *size)
int MPI_Comm_rank(MPI_Comm comm, int *rank)
int MPI_Bcast(void *buf, int count, MPI_Datatype datatype, int root, MPI_Comm comm)
int MPI_Send(void *buf, int count, MPI_Datatype datatype, int dest, int tag, MPI_Comm comm)
int MPI_Recv(void *buf, int count, MPI_Datatype datatype, int source, int tag, MPI_Comm comm, MPI_Status *status)

Although MPI contains a rich collection of message passing utilities, in our product of matrices program above we have used the complete list of MPI functions in which "a vast number of useful and efficient programs can be written," [Gropp, Lusk, Skjellum]. MPI function prototypes (APIs) are given in Table 3.

The call to MPI_INIT is required in every MPI program and must be the first MPI call. It establishes the MPI environment and begins program execution on the processors, which will be attached to the program. This initial group of processors is the "MPI_COMM_WORLD" group. All MPI messages are associated with a communication group. In general, subgroups of the initial set of processors can be established dynamically so that messages may be exchanged only within that subgroup.

To begin execution, a copy of the executable is placed on each processor; therefore all variables are local. Since the program is the same for all processors, variation in execution stems from conditional branches depending on the identity of each processor, use the MPI_COMM_RANK function as in Table 3 and discussed below.

All MPI calls produce an error code which is returned as the last argument of the Fortran prototype or the return value of the C prototype. This integer value is either MPI_SUCCESS or an implementation defined error code. For clarity we have not tested the return code in our example program. In practice, it is important to do this.

The number of processors associated with the named communications group is available via the MPI_COMM_SIZE function as the `size` argument. For the MPI_COMM_WORLD this will be the number of processors called for in the console invocation command.

As in the other parallel computational models, processors have a unique identity. In MPI, each processor attached to each communications group has an identity within that group, referred to in MPI as its "rank." The rank of a calling process with respect to the mentioned communications group is returned as the `rank` argument of the MPI_COMM_RANK function.

As discussed in Section 1.4, a broadcast is a communication sent by one member of the communications group to all other members. The details of how this is done depends on the implementation. The library is usually provided by the vendor to optimize for the topology of the installation. As in most other data transmission functions, `buffer` in the MPI_BCAST function refers to the data, which will be transmitted. This data is usually in multiple units of a simple or built-in data type, for example, an array of integers. The number of units is specified by the `count` argument, for example, the array size. Since the exact implementation of built-in data types can vary from machine to machine, MPI has a specification for its own purposes. The `datatype` argument referred to in the function is its MPI datatype, for example, MPI_INTEGER. In Table 4 we show the built-in datatypes recognized by MPI. One is not restricted to built-in datatypes; complicated user datatypes can be defined; however, this is beyond the scope of this tutorial.

The buffer sent by the MPI_BCAST function is that which resides on the processor specified by `root`. When calling for a broadcast in the program, all nodes of the communications group must refer to the same `root`. Hence the statement is the same for every processor. A broadcast is *blocking* which means each processor of the group waits at the broadcast statement until receiving its message. The broadcast function is an example of a *collective communication* in that it involves all the processors of the communications group.

Like the broadcast function, the `buffer`, `count`, and `datatype` arguments of the MPI_SEND function specify the data to be transmitted. But unlike a broadcast, MPI_SEND transmits the data to a single specific destination, `dest`, identified by its rank within the communications group `comm`. The remaining argument of MPI_SEND, `tag`, is a free parameter. Typically it is used to

Table 4. *Equivalent MPI data types*

MPI	Language (fertran/c)
Fortran	
MPI_CHARACTER	CHARACTER
MPI_COMPLEX	COMPLEX
MPI_DOUBLE_PRECISION	DOUBLE PRECISION
MPI_INTEGER	INTEGER
MPI_LOGICAL	LOGICAL
MPI_REAL	REAL
C	
MPI_CHAR	signed char
MPI_SHORT	signed short int
MPI_INT	signed int
MPI_LONG	signed long int
MPI_UNSIGNED_CHAR	unsigned char
MPI_UNSIGNED_SHORT	unsigned short int
MPI_UNSIGNED	unsigned int
MPI_UNSIGNED_LONG	unsigned long int
MPI_FLOAT	float
MPI_DOUBLE	double
MPI_LONG_DOUBLE	long double

catagorize messages when the receiver will be receiving messages of different types. But it can also be used to transmit additional information. For example, if the master has distributed different rows of a large matrix for processing, the `tag` parameter could specify the row corresponding to the data transmitted in `buffer`.

Finally, MPI_RECV is the dual to MPI_SEND. In addition to the usual data description and the communications group arguments, MPI_RECV uses a `source` argument to determine where the message is coming from and a `tag` argument to further identify the message. Unlike MPI_SEND, however, both the `source` and `tag` arguments are allowed to be wildcards; thus, the source field could be MPI_ANY_SOURCE and likewise the tag, field could be MPI_ANY_TAG if desired. The `status` argument is a structure with 3 members: source, tag, and error. For example, the source and tag can be accessed in Fortran via

```
status(MPI_SOURCE)
status(MPI_TAG)
```

and in C, use

```
status -> MPI_SOURCE
status -> MPI_TAG
```

The MPI_RECV call is blocking. In our example program `matrixMultiply` we take advantage of its blocking nature as a synchronization device that is called for by the fan-in DAG.

Nonblocking Communications and Other Features of MPI

As explained above, our example program uses blocking communications. But in many circumstances it is better that processors be allowed to continue computation and let, for example, communications coprocessors or at least background processes handle the communications. A nonblocking send/receive pair is MPI_ISEND and MPI_IRECV.

We illustrate these calls by modifying our example to incorporate them. Of course now we will have to explicitly synchronize the fan-in; MPI provides a barrier function and a WAIT function which can do that job for us. The modified code, lines 21f through 34f in Fortran, and lines 21c through 39c in C, are

```
20.5f  integer req(1)
21f   h = 1
22f   do 10 k = 2, r
23f   if( mod(myRank,2*h) .eq. 0 ) then
24f   call MPI_IRECV(recvdMat, Q*Q, MPI_DOUBLE_PRECISION, &
25f   myRank+h, 9, MPI_COMM_WORLD, req(1), ierr)
26f   call matProduct(myMat,recvdMat)
27f   else if( mod(myRank,2*h) .eq. h ) then
28f   call MPI_ISEND(myMat, Q*Q, MPI_DOUBLE_PRECISION, &
29f   myRank-h, 9, MPI_COMM_WORLD, req(2), ierr)
30f   ! after completeing its work, each proc still reports
      at barrier
31f   endif
32f   h = h*2
32.5f  call MPI_WAITALL(2,req,status_array,ierr)
33f   10 continue
34f
      and in C
20.5c  MPI_Request request;
21c   for(h=1, k=2; k<=r; ++k)
22c   {
23c   //send/receive to calculating node
24c   if( myRank %(2*h) == 0 )
25c   {
```

```
26c  //receive data from proc_myrank+h, tag is 9
27c  ierr = MPI_Irecv(recvdMat, Q*Q, MPI_DOUBLE,
28c  myRank+h, 9, MPI_COMM_WORLD, &request);
29c  //multiply with myMat
30c  matProduct(myMat,recvdMat);
31c  }
32c  else if( myRank %(2*h) == h )
33c  {
34c  ierr = MPI_Isend(myMat, Q*Q, MPI_DOUBLE,
35c  myRank-h, 9, MPI_COMM_WORLD,&request);
36c  //after completeing its work, each proc still reports
     at barrier
37c  }
38c  h *= 2;
38.5c  ierr = MPI_Barrier(MPI_COMM_WORLD);
39c  }
     or
38.5cAlt  ierr = MPI_Wait(&request,&status);
```

Note that processes in the communications group cannot die now until all the work is done, even though their part is done, because they must still report in at the barrier.

The final function we mention is MPI_REDUCE. In our example program we had to fan-in the matrix product by hand, but if the datatype were a scalar, for example, an integer, or floating point number, then we could have used the built-in reduce funtion. As with the communication calls, the built-in reduce function is optimized by the vendor for the achitechture and so should be used to give the best performance.

To illustrate the reduce function, we make another modification to our program. Suppose that for each matrix, we compute the sum of all its terms, subtract this from Q, and divide the result by Q; Q being the number of rows. This value represents the average rate of loss of probabililty mass to the given system of Q states on a single iteration of the chain,

$$\text{avg}_n = \left(Q - \sum_{i,j=1}^{Q} p_{i,j} \right) \Big/ Q \qquad \text{for } P_n = [p_{i,j}].$$

Further suppose we wish to add the averages over all N matrices.

```
16  <each proc computes avg_n for each matrix of its block>
17
18f  ! fan-in the averages
```

```
19f call MPI_REDUCE(mySum, sum, 1, MPI_DOUBLE_PRECISION, &
MPI_SUM,0,MPI_COMM_WORLD,ierr)
34f
```

    and in C

```
16 <each proc computes avgₙ for each matrix of its block sum>
17
18c // fan-in the averages
19c ierr = MPI_Reduce(&mySum, &sum, 1, MPI_DOUBLE, MPI_SUM,
    0, MPI_COMM_WORLD);
40c
```

As one can see from these examples, the prototype for the reduce function is: first the reference to the local value, next the reference to the variable into which the reduced value is to be placed, this is followed by the usual count of the number of these items and their datatype. The next argument is the kind of reduction operation to be performed (see Table 5 for other possible operations), then the node where the reduced value should be placed, and that is followed by the communications group.

One of the strong points of MPI is its debugging and execution-tracking facilities sometimes called *instrumentation*. Creating a logfile of events during an execution is done using the MultiProcessing Environment or MPE. MPE is a library of tools for measuring, understanding, and improving the performance of parallel programs. The tools include timing routines and a library to produce an event log for postmortem program visualization. Graphical depiction of a log file written by MPE is done using UPSHOT or JUMPSHOT.

Table 5. *MPI reduction data types*

Operation	MPI argument
Maximum	MPI_MAX
Minimum	MPI_MIN
Product	MPI_PROD
Sum	MPI_SUM
Logical and	MPI_LAND
Logical or	MPI_LOR
Logical exclusive or (xor)	MPI_LXOR
Bitwise and	MPI_BAND
Bitwise or	MPI_BOR
Bitwise xor	MPI_BXOR
Maximum value and location	MPI_MAXLOC
Minimum value and location	MPI_MINLOC

Table 6. *Timing comparisons for the Matrix Product program*

Blocking calls		Nonblocking calls	
nProcs	time (s)	nProcs	time (s)
1	26.3	1	26.3
2	13.3	2	13.3
4	13.2	4	13.2
8	13.0	8	12.9
16	13.2	16	12.9
32	13.3	32	13.2

If all that is needed is timing results, MPI_WTIME() in Fortran or MPI_Wtime() in C may be inserted around the section to be timed. See the source below for the example problem. Timing results for the blocking and nonblocking versions are presented in Table 6.

Matrix Product Source Code in C

```
1  /*
2    program to multiply N QxQ matrices, P_1*P_2*...*P_N
3    compile:
4      mpicc inhomogProduct.c -lm
5    use:
6      mpirun -np #procs  ./a.out
7    Note, #procs needs to be a power of 2
8  */
9  #include  <stdlib.h>
10 #include  <stdio.h>
11 #include  <math.h>
12 #include  <mpi.h>
13 #define  Q 6 /* matrix dimension as required */
14   //prototypes
15 void setMatrix(int , double *);
16 void printMat(double *);
17 void figureMyBlockbase1( int , int , int , int *,
      int *, int *);
18 void matProduct(double * , double * , double * );
19 main(int  argc, char  **argv)
20 {
```

```
21      int  N;  /* #terms to multiply, e.g. 2097152, runtime
        parameter */
22      int  r;  /* log base 2 of nProcs */
23      int  h;  /* helper to designate active branches of
        the fan-in */
24      int  n;  /* matrix index for block product */
25      int  nProcs;  /* user specifies via invocation */
26      int  myRank, err;
27      MPI_Status status;
28      MPI_Comm IWCOMM=MPI_COMM_WORLD;  //comm group = all
        procs
29      MPI_Init(&argc,&argv);
30      err = MPI_Comm_size(IWCOMM, &nProcs);
31        //find power of 2
32      h=1;  r=0;
33      while( h<nProcs ) { h *=2;  r++;}
34        //ranks are 0,1,..,nProcs-1
35      err = MPI_Comm_rank(IWCOMM, &myRank);
36      char  ipstring[16];
37        //read #terms from keyboard
38      if ( myRank == 0 )
39      {
40        printf ("enter N" );
41        gets (ipstring);  sscanf (ipstring,"%d",&N);
42      }
43        //distribute N;  blocks each proc until received
44      MPI_Bcast(&N,1,MPI_INTEGER,0,IWCOMM);
45        //get BlockSize, FirstBlock, LastBlock
46      int  myBlockSize, myFirst, myLast;
47      figureMyBlockbase1(
48        N, nProcs, myRank, &myBlockSize, &myFirst, &myLast);
49        //allocate space for  the matrices
50      double *myMat = (double *)malloc(Q*Q*sizeof(double));
51      double *recvdMat = (double *)malloc(Q*Q*sizeof(double));
52      double  *c = (double *)malloc(Q*Q*sizeof(double));
        //hold matrix prod
53      double  starttime = MPI_Wtime();  //for  timing
54        //multiply the block
55      setMatrix(myFirst,myMat);  //initialize to matrix
                                  //P_{myFirst}
```

```
56    for ( n=myFirst+1;  n<=myLast;  ++n )
57    {
58      setMatrix(n, recvdMat);  //use recvdMat for  the
                                   //2nd argument
59      matProduct(myMat,recvdMat,c);  //result copied back
                                        //to 1st arg
60    }
61      //now fan-in the products via binary tree
62    int  k;
63    for ( h=1, k=2;  k<=r;  ++k)
64    {
65        //send/receive to calculating node
66      if ( myRank%(2*h) == 0 )
67      {
68          //receive data from proc_{myrank+h}, tag is 9
69        err = MPI_Recv(
70            recvdMat, Q*Q, MPI_double , myRank+h, 9,
               IWCOMM, &status);
71          //combine, as per reduction
72        matProduct(myMat,recvdMat,c);
73      }
74      else  if ( myRank%(2*h) == h )
75      {
76        err = MPI_Send(myMat, Q*Q, MPI_double , myRank-h,
             9, IWCOMM);
77        break;  //now this process can vanish
78      }
79      h *= 2;
80    }
81    double  stoptime = MPI_Wtime();
82    if ( myRank == 0 )
83    {
84      printf ("Time req'd= %lf\n" ,(stoptime-starttime));
85      printf ("the product of %d transition matrices
           is\n" ,N);
86      printMat(myMat);
87    }
88    MPI_Finalize();
89  }
90
```

3.6 Vector Parallelization on the Cray

Machine Vectors

A machine vector is a list of floating point data, single or double precision, that can enter the vector registers sequentially one per clock cycle. At one time this required the data be contiguous in memory, but this is no longer an issue. Noncontiguous data must be selectively fetched and routed to the vector registers: an operation called a *gather*. If the spacing between gathered data is uniform, it is called the *stride*. A dual problem is that of storing calculated data back into memory noncontiguously and is called a *scatter*.

Gather and scatter operations occur quite naturally in scientific computing. Consider a rectangular array A of dimension $m \times n$ stored in column order, that is sequential memory locations contain

$$a_{11}, a_{21}, \ldots, a_{m1}, a_{12}, \ldots, a_{mn},$$

respectively (this is the method used by Fortran, that is the left most indices cycle faster). Then accessing the rows of A will result in a gather operation with constant stride of m. By contrast, if A is stored row first, the method used by C, then accessing the columns will require a gather with constant stride n.

On the Cray Y-MP hardware devices, perform gather and scatter operations transparently, even if the stride is not constant.

Note from the Cray architecture diagram that data does not flow directly from memory to the vector pipes. Instead there are vector registers inbetween. Data flows from memory to the vector registers, then to the pipes, then back to the vector registers, and finally back to main memory. The vector registers can hold 64 terms and therefore vector operations are chunked into 64 length chunks. A chunk must be cycled through the vector register before the next chunk can be processed.

An alternative architecture would have the data stream from memory to the vector pipes and back to memory.

Writing Vector Code

To specify vector processing, nothing special is required, code as usual. Rather it is the compiler that inserts vector instructions. Consequently, programs not necessarily written with vectorization in mind only need to be recompiled to benefit from this advanced processing. Of course, different coding techniques take advantage of the hardware to a greater or lesser degree often with dramatic

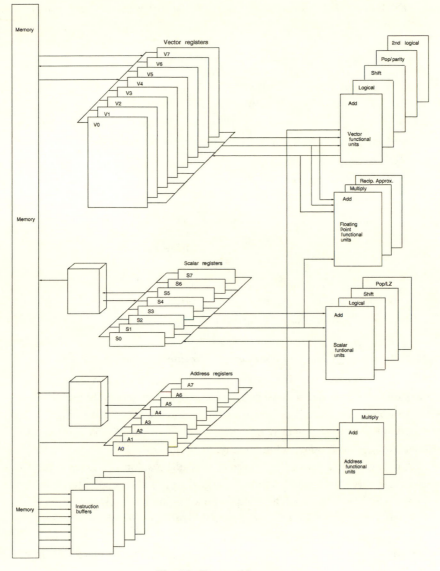

Fig. 16. Cray architecture.

results. Consequently, it is desirable to understand how the compiler affects vectorization.

To begin with, the only construct to be examined for possible vectorization is an innermost loop. Furthermore, the loop must be of the indexed kind, that is a DO loop in Fortran or a for($i = \ldots$) loop in C. The following simple loop vectorizes,

```
loop i = 1,...,n
    cᵢ ← aᵢ + bᵢ
    dᵢ ← cᵢ * aᵢ
endloop
```

where a, b, c, and d are floating point arrays. Vector processing of the loop proceeds in a manner different from that of the von Neumann execution as seen as follows.

$c_1 = a_1 + b_1$	$c_1 = a_1 + b_1$
$d_1 = c_1 * a_1$	$c_2 = a_2 + b_2$
$c_2 = a_2 + b_2$	$c_3 = a_3 + b_3$
$d_2 = c_2 * a_2$	$\ldots$
$\ldots$	$c_n = a_n + b_n$
$\ldots$	$d_1 = c_1 * a_1$
$\ldots$	$\ldots$
$d_n = c_n * a_n$	$d_n = c_n * a_n$
von Neumann calculation	Vector calculation

Pseudovectorization

As we have seen, an operation such as dot product will not vectorize because it is not a vector operation. The same holds true for other fan-in operations. However, the Cray compiler can still optimize such operations through a technique called *pseudo-vectorization*. Suppose that the sum of the terms of a 64 length vector is called for. This is done, automatically, by dividing the list into two 32 length vectors and doing a vector add on them. Next the resulting 32 length vector is divided into two 16 length vectors and added; hence at this point the resulting vector length is 16 but each term represents the sum of 4 original terms. This technique is repeated until the vector–scalar break-even point is reached and the remainder is added in scalar mode.

Besides dot product, there are many built-in fan-in operations, for example, *max* and *min*.

Chaining

A vector calculation which uses two different arithmetic operations is called a *linked-triad*. The most typical example is a saxpy or scalar alpha x plus y

$$\mathbf{z} = \alpha * \mathbf{x} + \mathbf{y},$$

where α is a scalar, effectively a constant vector to the computer. A vector computer can *chain* the calculation of a linked-triad meaning the intermediate results, here $\alpha * x_i$, are not returned to main memory but instead are re-sent through the vector arithimetic logic unit as long as there are remaining operations to perform. For this to occur, the operations must be different and must be among the basic operations performed by the vector ALU, for example, multiplication and addition. The following loop will chain.

```
loop i = 1,...,n
    cᵢ ← aᵢ + rᵢ*bᵢ
endloop
```

Memory Contention

Main memory is spread over 64 boards or *banks* and is arranged so that sequential addresses occur on different banks. Physical limitations make it impossible for a memory board to fetch or store data on successive clock cycles. On the Cray X-MP, a memory board can be accessed maximally every 8 cycles. On the Cyber 990 it is every 4 cycles. Multiple banks make it possible to fetch contiguous data one per clock cycle despite this limitation. However, now a gather or scatter operation with a stride equal to some multiple of 64 will suffer memory contention. In such a case the problem may be averted by simply increasing the offending dimension by 1 in the declarations, but using the true dimension in the code. For example, suppose that A and B are 64×64 arrays, but are declared to be 65×65 dimensional. Then the following transpose computation suffers no memory contention.

```
loop i = 1,...,64
    loop j = 1,...,64
        bᵢⱼ ← aⱼᵢ
    endloop
endloop
```

Instruction Buffering

Instruction buffering refers to making small subroutines so that the entire subroutine code fits in fast memory. This obviates the need for swapping pages of memory in and out from the disk or from slow memory.

Loop Unrolling

It may be advantageous to unroll the innermost loop by two or even three in order to balance the vector arithmetic with the loads and stores, which must occur at both the beginning and end of loops.

Vectorization

An innermost loop will fail to vectorize for any of the following reasons.

- No vector is being calculated in the loop; that is, there is no vector array reference on the left-hand side of an equal sign.
- There is a call to a subprogram (subroutine).
- There is an unconditional backward branch within the loop.
- Input/output is done within the loop.
- There is a "nonbenevolent" conditional branch within the loop.
- There is a vector dependency.

Vector Dependencies

There are three different types of vector dependencies: recursion, result not ready, and value destroyed. The three are illustrated by the following examples. While these examples are somewhat artificial, they have been distilled down from real examples to show the essence of the problem.

Recursion.

```
loop i = 2,...,n
   bᵢ ← aᵢ₋₁
   aᵢ ← cᵢ
endloop
```

The von Neumann execution of this loop produces the following results:

$$b_2 = a_1$$
$$a_2 = c_2$$
$$b_3 = a_2(= c_2)$$
$$a_3 = c_3$$
$$b_4 = a_3(= c_3)$$
$$a_4 = c_4$$
$$\vdots$$

However, the vectorized execution gives

$$b_2 = a_1$$
$$b_3 = a_2$$
$$b_4 = a_3$$
$$\vdots$$
$$a_2 = c_2$$
$$a_3 = c_3$$
$$a_4 = c_4$$
$$\vdots$$

Here the b's get the old values of the a's and not the new ones. Thus the result is wrong.

The problem is that previous subscripts of the a array are referenced in the earlier part of the loop but those values are set in a later part of the loop. We will see below that the "ABC" test detects this dependency.

The reader should work out the next examples in the same manner as above to see that the results are wrong if the loops are executed in vector mode.

Result not ready. *(Recall the arithmetic pipe is 8 segments long, cf. Fig. 4.)*

```
loop i = 1,...,n
   a_{i+2} ← a_i + b_i
endloop
```

Value destroyed.

```
loop i = 1,...,64
   a_i ← 2 * b_i
   a_{i+1} ← c_i
endloop
```

ABC test

The need for detecting data dependencies in loops to make for "smart compilers" has led to much research in this area. For an in-depth discussion of this topic, see [6]. Here we will explain the "ABC" test to determine whether or not the compiler will vectorize an innermost loop. This test is very simple and conservative.

The test is applied to every pair of references in the loop to the same array. The test is applied only when at least one array of the pair, the "key," is being calculated in the loop, that is, appears on the left-hand side of an equal sign. For this pair, define the code on the right-hand side of this equal sign and the code within the innermost loop above the equal sign as the "previous" region of the loop. Define the code below the line on which the key appears as the "subsequent" region.

Count A as 0 if the indices of both arrays of the pair are increasing and 1 if both are decreasing. (If the indices are changing in opposite directions, then this pair passes the ABC test.)

Count B as 0 if the "other" array appears in the previous part of the loop and 1 if it appears in the subsequent part. If B is 1, the pair passes the test.

Finally count C as 0 if the subscript of the other array is greater than the key and 1 if less than the key. (If the two are equal, then again this pair passes the test.)

The pair fails the ABC test and the loop will not vectorize if B is 0 and A and C are opposite.

The three examples above fail the ABC test with values of 001 in each case.

Conditional Branching

Bit vector model,

where $bitvector_i = 1$
    vector assignment
else
    vector assignment
endwhere

Both vector assignment codes are executed; the result of the calculation is not written if the bitvector for that bit is 0 in the first line or 1 in the second.

Programming Aids

An excellent performance utility is the hardware performance monitor or hpm. This utility gives information about execution, memory usage, vectorization, and many other aspects of the execution of a program. Invoke hpm on your executable a.out with hpm -g x a.out > prog.hpm, where x is either 0,1,2, or 3. Use 0 for an execution summary, 1 for hold issue conditions, 2 for memory information such as faults, and 3 for a vectorization summary. The program will be executed and the performance will be written as the ASCII file prog.hpm. See man hpm for more information.

The Cray also offers a bit-bucket profiling tool, prof, such as we mentioned in the last chapter. To use the profiler, compile with

$$cc\ -p\ prog.c$$

or

$$cc\ -gp\ prog.c$$

The former produces a mon.out file corresponding to a run, which counts the number of times subroutines are called. The latter produces a gmon.out file, which gives a histogram corresponding to execution time spent in small uniformly divided sections of the (object) code.

The Cray has another utility, flowtrace, which traces and times procedure (subroutine/function) calls. To invoke flowtrace (see man flowtrace), use

```
cf77 -F yourcode.f
a.out
flowview -Luch > flow.report
```

Flowtrace reports accumulate CPU time and enables one to determine the amount of time spent in each procedure. In addition, flowtrace makes it possible to determine the calling tree during execution.

To get optimum performance, use built-in subroutines whenever possible. See man SCILIB for information on the vector library routines.

The Cray compiler will modify source code to optimize its execution. It is possible to get a listing of compiler modified Fortran source code using the -M compile option. Thus

```
cf77 -M bandmult.f
```

will produce the file bandmult.m, which contains the modified code. Alternatively, cf77 -J -Zp bandmult.f does the same.

On the next two pages we present some "before" and "after" examples of code modification the programmer can use to improve performance on a vector computer.

Before

```
loop j=1 to 1000              loop  i=1 to 100
   lots_of_work;                 if ( aᵢ < 0) aᵢ ← 0;
   loop i=1 to 3                 bᵢ ← √aᵢ ;
      xᵢ ← xᵢ + 1;            end  loop
```

```
    end loop                          loop  i=2 to 100
  end loop                              aᵢ ← bᵢ + cᵢ;
                                        dᵢ ← dᵢ₋₁ * aᵢ + cᵢ;
                                      end  loop
  loop j=1 to m
    loop i=1 to 3
      aⱼ ← aⱼ + bᵢⱼ;                  loop  i=1 to 10000
    end  loop                           aᵢ ← bᵢ * c * dᵢ + e + fᵢ;
  end  loop                           end  loop

  /* 3 memory references, 1 flop */


  loop  i= 1 to 100
    cᵢ ← aᵢ + bᵢ;
  end  loop
  loop  i=1 to 100
    zᵢ ← xᵢ * yᵢ;
  end  loop


  loop  j=1 to n
    loop  i=1 to n
      if ( i ≠ j )
        cᵢ ← aᵢ + bᵢ;
    end  loop
  end  loop
```

After

```
  loop  j=1 to 1000                   loop  i=1 to 100
    lots_of_work;                       aᵢ ← max(aᵢ,0);
    x₁ ← x₁ + 1;                        bᵢ ← √aᵢ;
    x₂ ← x₂ + 1;                      end  loop
    x₃ ← x₃ + 1;
  end  loop                           /* Use a built-in vector
                                      function when possible */
  /* Unroll a short loop */
                                      loop  i=2 to 100
  loop  j=1 to m                        aᵢ ← bᵢ + cᵢ;
    aⱼ ← aⱼ + b₁ⱼ + b₂ⱼ + b₃ⱼ;        end  loop
  end  loop
```

```
/* 5 memory references,
   3 flops */

loop  i=1 to 100
   c_i ← a_i + b_i;
   z_i ← x_i * y_i;
end  loop

/* Combine loops saves certain
index overhead calculations */

loop  j=1 to n
   temp ← c_j;
   loop  i= 1 to n
      c_i ← a_i + b_i;
   end  loop
   c_j ← temp;
end  loop
/* The loop now vectorizes */
```

```
loop  i=2 to 100
   d_i ← d_{i-1} * a_i + c_i;
end  loop

/* The first calculation
now vectorizes */

loop  i= 1 to 10000
   a_i ← b_i*c*d_i + (e + f_i);
end  loop

/* The calculation now
chains. */
```

3.7 Quantum Computation

Qubits

A quantum computer utilizes and manipulates *qubits*. Physically, qubits can be implemented in "hardware" in a variety of ways, one of which uses the spin of an electron, while another uses the polarization state of a photon. In this discussion we will model qubits by photons.

A qubit's behavior is described by, and obeys, the laws of the mathematical theory of Hilbert Spaces; thus, we say a qubit "lives" in Hilbert Space. A Hilbert Space consists of vectors, denoted $|label\rangle$, called *kets* (in Quantum Mechanics). In this, *label* is some label designating the quantum state. Kets can be added, one to another, to produce another ket. Kets can be multiplied by complex numbers to produce a ket. Complex numbers are referred to as *scalars* and will be denoted by Greek letters, for example, α. This operation on kets is called *scalar multiplication*. Finally a ket may be multiplied by another ket to produce a scalar. This multiplication is called *inner* or *dot product*.

In what follows, the space will be only finite dimensional. For a single qubit, the dimension is 2, meaning all kets in the space can be represented as a linear combination of 2 designated, fixed qubits, for example $\alpha|0\rangle + \beta|1\rangle$, where the kets $|0\rangle$ and $|1\rangle$ have been chosen as the basis.

Besides the $|\cdot\rangle$ notation, a ket can also be represented as a column vector, thus for a single qubit,

$$|0\rangle = \begin{bmatrix} 1 \\ 0 \end{bmatrix} \qquad |1\rangle = \begin{bmatrix} 0 \\ 1 \end{bmatrix}.$$

To implement a qubit using a photon, recall that a photon exists in a polarized state. Plane polarization is when the electric component of the wave lies in a single plane along the axis of propagation. The plane can lie at any angle; we arbitrarily designate a horizontally plane polarized photon, $|\leftrightarrow\rangle$, as "0" and a vertically plane polarized photon, $|\updownarrow\rangle$, as a "1." Then a diagonally polarized photon is represented as

$$|\nearrow\rangle = \frac{1}{\sqrt{2}}\left(|0\rangle + |1\rangle\right).$$

Note that a horizontally polarized photon and a vertically polarized one are *orthogonal* and so their dot product is 0. Physically, if a photon is first passed through a horizontally polarizing filter and then through a vertically polarizing filter, the photon is blocked.

There are other polarization possibilities besides plane polarization. For example, if the electric wave spirals around the axis of propagation in helical fashion, then the wave is *circularly polarized*, and we designated this by $|\bigcirc\rangle$. With respect to the horizontal and vertical polarization basis, a counterclockwise (CCW) circularly polarized photon has the representation

$$|\bigcirc_{\mathrm{CCW}}\rangle = \frac{1}{\sqrt{2}}\left(|0\rangle + i|1\rangle\right),$$

while the clockwise (CW) circularly polarized photon is given by

$$|\bigcirc_{\mathrm{CW}}\rangle = \frac{1}{\sqrt{2}}\left(|0\rangle - i|1\rangle\right).$$

Here $i = \sqrt{-1}$.

In the representation of polarization as vectors, the length or *norm* of the vector must always be 1 since a given polarization cannot be more or less in effect. The norm of a vector is denoted by $\|\cdot\|$ and if the vector is given as a linear combination of an orthogonal basis, then it is calculated as the square root of the sum of the squares of the coefficients. Thus if $|v\rangle = \alpha_0|0\rangle + \alpha_1|1\rangle$, then

$$\||v\rangle\| = \sqrt{|\alpha_0|^2 + |\alpha_1|^2} = 1,$$

where $|\gamma|$ is the complex modulus of γ for a complex scalar. Since the norm of a ket is always 1, it lies on the surface of the unit sphere in the space.

Notice that the terms $|\alpha_i|^2$, summed over all the coeffients, equals 1 (without the square root too). The value $|\alpha_i|^2$ is called the *probability amplitude* of its term in the superposition. We will see that it is the probability that a measurement will find the system in state i.

Superposition of States – Quantum Reality

The famous *two-slit experiment* shows that each single photon travels through both slits and interfers with itself. However, if a photon is queried as which slit it passes through, as for example by a measuring device placed at one of the slits, then it makes a choice 50–50 and goes through only the slit it has chosen. This leads to the Quantum Measurement Postulate.

Quantum Measurement Postulate. *When a measurement is made, the system makes a random selection among the possibilities and chooses one. The ith state is chosen with probability given by its probability amplitude. After the measurement, the system is in the state that always gives that choice; the other possibilities have gone away.*

Consider a modification to the polarizing filter experiment described above. Recall that no light passes through a pair of polarizing filters that are placed at right angles. But if a third filter is placed between these two, and it is oriented diagonally to them, then light passes through all three. How can there be more light when an additional filter is added?

The quantum mechanical explaination is that after passing the first polarizer, a photon is of course vertically polarized, but this state can be represented as a linear combination of a NorthEast/SouthWest polarization and a North-West/SouthEast polarization,

$$| \updownarrow \rangle = \frac{1}{\sqrt{2}}(| \nearrow \rangle + | \searrow \rangle).$$

Thus we are now using these diagonal polarizations as a basis. Note that these two basis states are orthonormal just as the vertical and horizontal states are. An interpretation of the representation is that the photon is a superposition of both these states; that is to say, it is in both these states *simumltaneously*. Encountering the diagonal polarizer, which acts as a measuring device, the photon must make a choice between the two with one-half chance of selecting each. If it chooses the diagonalization in the same direction as the middle filter, then it passes through; otherwise, it is blocked. Hence 50% of the photons (which pass the vertical filter) pass through the diagonal filter. Now the situation at the third, horizontal filter is just the same, any single photo has a 50% chance of passing through and a 50% chance of being blocked.

Thus we have the key observation that any quantum system, which is the superposition of basis states, is in each of the basis states simultaneously and, when subjected to measurement, chooses one of the states according to predetermined probabilities.

Before leaving the qubit, we note another reality of quantum mechanics, a qubit, or set of qubits, cannot be copied, for if it is measured, then the superposition degenerates into one of the possible states.

Adding More Qubits

Let $\mathcal{H}_0$ be a 2-dimensional Hilbert space with an arbitrarily selected orthonormal basis designed by $|0_0\rangle$ and $|1_0\rangle$. Similarly let $\mathcal{H}_1$ be the another 2-dimensional Hilbert Space with basis $|0_1\rangle$ and $|1_1\rangle$. Let these two spaces be separately prepared without interacting. Then the quantum system $\mathcal{Q}$ consisting of $\mathcal{H}_0$ and $\mathcal{H}_1$ is called the *juxtaposition* of $\mathcal{H}_0$ and $\mathcal{H}_1$. Mathematically $\mathcal{Q}$ is the *tensor product* of the separate spaces, written

$$\mathcal{Q} = \mathcal{H}_1 \otimes \mathcal{H}_0.$$

The properties of a tensor product are that if $|a_0\rangle \in \mathcal{H}_0$ and $|a_1\rangle \in \mathcal{H}_1$ then there is an element of the tensor product denoted

$$|a_1\rangle \otimes |a_0\rangle \qquad \text{or just} \quad |a_1 a_0\rangle.$$

Further, $\otimes$ is linear is each of its arguments, for example,

$$(|a_1\rangle + |b_1\rangle) \otimes |a_0\rangle = |a_1\rangle \otimes |a_0\rangle + |b_1\rangle \otimes |a_0\rangle.$$

As a consequence, if $\{|a_{10}\rangle, |a_{11}\rangle\}$ is a basis for $\mathcal{H}_1$ and $\{|a_{00}\rangle, |a_{01}\rangle\}$ is a basis for $\mathcal{H}_0$, then the set

$$\{|a_{1i}\rangle \otimes |a_{0j}\rangle \ : \ i = 0, 1, \ j = 0, 1\}$$

$$= \{a_{10} \otimes |a_{00}\rangle, \ |a_{10}\rangle \otimes |a_{01}\rangle, \ |a_{11}\rangle \otimes |a_{00}\rangle, \ |a_{11}\rangle \otimes |a_{01}\rangle\}$$

is a basis for $\mathcal{Q}$. Hence $\mathcal{Q}$ is 4-dimensional. In column vector notation, if $\begin{bmatrix} \alpha_1 \\ \beta_1 \end{bmatrix} = \alpha_1 |a_{10}\rangle + \beta_1 |a_{11}\rangle$ and $\begin{bmatrix} \alpha_0 \\ \beta_0 \end{bmatrix} = \alpha_0 |a_{00}\rangle + \beta_0 |a_{01}\rangle$, then

$$\begin{bmatrix} \alpha_1 \\ \beta_1 \end{bmatrix} \otimes \begin{bmatrix} \alpha_0 \\ \beta_0 \end{bmatrix} = \begin{bmatrix} \alpha_1 \begin{bmatrix} \alpha_0 \\ \beta_0 \end{bmatrix} \\ \beta_1 \begin{bmatrix} \alpha_0 \\ \beta_0 \end{bmatrix} \end{bmatrix}$$

$$= \begin{bmatrix} \alpha_1 \alpha_0 \\ \alpha_1 \beta_0 \\ \beta_1 \alpha_0 \\ \beta_1 \beta_0 \end{bmatrix}$$

in the basis $|a_{10}a_{00}\rangle, |a_{10}a_{01}\rangle, |a_{11}a_{00}\rangle, |a_{11}a_{01}\rangle$.

Dot product in $\mathcal{Q}$ is defined for product kets as the product of their component inner products; that is,

$$|a_1 a_0\rangle \cdot |b_1 b_0\rangle = (|a_1\rangle \cdot |b_1\rangle)(|a_0\rangle \cdot |b_0\rangle).$$

Since every ket in $\mathcal{Q}$ can be represented as the sum of product kets, this definition may be used to figure the dot product of any pair.

Now a typical ket in $\mathcal{Q}$ is the superposition of the 4 basis kets and therefore represents 4 qubits simultaneously, namely $|00\rangle$, $|01\rangle$, $|10\rangle$, and $|11\rangle$. As in classical computing, we identify these as the digits 0, 1, 2, and 3, respectively.

Proceeding in this fashion, n 2-dimensional quantum spaces, $\mathcal{H}_{n-1}, \ldots, \mathcal{H}_1$, $\mathcal{H}_0$ juxtaposed produces a space in which typical kets represent 2^n qubits simultaneously which we take to be the integers 0 up to $2^n - 1$. A collection of n qubits is called a *quantum register* of size n.

Entanglement

Not all states of $\mathcal{H}_1 \otimes \mathcal{H}_0$ are products of a qubit in $\mathcal{H}_1$ with one in $\mathcal{H}_0$. The superposition

$$\frac{1}{\sqrt{2}} (|00\rangle - |11\rangle),$$

called a *EPR pair*, is not. It cannot be written as a tensor product. A state which cannot be written as a tensor product is said to be *entangled*.

The EPR pair can be constructed as follows. Start with the juxtaposition

$$\frac{1}{\sqrt{2}} (|0\rangle - |1\rangle) \otimes |0\rangle = \frac{1}{\sqrt{2}} (|00\rangle - |10\rangle).$$

To this, apply the *controlled NOT* gate, see the next section and the exercises, and the result is the EPR pair above.

Entangled states can have perplexing properties. The following experiment was first suggested by Albert Einstein, Boris Podolsky, and Nathan Rosen in 1936, and is known as the EPR experiment.[2] Suppose one of the qubits of the superposition displayed above, as implemented as a polarized photon, is sent into deep space while the other is stored, undisturbed, close at hand. After some time, this local one is measured, causing it to choose, at that moment, to be either $|0\rangle$ or $|1\rangle$. Instantly the distant qubit must now also be the same, $|0\rangle$ or $|1\rangle$, respectively.

Quantum Computation

Since a quantum computation cannot create or destroy qubits during a calculation; a calculation will be a transformation, U, which preserves norm,

$$\|Ux\| = \|x\| \qquad \text{for all kets } x.$$

Such a transformation is called a *unitary transformation*. If the column vector notation is used to represent a ket, then a square matrix is used to represent a transformation.

In addition to preserving norm, it is necessarily true that the *adjoint U^** of a unitary transformation is its inverse. Thus U satisfies the operator equation

$$U^*U = UU^* = I,$$

where I is the identity operator. When U is represented as a matrix, its adjoint U^* is the conjugate transpose of that matrix; that is, U^* is the matrix whose columns are the complex conjugates of the rows of U.

A *quantum logic gate* is a unitary transformation on a quantum register, and a *quantum network* or *program* is the succession of quantum logic gates. Thus the output register of a gate becomes the input register to the next gate in the succession. The *size of the network* is the number of gates it contains.

One of the most useful gates on a qubit is the *Hadamard gate* given by the matrix

$$H = \frac{1}{\sqrt{2}} \begin{bmatrix} 1 & 1 \\ 1 & -1 \end{bmatrix}.$$

---

[2] The EPR experiment as suggested uses electron spin instead of photon polarization, but the principle is the same.

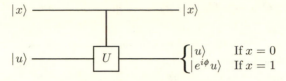

Fig. 17. Controlled U gate.

Acting on $|0\rangle = \begin{bmatrix} 1 \\ 0 \end{bmatrix}$ and on $|1\rangle = \begin{bmatrix} 0 \\ 1 \end{bmatrix}$ the outputs are

$$H \begin{bmatrix} 1 \\ 0 \end{bmatrix} = \frac{1}{\sqrt{2}} (|0\rangle + |1\rangle), \quad H \begin{bmatrix} 0 \\ 1 \end{bmatrix} = \frac{1}{\sqrt{2}} (|0\rangle - |1\rangle).$$

The tensor product of three such transformations (on $|0\rangle$'s) gives

$$\frac{1}{\sqrt{2}} (|0\rangle + |1\rangle) \otimes \frac{1}{\sqrt{2}} (|0\rangle + |1\rangle) \otimes \frac{1}{\sqrt{2}} (|0\rangle + |1\rangle),$$

which is the superpostion of $|000\rangle$ through $|111\rangle$ or a representation of the integers 0 through 7.

A second transformation we shall need to consider is the 2-qubit *controlled U gate*. This is illustrated schematically in Fig. 17. The first qubit acts as the *control* while the second is the target. In this, U is any single qubit unitary transformation; let $e^{i\phi}$ denote its eigenvalue.

Although the quantum mechanical implementation of the gate depends on the medium (for an implementation in chloroform, see [7]), the conceptual effect of the gate is as follows. If the control qubit $|x\rangle$ is $|0\rangle$, the target is unchanged, but if the control is $|1\rangle$, then the target is multiplied by its eigenvalue. Thus

$$|u0\rangle \mapsto |u0\rangle$$
$$|u1\rangle \mapsto |e^{i\phi}u1\rangle = e^{i\phi}|u1\rangle.$$

Programming a quantum computer consists in designing a sucession of unitary transformations leading to the desired output.

Capturing the output is a matter of measuring the quantum register at the end of the calculation. Since this forces a selection of one of the superpositioned states according to its probability amplitude, it is necessary to arrange that the amplitude of the desired term be made large, larger than $1/2$, for example. By running the computation several times, the chance of not observing the desired term is made arbitrarily small.

Grover's Algorithm for the Password Problem

Suppose that we are given a boolean function f_k, defined on the integers 0 to $2^n - 1$, whose value $f_k(x) = 0$ except when $x = k$, the password, where its value is 1. We envision a program for finding k, by trying integers in the domain and checking the function values. If we try half the domain, 2^{n-1} integers, either randomly or in some order, the probability of finding k is 50%. (Taking half the domain in some order, we have a 50% chance k is in the half we select. Randomly, there is a 1 in 2^n expectation on each try, so after 2^{n-1} trys the expectation is $1/2$.)

By contrast, a quantum computer needs only $O(2^{n/2})$ function evaluations using Grover's Algorithm. If there are about a billion possible passwords, 2^{30}, then a quantum computer needs only complexity on the order of 2^{15} or 33,000.

A Grover Iteration programmatically consists of Hadamard transformations and controlled U gates where U is affected by the function f. Analyzing the operation is somewhat involved and beyond our scope (see [8]) but the output is the rotation in space of the n register input by an angle 2ϕ toward the desired answer $|k\rangle$. In this, ϕ is given by $\sin \phi = 1/2^{n/2}$. Grover's Algorithm consists in repeating the iteration, say m times, where we calculate m as follows. In the worst case, the total angle through which the input must be rotated is $\pi/2$, and so we want

$$m2\phi \approx \frac{\pi}{2}$$

or $m = \pi/(4\phi)$. For large n, $\phi \approx \sin \phi = 1/2^{n/2}$. So

$$m \approx \frac{\pi}{4}2^{n/2} = O(2^{n/2}).$$

After each iteration the coefficient of the resultant ket in the direction of the solution $|k\rangle$ has been changed by $\cos 2\phi$ and so the new probability amplitude is $\cos^2(2\phi)$. If n is large, this is approximately 1 and so even after m Grover Iterations the probability amplitude of the output will exceed $1/2$.

Shor's Algorithm to Break an RSA Code in Polynomial Time

The problem is: given a very large integer n, we want to find integers p and q, $1 < p < n$, so that $pq = n$. We will outline how Shor's Algorithm solves this problem but we leave it for the reader to explore the algorithm in depth.

From Number Theory, if a and n have no common factors, then the function $F(x) = a^x \mod n$, $x = 0, 1, 2, \ldots$, is periodic; let the period be r, thus $F(x + r) = F(x)$. (What if a and n do have a common factor (other than 1 of course)?) It is in this step of finding the period that quantum computation is used. Continuing, if r is odd or if $a^{r/2} = -1 \mod n$, then discard this a and try another. Otherwise the greatest common divisor (gcd) of n and $a^{r/2} + 1$ is a solution to the problem; so is $\gcd(a^{r/2} - 1, n)$.

Shor's method for finding the period r has complexity $O(\log^3 n)$.

Decoherence

Creating and maintaining perfect qubits is a daunting challenge. If qubits interact with the environment, they immediately become useless for a quantum calculation. This is called *decoherence*.

One view of decoherence is that through the interaction, the environment can be regarded as making a measurement of the system and thereby destroying its superpositions. Schrödingers cat might be a superposition of being both dead and alive for nanoseconds or less of time, but light, air, particles of dust, and so on are constantly interacting with the cat. The resulting decoherence chooses "alive" with overwhelming probability.

Alternatively, decoherence can be viewed as an entanglement with the environment so that superpositions must now include its states as well. Either way, the intended quantum calculation is destroyed.

At the time this is written, the state of the art is that 4 qubits can be kept perfect for a few nanoseconds. Decoherence proceeds exponentially fast in the number of particles. For the Shor calculation on 200 digit keys n, 3,500 perfect qubits are required over the duration of the calculation.

Exercises

1. (3) In pseudocode, show how to add the terms of the harmonic series $(1 + \frac{1}{2} + \frac{1}{3} + \frac{1}{4} + \cdots)$ using 4 threads. Stop adding terms when they become smaller than $\epsilon = 10^{-5}$.
2. (3) Show how to form the quantum register containing the superposition of 3 and 7, that is, $|011\rangle$ and $|111\rangle$.
3. (3) Show that the transformation C_ϕ, called the *phase shift gate*, defined by

$$C_\phi = \begin{bmatrix} 1 & 0 \\ 0 & e^{i\phi} \end{bmatrix}, \quad 0 \le \phi \le 2\pi,$$

   is a unitary transform on 2-dimensional Hilbert Space.
4. (4) Show that the effect on $|0\rangle$ of the quantum program: apply H (Hadamard transformation), follow with $C_{2\theta}$, a phase shift gate (see above), and follow that with H is to produce

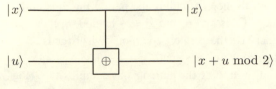

Fig. 18. Controlled NOT gate.

$$\cos\theta\,(\cos\theta + i\sin\theta)\,|0\rangle + \sin\theta\,(\sin\theta - i\cos\theta)\,|1\rangle$$
$$= e^{i\theta}\,(\cos\theta|0\rangle - i\sin\theta|1\rangle).$$

The leading factor $e^{i\theta}$ represents the global phase of the system and cannot be observed (and therefore can be ignored).

5. (5) Apply the phase shift gate $C_{\frac{\pi}{2}+\phi}$ to the quantum program above and show that the result is an arbitary qubit $\alpha|0\rangle + \beta|1\rangle$. What do θ and ϕ have to be given α and β?

6. (5) What is the matrix representation of the controlled U gate (in the basis $|00\rangle, |01\rangle, |10\rangle$ and $|11\rangle$). (Hint: a matrix element c_{jk} is the dot product of the jth basis vector with the transform of the kth basis vector.)

7. (5) The controlled NOT gate (see Fig. 18), behaves as follows. If the control bit is $|0\rangle$, then the target is unchanged; but if the control bit is $|1\rangle$, then the target bit is flipped. (a) What is the matrix of the controlled NOT gate? (b) Show that the controlled NOT gate transforms the 2-qubit $\frac{1}{\sqrt{2}}\,(|00\rangle - |10\rangle)$ to the EPR pair.

Programming Exercises

8. (6) Use a random number generator (RNG) to place 1000 "stars" in a galaxy occupying a volume of $10 \times 10 \times 10$ (in appropriate units). Give each star a mass between 1 and 12 (also in appropriate units). For star number 1, calculate the gravitational pull on it due to every other star (direction and magnitude). Calculate the net vector sum of these gravitational pulls.

9. (4) Using your program above, do the calculation for every star in the galaxy.

10. (6) Let temperature T at each point of a volume $10 \times 10 \times 10$ be given by

$$T = \sum_{i=1}^{20} \frac{K_i}{(x - a_i)^2 + (y - b_i)^2 + (z - c_i)^2 + d_i}.$$

(This is called a *Shekel function*.) Choose the real values a_i's, b_i's, c_i's and d_i's randomly between 0 and 10. Likewise choose the K_i's randomly between 1 and 20. The problem is to estimate the maximum value of T as follows. Divide the space into blocks, say $1 \times 1 \times 1$. Evaluate the function at the center of each block. Where does the maximum occur? Now divide each block in half in each direction and redo the calculation. Does the new maximum point occur inside the same block?

11. (6) Devise a parallel algorithm to sieve $N = 1000000$ positive integers for primes. (Sieving means for $k = 2, 3, \ldots$, delete all multiples of k in the range 2 to N.)

12. (6) Use a random number generator to place 10000 points in the volume $10 \times 10 \times 10$. (a) Rotate each point around the z-axis by 30°. (b) Rotate each point around an axis up from the xy plane by 60° and in the vertical plane $y = (1/\sqrt{3})x$. In (b) how many points move from above the xy plane to below it?

PART II
Linear Systems

4

Building Blocks – Floating Point Numbers and Basic Linear Algebra

Many problems in scientific computation can be solved by reducing them to a problem in linear algebra. This turns out to be an extremely successful approach. Linear algebra problems often have a rich mathematical structure, which gives rise to a variety of highly efficient and well-optimized algorithms. Consequently, scientists frequently consider linear models or linear approximations to nonlinear models simply because the machinery for solving linear problems is so well developed.

Basic linear algebraic operations are so fundamental that many current computer architectures are designed to maximize performance of linear algebraic computations. Even the list of the top 500 fastest computers in the world (maintained at www.top500.org) uses the HPL benchmark for solving dense systems of linear equations as the main performance measure for ranking computer systems.

In 1973, Hanson, Krogh, and Lawson [9] described the advantages of adopting a set of basic routines for problems in linear algebra. These basic linear algebra subprograms are commonly referred to as the Basic Linear Algebra Subprograms (BLAS), and they are typically divided into three heirarchical levels: level 1 BLAS consists of vector–vector operations, level 2 BLAS are matrix–vector operations, and level 3 BLAS are matrix–matrix operations. The BLAS have been standardized with an application programming interface (API). This allows hardware vendors, compiler writers, and other specialists to provide programmers with access to highly optimized kernel routines adapted to specific architectures. Profiling tools indicate that many scientific computations spend most of their time in those sections of the code that call the BLAS. Thus, even small improvements in the BLAS can yield substantial speedups. Programmers who use higher level languages such as C and Fortran benefit by relying on optimally tuned and standardized libraries like BLAS for a large portion of their performance.

BLAS algorithms are available for download from www.netlib.org/blas.

4.1 Floating Point Numbers and Numerical Error

In computation, a distinction is made between integer numbers and noninteger real numbers, and they are stored in the computer in different ways. Integers are exact and can be tested for equality, for example,

```
int i = 0;
...
if( i == 3 ) {
...
}
```

Mathematically an *integer* is one of the numbers $0, \pm 1, \pm 2, \pm 3, \ldots$, and is a *countably infinite* set. Computer integers form a finite subset of this centered around 0.

The most widely used method for storing integers is *fixed width two's complement* binary storage using either 32 or 64 bits; 32 bits for a standard integer and 64 bits for a long integer. In the representation, one bit is used for the arithmetic sign of the number, the left-most, and the remaining bits are the number itself mathematically written in base 2; at least for nonnegative integers. For clarity we illustrate the method, using only 8 bits, but the ideas extend without trouble to any number of bits.

A sign bit of 0 expresses a positive integer or 0 while a sign bit of 1 indicates a negative integer. First, take it to be 0. Then, as stated, the remaining 7 bits, $b_6 b_5 \ldots b_1 b_0$, are the base 2 representation of the number, thus

$$(b_6 b_5 \ldots b_1 b_0)_2 = b_6 2^6 + b_5 2^5 + \cdots + b_1 2 + b_0.$$

In particular, (0000000) represents the integer 0, (0000001) is 1, (0000010) is 2, and so on up to (1111111), which is

$$1 \cdot 2^6 + 1 \cdot 2^5 + \cdots + 1 \cdot 2^1 + 1 \cdot 2^0 = \frac{2^7 - 1}{2 - 1}$$

or 127. In the general case using w bit representation, with therefore $w - 1$ bits available for the nonnegative integers, the maximum representable integer is

$$\text{maximum positive integer} = 2^{w-1} - 1.$$

For $w = 32$ this is 2,147,483,647 and for $w = 64$ we have 9,223,372,036,854, 775,807 or over 9×10^{18}.

Now assume the sign bit is 1. The guiding principle behind two's complement storage is that, when the negative number is added to its positive counterpart in binary, the result should be 0, thus $-x + x = 0$ ignoring overflow. In our 8-bit example this means that (10000001) represents -127 because, in binary arithmetic

$$
\begin{array}{r}
(10000001) \\
+(01111111) \\
\hline
1(00000000) \rightarrow (00000000)
\end{array}
$$

In this, the overflow into the 9th bit was dropped (automatically since there are only 8 bits). In the same way, the arrangement that represents -1 is seen to be (11111111) because adding 1 results in a carry into each place giving an all 0 result for the 8 bits.

What then does (10000000) code for? The answer is -128 since it is one less than (10000001). It is convenient to think of the two's complement integers as on a giant circle. Starting at $0 = (000\ldots00)$ and adding 1 repeatedly leads to the maximum positive representable integer, $(011\ldots11)$. But now, adding the next 1 gives the smallest representable integer, $(100\ldots00)$. Continuing to add 1 brings us step by step to $-1 = (11111111)$ and adding the final 1 gives back 0.

In the general case of w-width integers, the smallest representable one is -2^{w-1}, which is $-2,147,483,648$ for $w = 32$ and $-9,223,372,036,854,775,808$ for $w = 64$. Thus the 2^w possible combinations of w 0's and 1's divide themselves up into 2^{w-1} negative integers and 2^{w-1} nonnegative integers.

Note that the rule for producing the negative of a number in two's complement is to complement or flip all the bits and then add 1. The one exception to this is $(100\ldots00)$. By comparison, *one's complement* is to flip all the bits only.

Floating Point Numbers

While integers are just right for special purposes on the computer such as counting in loops and indexing arrays, they cannot represent fractions and they lack the ability to represent really big or small numbers. For this we need the *floating point* numbers. The floating point number representation is much like scientific notation; the decimal or binary point is moved to the right of the first significant digit and the result is multiplied by the appropriate power of 10 or 2. For example, in base 10, the number $x = 527.2$ is written as 5.272×10^2 in scientific notation. But computers use base 2 and it is easy to convert this number to base 2 giving

$$
\begin{aligned}
(527.2)_{10} &= \\
2^9 + 2^3 + 2^2 + 2^1 &+ 2^0 + 0 \cdot 2^{-1} + 0 \cdot 2^{-2} + 1 \cdot 2^{-3} + 1 \cdot 2^{-4} + \cdots \\
&= (1000001111.0011\cdots)_2 = (1.0000011110011\cdots)_2 \times 2^9.
\end{aligned}
$$

Table 7. *IEEE 754 Specifications*

	Sign	Exponent	Fraction	Bias
Single precision	1 [31]	8 [30–23]	23 [22–0]	127
Double precision	1 [63]	11 [62–52]	52 [51–0]	1023

Unfortunately $(527.2)_{10}$ cannot be represented exactly in base 2, those that can are called *binary rational numbers*, and so our representation must settle for an approximation to the actual number. The error incurred in the floating point storage of an exact real number is called *round-off error*; controlling round-off error is a fundamental issue in scientific computation.

In floating point notation a number has two components, the *exponent* is the power of 2 in the representation and the *mantissa* is the part of the number which the power of 2 multiplies. In storing this and other binary floating point numbers using a fixed number of bits, say 64, a decision must be made as to how many bits to allocate to the mantissa and how many to the exponent. It should be clear that the mantissa governs the extent of round-off error, that is, the precision of the representation, while the exponent controls the range of the numbers that can be represented. An agreement about this is incorporated into the IEEE standard 754 giving us the following Table 7 for single precision floating point, which uses 32 bits, and double precision floating point, which uses 64 bits. We will see that, in storage, we get one free mantissa bit, so the bits actually stored for the mantissa are called the *fraction bits*.

As shown, the leftmost bit codes for sign, the next set of bits from the left code for exponent and the rightmost bits code for fraction. We will explain "bias" shortly. The sign bit however is simpler here than for integers; if x is the value coded for by the exponent and fraction bits, then a sign bit of 0 codes for $+x$, and a sign bit of 1 codes for $-x$. In particular, $x = 0$ exits as $+0$ and -0 but the two are rendered the same via software, for example $+0 = -0$.

For the purposes of illustration, assume a 10-bit floating point system with 4 bits for exponent, 5 bits for fraction, a bias of 7 and 1 bit for sign as usual; we denote this as $\mathcal{F}(5, 4, 7)$. First consider the exponent. Both positive and negative exponents can arise but it would be wasteful to allocate an exponent bit for this purpose. Instead a fixed value called the *bias* is added to make the stored value of all exponents positive. Conversely, given a stored value of the exponent, the bias is subtracted to get the actual exponent. For example, using 4 bits for the exponent allows for $2^4 = 16$ stored exponent values ranging from 0 to 15. We will see below that two of these, namely 0 all of whose bits are 0 and 15 all of whose bits are 1, have special purposes so throw out 0 and 15. With a bias of 7, actual exponents may range from -6 to 7. In particular, the stored exponent equal to the bias, 7, codes for an actual exponent of 0. In general then, using e exponent bits and a bias of b, the range of exponents is

$$\text{smallest exponent} = 1 - b, \quad \text{largest exponent} = 2^e - 2 - b,$$

and 2^0 is coded by the bias b itself.

Now consider the mantissa. Since we have assumed the binary point to be to the right of the first significant digit, the first mantissa bit is always 1 (except for $x = 0$) and so there is no need to write it. For $x = 0$ itself, a special provision is made, all exponent and fraction bits equal to 0 codes for $x = 0$. With this provision, we actually achieve an additional bit of precision. Thus using f fraction bits the smallest mantissa (in base 2) is $(1.0\ldots0)_2$ with a 1 and f 0's and the largest is $(1.1\ldots1)_2$ with $1 + f$ 1's.

Let us consider the range of real numbers representable in our $\mathcal{F}(5, 4, 7)$ system. The largest is coded for by (0111011111) meaning $+(1.11111)_2 \times 2^{(1110)_2 - 7}$ or $(2 - 2^{-5}) \times 2^7 = 252$. In general, an $\mathcal{F}(f, e, b)$ floating point system will have a maximum value of

$$(1 + 2^{-1} + \cdots + 2^{-f}) \times 2^{2^e - 2 - b} = (2 - 2^{-f}) \times 2^{2^e - 2 - b}.$$

In particular, this is about 3.4×10^{38} for the single precision IEEE standard and 1.7×10^{308} for double precision. An attempt to represent a real number bigger than the maximum possible results in a *positive overflow*. An attempt to represent a real number smaller than the negative of this results in a *negative overflow*.

Consideration of the smallest positive representable number is complicated by the application of *denormalization*. This is another special case which does away with the assumed leading 1 if the exponent bits are all zero but one or more of the fraction bits are not. Without denormalization the smallest positive number is $(1.0\ldots0)_2 \times 2^{1-b}$, this being 2^{-6} in our $\mathcal{F}(5, 4, 7)$ system. But under denormalization the range $(0.11\ldots1)_2 \times 2^{1-b}$ down to $(0.00\ldots1)_2 \times 2^{1-b}$ is also represented. For our example this is $(1 - 2^{-5}) \times 2^{-6}$, picking up where the normalized system leaves off, down to $2^{-5} \times 2^{-6} = 2^{-11}$. Note that the denormalized exponent is taken as -6 and not -7 because otherwise the range from 2^{-6} down to 2^{-7} would not be covered. In general, the smallest positive real number in an $\mathcal{F}(f, e, b)$ system is

$$2^{1-b-f}.$$

For 32-bit IEEE this is $2^{-149} \approx 1.6 \times 10^{-45}$ and $2^{-1074} \approx 5 \times 10^{-324}$ for 64 bits.

Table 8. *Extended Arithmetic*

Operation	Result
$\dfrac{x}{\pm\infty}$	0
$\pm\infty \times \pm\infty$	$\pm\infty$
$\dfrac{\pm\text{nonzero}}{0}$	$\pm\infty$
$\infty + \infty$	∞
$\dfrac{\pm 0}{\pm 0}$	NaN
$\infty - \infty$	NaN
$\dfrac{\pm\infty}{\pm\infty}$	NaN
$\pm\infty \times 0$	NaN

Positive real numbers too small to represent are said to *underflow* (positively or negatively).

Infinity and Not a Number (NaN)

It can be desirable to allow the numbers $\pm\infty$ to be part of the floating point system; for example, $1/\infty = 0$ would be sensible. At other times operations with infinity must be handled with care by the programmer and usually depend on rates of convergence; for example, $\infty - \infty$. Table 8 defines these extended operations.

Infinity is encoded as all exponent bits 1 and all fraction bits 0. The sign is determined by the sign bit. Not a number, NaN, is represented with all exponent bits 1 and not all fraction bits 0.

Density of Floating Point Numbers and Round-off Error

Now fix the (actual) exponent, say at 0, and consider the effect of the fraction bits. If there are f fraction bits then combinatorially 2^f mantissas are possible. In our $\mathcal{F}(5, 4, 7)$ system, the possible exactly representable real numbers are $(1.00000)_2 \times 2^0$ up to $(1.11111)_2 \times 2^0$ in steps of 2^{-5}; this is the precision in the exponential band 2^0 to 2^1. But in the normalized case every exponential band, say 2^k to 2^{k+1}, has the same number of representatives, namely 2^f; the precision in this band is 2^{k-f}.

Given a real number x in this exponential band, let x^* be its floating point representation. Most computers form x^* by *truncation*; that is, if f fraction bits are being used, then the binary bits of x beyond f in the floating point

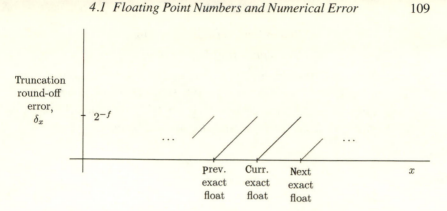

Fig. 19. Floating point relative truncation error.

representation are ignored. Hence, from above, the maximum difference between x and x^* is 2^{k-f}. Let δ_x be the relative error in the floating point representation of x, that is,

$$\delta_x = \frac{x - x^*}{x}.$$

Since the smallest value of x in this range is 2^k, the maximum round-off error is

$$\delta_x < \frac{2^{k-f}}{2^k} = 2^{-f}.$$

The graph of δ_x is saw-tooth, being 0 for exactly representable real numbers and then increasing linearly up to 2^{-f} just before the next representable real number (see Fig. 19).

In the denormalized case, there are $2^{-f} - 1$ different mantissas since all fraction bits equal to 0 are not allowed. And as we have seen above, they range from $(0.11 \ldots 1)_2 \times 2^{1-b}$ down to $(0.00 \ldots 1)_2 \times 2^{1-b}$ in steps of 2^{1-b-f} and this is the precision. Of course, for x near 0, the absolute value of $x - x^* \approx 2^{1-b-f}$ is on the same order of magnitude as x itself, so the relative error is large here.

Round-off error is closely related to *machine epsilon*, ϵ_m. Precisely, machine epsilon is defined as the smallest positive floating point number which, when added to 1, gives a result strictly bigger than 1. For an $\mathcal{F}(f, e, b)$ system using truncation, machine epsilon is the next number bigger than 1, hence $\epsilon_m = (1 + 2^{-f}) - 1 = 2^{-f}$.

4.2 Round-off Error Propagation

Adding Numbers of Different Sizes

Assume now a base 10 floating point system that uses 4 mantissa digits and 3 exponent digits, we will denote this by $S(4, 3)_{10}$. Consider adding the two numbers 125.0 and 0.02. The first is represented as 1.250×10^2 and the second as 2.000×10^{-2}. In calculating their sum, the decimal points must be aligned,

$$1.250|0 \times 10^2$$

$$0.000|2 \times 10^2$$

but since there are only 4 precision digits available, all digits after the 4th are truncated and so the 2 is discarded. Hence, in this system $125.0 + 0.02 = 125.0$.

This shows the problem of adding numbers of different sizes. In another example, suppose that it is desired to calculate the sum of the infinite series $\sum_k 0.4^k$. In our $S(4, 3)_{10}$ system we get

k	$(.4)^k$ (exact)	sum k increasing	sum k decreasing
0	1.0	1.0	1.666
1	0.4	1.4	0.6665
2	0.16	1.56	0.2665
3	0.064	1.624	0.1065
4	0.0256	1.649	0.04259
5	0.01024	1.659	0.01699
6	0.004096	1.663	0.006756
7	0.0016384	1.664	0.002660
8	0.00065536	1.664	0.001022
9	0.000262155	1.664	0.0003669
10	0.000104858	1.664	0.0001048

The correct answer in this floating point system is 1.666 for the exact value of $(1 - 0.4^{11})/(1 - 0.4)$. The relative error adding from bigger to smaller numbers is 0.12%, but there is no error, in this case, adding from smaller numbers to the bigger ones.

Subtracting Numbers About the Same Size

Suppose that two numbers are generated in the course of a computation and we must calculate their difference; say the numbers are 125.68 and 125.31. If arithmetic were exact, the result would be 0.37. But let us suppose we calculate the difference in a $S(4, 3)_{10}$ (decimal) system. Because of the roundoff error imposed by the system, the first is taken to be 1.256×10^2 and the second 1.253×10^2. Then their floating point difference is 0.3 instead of 0.37. This is an unavoidable error of 23% (0.07/0.3). But in addition to that, whereas the original floating point representations had 4 digits of precision (possibly the last digit of each operand is wrong), the floating point difference has only 1 (or none if the last digits of the operands were indeed wrong). This type of problem is ever present in the numerical calculation of derivatives.

Condition

The *condition*, cond($f(x)$), or *condition number* of a calculation $f(x)$ measures its sensitivity to changes in the argument x. Condition is defined by

$$\text{cond}(f(x)) = \frac{\left(\frac{\Delta f}{f}\right)}{\left(\frac{\Delta x}{x}\right)} = \max_{|x-y| \text{ small}} \frac{\left|\frac{f(x)-f(y)}{f(y)}\right|}{\left|\frac{x-y}{y}\right|} \approx \left|\frac{f'(x)x}{f(x)}\right|.$$

A calculation is *well-conditioned* if cond($f(x)$) is small and *ill-conditioned* if it is large.

For example, let $f(x) = 10/(1 - x^2)$, then

$$\text{cond}(f(x)) = \frac{2x^2}{|1 - x^2|}$$

so the calculation is ill-conditioned near $x = 1$.

In another example, consider the calculation $f(x) = \sqrt{x+1} - \sqrt{x}$ for $x = 12345$. Calculating the condition of f directly, we get

$$\text{cond}(f(x)) = \left|\frac{\frac{x}{2}\left(\frac{1}{\sqrt{x+1}} - \frac{1}{\sqrt{x}}\right)}{\sqrt{x+1} - \sqrt{x}}\right|$$

$$= \left|\frac{x}{2\sqrt{x+1}\sqrt{x}}\right|\Bigg|_{x=12345} \approx \frac{1}{2}.$$

Seemingly a well-conditioned calculation. But if this computation is performed in a $S(15, 9)$ base 2 floating point system, the relative error is 173%, why?

Consider the DAG of the calculation as shown in Fig. 20. Ones sees that in the computer the calculation is actually carried out in several steps, each step having its own condition. Therefore we compute the condition for each step.

Step (1) $x_0 = 12345$.

Step (2) $x_1 = x_0 + 1$; with $g(x) = x + 1$ the condition is
$$\text{cond}(g(x)) = \frac{g'(x_0)x_0}{g(x_0)} = \frac{x_0}{x_0+1} = \frac{12345}{123456} \approx 1.$$

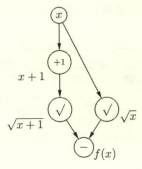

Fig. 20. DAG for $\sqrt{x+1} - \sqrt{x}$.

Step (3) $x_2 = \sqrt{x_0}$; here $g(x) = \sqrt{x}$,

$\quad$ $\text{cond}(g(x)) = \frac{\frac{1}{2\sqrt{x}}x}{\sqrt{x}} = \frac{1}{2}$.

Step (4) $x_3 = \sqrt{x_1}$; as above, the condition of this step is $\frac{1}{2}$.

Step (5) $x_4 = x_3 - x_2$; here $g(x) = x - c$ with $c = \sqrt{12345}$,

$\quad$ $\text{cond}(g(x)) = \frac{x}{x-c} = \frac{\sqrt{12346}}{\sqrt{123456} - \sqrt{12345}} = 22,200$.

From the last line, any error present at Step 5, round-off, for instance, will be magnified approximately 22,200 times by that step. This exercise shows that a step-by-step condition calculation can quantitatively pinpoint numerically unstable computation problems.

$\quad$ Obviously we would like to do something to alleviate the bad condition problem in this example if possible; we try restructuring the calculation,

$$\sqrt{x+1} - \sqrt{x} = \frac{(\sqrt{x+1} - \sqrt{x})(\sqrt{x+1} + \sqrt{x})}{\sqrt{x+1} + \sqrt{x}}$$

$$= \frac{1}{\sqrt{x+1} + \sqrt{x}}.$$

$\quad$ The step-by-step condition is recalculated for this form. Steps 1–4 are the same as before.

Step (5) $x_4 = x_3 + x_2$; take $g(x) = x + c$ with $c = \sqrt{12345}$,

$\quad$ $\text{cond}(g(x)) = \frac{x}{x+c} = \frac{\sqrt{12346}}{\sqrt{123456} + \sqrt{12345}} \approx \frac{1}{2}$.

Step (6) $x_5 = \frac{1}{x_4}$; here $g(x) = \frac{1}{x}$,

$\quad$ $\text{cond}(g(x)) = \frac{\frac{1}{x^2}x}{\frac{1}{x}} = 1$.

This is a very different result; the condition of the restructured calculation is satisfactory.

4.3 Basic Matrix Arithmetic

BLAS are at the heart of every computer program that calculates with (mathematical) vectors or matrices. That being the case, one sees that by optimizing the BLAS tasks, all vector and matrix programs benefit. The BLAS Level 1 tasks deal with vector–vector operations such as dot product, scalar–vector product, and vector addition, BLAS Level 2 tasks deal with matrix–vector operations, and BLAS Level 3 tasks deal with matrix–matrix operations such as matrix–matrix multiply and matrix powers.

Our purpose here is to regard the computational problem from the point of view of parallelization or vectorization and to examine alternatives for the calculation, especially for the Levels 2 and 3 tasks.

With respect to the BLAS tasks, parallelizability and vectorizability are essentially the same thing. The work to achieve these tasks is performed in one or more nested, tight loops free of recursion.

Dot Product

Mathematically, the dot or inner-product of two vectors $\mathbf{x}$ and $\mathbf{y}$ is given by $\text{dot} = \sum_{i=1}^{n} x_i y_i$. In pseudocode this is calculated as

```
dot ← 0;
loop  i=1 to n
      dot ← dot + xᵢ * yᵢ;
end  loop
```

As we have seen, this does not parallelize. It is the basic fan-in calculation which can be performed by pseudovectorization on a vector machine.

Complexity: $O(\log n)$ time using $n/2$ processors (see the problems).

Scalar–Vector Product

Mathematically, this is the calculation $\mathbf{y} = a\mathbf{x} = (ax_1, ax_2, \ldots, ax_n)$, where a is a scalar (real or complex) and $\mathbf{x}$ is a vector. In pseudocode this is calculated as

```
loop  i=1 to n (in parallel)
      yᵢ ← x a*xᵢ;
end  loop
```

This operation parallelizes completely; throughout this chapter we indicate parallelization in our pseudocode as in this example.

Complexity: $O(1)$ time using n processors.

Vector Addition

For vectors $\mathbf{x}$ and $\mathbf{y}$, mathematically their sum is $\mathbf{z} = \mathbf{x} + \mathbf{y}$ component by component.

```
loop i=1 to n (in parallel)
   zᵢ ← xᵢ+yᵢ;
end loop
```

This operation parallelizes. A DAG of this computation is was given in Fig. 13 of Chapter 2. As above, the loop parallelizes.

Complexity: O(1) time using n processors.

Sum of n Vectors, Each m × 1

This is the operation $\mathbf{y} = \mathbf{x}_1 + \mathbf{x}_2 + \cdots + \mathbf{x}_n$, where $\mathbf{x}_i$ is an m-dimensional vector

$$\mathbf{x}_i = [\,x_{i1} \quad x_{i2} \quad \ldots \quad x_{im}\,]^T.$$

The computation looks like this.

```
loop i=1 to n (in parallel)
   dotᵢ ← 0;
   loop j=1 to m
      dotᵢ ← dotᵢ + xᵢⱼ;
   end loop
   yᵢ ← dotᵢ;
end loop
```

The inner loop is a fan-in calculation for each component; hence, it does not parallelize, but each component can be done in parallel with the other components. A DAG for this calculation is given in Fig. 21.

Complexity: O($\log n$) time using $mn/2$ processors.

Sum of n Matrices, Each m × m

This is the same problem as above since a matrix can be viewed as a vector if listed row-by-row for example. As above, this is a fan-in calculation in each matrix position i, j but can be parallelized with respect to the other positions.

Complexity: O($\log n$) time using $m^2n/2$ processors.

Partition the data by components

Sum the first components   Sum the second components $\cdots$

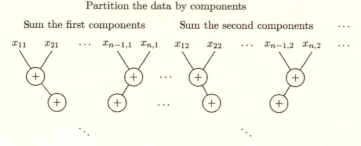

Fig. 21. DAG for the sum of vectors.

Matrix–Vector multiply

Let A be an $m \times n$ matrix and $\mathbf{x}$ an $n \times 1$ vector and put $\mathbf{y} = A\mathbf{x}$. The calculation consists of m inner products, one for each row of the matrix, each of which is n components long. Therefore the complexity is O($\log n$).

If only m processors are available, using one per row leaves each fan-in to be done by a single processor and so requires an order n time. On the other hand, with only 1 processor overall, the time is on the order of mn.

Complexity: O($\log n$).
Time: O($\log n$) using $mn/2$ processors.
Time: O(n) using m processors, one per row.
Time: O(mn) using 1 processor.

Computing a matrix–vector product can be accomplished in two different ways, by the *inner-product model* or by the *linear combination of columns* model.

Inner Product Model

Let $\mathbf{a}_{i\cdot}$ denote the ith row of A. Then A may be regarded as an $m \times 1$ matrix of these row vectors. This is called a *partition* of A. In terms of the partition, the matrix–vector product can be written as

$$
A\mathbf{x} = \begin{bmatrix} \mathbf{a}_{1\cdot} \\ \mathbf{a}_{2\cdot} \\ \vdots \\ \mathbf{a}_{m\cdot} \end{bmatrix} \mathbf{x} = \begin{bmatrix} \mathbf{a}_{1\cdot} \cdot \mathbf{x} \\ \mathbf{a}_{2\cdot} \cdot \mathbf{x} \\ \vdots \\ \mathbf{a}_{m\cdot} \cdot \mathbf{x} \end{bmatrix}.
$$

In this, each resultant component, $y_i = \mathbf{a}_{i\cdot} \cdot \mathbf{x}$, is calculated in its entirety before moving to the next component.

Pseudocode for the calculation is

```
loop  i=1 to m (in parallel)  // outer loop on the rows
of A
  yᵢ ← 0;
  loop  j=1 to n   // inner loop on the components of x
    yᵢ ←  yᵢ + aᵢⱼ * xⱼ;
  end  loop
end  loop
```

The inner-most loop does not parallelize or vectorize; there is no vector array reference on the left-hand side in the inner-most loop. In fact, as we have observed above, this is an inner-product calculation and so only pseudovectorizes. In addition, it is best to use a temporary variable, like "sum," to accumulate the sum in the inner loop rather than recalculating the y_j address repeatedly. Most modern optimizing compilers will detect this and do it automatically.

Linear Combination of Columns Model

Now let $\mathbf{a}_{.j}$ denote the jth column of A, and partition A into the $1 \times n$ matrix of its columns. The column vector $\mathbf{x}$ must be partitioned as a $1 \times n$ vector of scalars to be compatible. The matrix vector product now becomes

$$A\mathbf{x} = [\, \mathbf{a}_{.1} \quad \mathbf{a}_{.2} \quad \cdots \quad \mathbf{a}_{.n} \,] \begin{bmatrix} x_1 \\ x_2 \\ \vdots \\ x_n \end{bmatrix} = x_1 \mathbf{a}_{.1} + x_2 \mathbf{a}_{.2} + \cdots + x_n \mathbf{a}_{.n}.$$

In this form we accumulate the resultant y's piecemeal.

In pseudocode,

```
loop  i=1 to n (in parallel)
  yᵢ ← 0;
  end  loop
loop  j=1 to n  // outer loop on the components of x
  loop  i=1 to m (in parallel)  // inner loop on the rows
  of A for a fixed column
    yᵢ ← yᵢ + xⱼ * aᵢⱼ; // scalar multiply the jth A vector
  end  loop
end  loop
```

Here the innermost loop parallelizes and vectorizes, but n sums must still be done.

A modification of this algorithm is to unroll the inner loop, say to a depth of 2. The value of this is to balance the time for fetch operations with the time for the vector addition. Thus

```
loop  i=1 to n (in parallel)
   yᵢ ← 0;
end  loop
loop  j=1 to n
   loop  i=1 to m increment by 2 (in parallel)
      yᵢ ← yᵢ + xⱼ * aᵢⱼ + xⱼ * aᵢ₊₁,ⱼ;
   end  loop
end  loop
```

Matrix–Matrix Multiply, ijk-Forms

The task is to multiply an $m \times n$ matrix A into an $n \times \ell$ matrix B to produce an $m \times \ell$ matrix C. From a complexity standpoint, the calculation consists of $m\ell$ inner products, each n long. Thus we get a complexity of $\log n$, using $mn\ell/2$ processors.

Suppose now $m = \ell = n$ and we have only n^2 processors. We can allocate one per product and so the time will be $n - 1$. Alternatively we can allocate one per column (of the second matrix) in which case the computation is that of n matrix–vector multiplies each using n processors; this takes $n - 1$ time or the same as before. (Allocating one processor per row gives the same result.)

If we have only n processors, then again we can allocate one per column (or row) and do the matrix–vector calculations now with only one processor. This requires $n(n - 1)$ time (or order n^2 time).

Summarizing
Complexity: $O(\log n)$ using $O(mn\ell)$ processors
If $m = \ell = n$,
Time: $O(\log n)$ time using $O(n^3)$ processors.
Time: $O(n)$ time using $O(n^2)$ processors.
Time: $O(n^2)$ time using $O(n)$ processors.

The most direct calculation of the matrix product $AB = C$ is given by

$$c_{ij} = \sum_{k=1}^{n} a_{ik} * b_{kj} \qquad 1 \le i \le m, \quad 1 \le j \le \ell.$$

Implementing this requires three loops, on i, j, and k. But since only finite sums are involved, the loops may be done in arbitrary order. There are $3! = 6$

different ways to order i, j, and k; they are ijk, jik, ikj, jki, kij, and kji. These are called the ijk-*forms*. In the following we will see that the type of calculation performed depends on the position of k in the form. This being so, we expect that the computational time for this task varies from one of the six forms to the next. This is indeed so; it is especially true for the implementation on vector computers. We will investigate the timing of the calculation in the Exercises.

Partition matrices may be used to study the calculation. We first decompose according to the first index, then according to the second. Note that i corresponds to the rows of A, j to the columns of B and k to both the columns of A and the rows of B.

Inner-Product Model, Forms ijk and jik

Corresponding to ijk, first decompose A on i,

$$ AB = \begin{bmatrix} \mathbf{a}_{1\cdot} \\ \mathbf{a}_{2\cdot} \\ \vdots \\ \mathbf{a}_{m\cdot} \end{bmatrix} B $$

then B on j

$$ AB = \begin{bmatrix} \mathbf{a}_{1\cdot} \\ \mathbf{a}_{2\cdot} \\ \vdots \\ \mathbf{a}_{m\cdot} \end{bmatrix} \begin{bmatrix} \mathbf{b}_{\cdot 1} & \mathbf{b}_{\cdot 2} & \cdots & \mathbf{b}_{\cdot \ell} \end{bmatrix}. $$

This is an $m \times 1$ "column vector" times a $1 \times \ell$ "row vector." The result is $m\ell$ products of row vectors of A with column vectors of B, that is $m\ell$ inner products. The inner-most loop calculation gives this method its name. The outer loops can proceed along the columns j of C for each fixed row i giving an ijk order, or along the rows of C for each fixed column giving a jik order.

Reversing the order of i and j leads to the same decomposition. In terms of code these give the following. The first step is to initialize all elements of C to zero which we indicate by $C = 0$.

ijk-form	jik-form

```
C ← 0;
  loop  i=1 to m (in parallel)
    loop  j=1 to ℓ (in parallel)
      loop  k=1 to n
        c_ij ← c_ij+ a_ik* b_kj;
```

```
C ← 0;
  loop  j=1 to ℓ (in parallel)
    loop  i=1 to m (in parallel)
      loop  k=1 to n
        c_ij ← c_ij+ a_ik* b_kj;
```

```
            end  loop                        end  loop
          end  loop                        end  loop
        end  loop                        end  loop
```

(a) Inner product   (b) Dual inner product

Middle-Product Model, Forms ikj and jki

Corresponding to ikj, first decompose with respect to i,

$$AB = \begin{bmatrix} \mathbf{a}_1. \\ \mathbf{a}_2. \\ \vdots \\ \mathbf{a}_m. \end{bmatrix} \quad B = \begin{bmatrix} \mathbf{a}_1.B \\ \mathbf{a}_2.B \\ \vdots \\ \mathbf{a}_m.B \end{bmatrix}.$$

Next decompose on k, each term $\mathbf{a}_i.B$ becomes

$$\mathbf{a}_i.B = \begin{bmatrix} a_{i1} & a_{i2} & \cdots & a_{in} \end{bmatrix} \begin{bmatrix} \mathbf{b}_1. \\ \mathbf{b}_2. \\ \vdots \\ \mathbf{b}_n. \end{bmatrix} = a_{i1}\mathbf{b}_1. + \cdots + a_{in}\mathbf{b}_n..$$

So the operation in the inner-most loop is the scalar times vector product $a_{ik}\mathbf{b}_k..$
For jki we get,

$$AB = A\begin{bmatrix} \mathbf{b}_{.1} & \mathbf{b}_{.2} & \cdots & \mathbf{b}_{.\ell} \end{bmatrix} = \begin{bmatrix} A\mathbf{b}_{.1} & A\mathbf{b}_{.2} & \cdots & A\mathbf{b}_{.\ell} \end{bmatrix}$$

This is a 1×1 "scalar," A, times a $1 \times \ell$ "vector" giving a $1 \times \ell$ "vector" C.
Each of these components of C is an $m \times n$ by $n \times 1$ matrix–vector product.
Now these products are computed by the linear combination of vectors model
as above

$$A\mathbf{b}_{.j} = b_{1j}\mathbf{a}_{.1} + \cdots + b_{nj}\mathbf{a}_{.n}.$$

Hence in each case, the innermost loop will be scalar products of vectors.

ikj-form   jki-form

```
C ← 0;                                  C ← 0;
 loop  i=1 to m (in parallel)            loop  j=1 to ℓ (in parallel)
  loop  k=1 to n                          loop  k=1 to n
    loop  j=1 to ℓ (in parallel)            loop  i=1 to m (in parallel)
      cᵢⱼ ← cᵢⱼ + aᵢₖ * bₖⱼ;                   cᵢⱼ ← cᵢⱼ + aᵢₖ * bₖⱼ;
     end loop                               end loop
    end loop                              end loop
   end loop                             end  loop
```

(a) Middle product   (b) Dual middle product

Outer-Product Model

Corresponding to kij, first decompose with respect to k,

$$AB = [\, \mathbf{a}_{.1} \quad \mathbf{a}_{.2} \quad \cdots \quad \mathbf{a}_{.n}\,]
\begin{bmatrix} \mathbf{b}_{1.} \\ \mathbf{b}_{2.} \\ \vdots \\ \mathbf{b}_{n.} \end{bmatrix}.$$

This is a $1 \times n$ "row vector" times an $n \times 1$ "column vector" giving a sum of products of $m \times 1$ column vectors by $1 \times \ell$ row vectors. Each of these products is called an outer product of vectors and gives an $m \times \ell$ matrix; C is the sum of these matrices. As in the middle-product model, the inner-most loop is a vector operation.

kij-form	kji-form

```
C ← 0;                          C ← 0;
loop k=1 to n                   loop k=1 to n
   loop i=1 to m (in parallel)     loop j=1 to ℓ (in parallel)
   loop j=1 to ℓ (in parallel)     loop i=1 to m (in parallel)
      cᵢⱼ ← cᵢⱼ + aᵢₖ * bₖⱼ;          cᵢⱼ ← cᵢⱼ + aᵢₖ * bₖⱼ;
      end loop                       end loop
   end loop                       end loop
end loop                        end loop
```

(a) Outer product	(b) Dual Outer product

Matrix Powers

From Section 2.2 we saw that the time complexity for squaring an $m \times m$ matrix is $O(\log m)$ using $O(m^3)$ processors. Furthermore, to calculate all powers of A from A^2 through A^n, we may proceed as in Fig. 15, the Russian Peasant Algorithm. Therefore for the entire calculation we have,

Complexity: O $\lceil \log n \rceil (1 + \lceil \log m \rceil)$

using $p = \frac{n}{2} m^3$ processors.

4.4 Operations with Banded Matrices

A banded matrix A, with semibandwidth α, is one for which

$$a_{ij} = 0 \qquad \text{if } |i - j| > \alpha.$$

For example, for a matrix with semibandwidth 1, the elements of the first row, a_{1j}, are all zero except, possibly, a_{11} and a_{12}. In the second row, only a_{21}, a_{22}, and a_{23} can be nonzero, and so on. In general, all diagonals except the main diagonal and the one immediately above and below it are zero. A matrix with semibandwidth 1 is called a *tridiagonal matrix*.

Banded Matrix–Vector Product by Diagonals

If the semibandwidth α is small, it is much more efficient to store the matrix by diagonals and also to multiply with the matrix by diagonals. For example, a 100×100 tridiagonal matrix has only $100 + 2 \cdot 99 = 298$ nonzero elements, the other $100^2 - 298$ elements are zero and there is no need to store them or compute with them.

We name the diagonals of an $n \times n$ matrix, as shown in Eq. (2), by A_0 for the main diagonal, then $A_1, A_2, \ldots, A_{n-1}$, for successively the first superdiagonal, the second superdiagonal, and so on. The first subdiagonal is A_{-1}, the second is A_{-2}, and so on until the last, A_{-n+1}.

$$
\begin{matrix}
A_0 & A_1 & A_2 & A_3 & \cdots & A_{n-1} & & \\
\end{matrix}
$$

$$
\begin{matrix}
A_{-1} \\
A_{-2} \\
\vdots \\
A_{-n+1} \\
\\
\end{matrix}
\begin{bmatrix}
a_{11} & a_{12} & a_{13} & \cdots & a_{1,n-1} & a_{1n} \\
a_{21} & a_{22} & a_{23} & \cdots & a_{2,n-1} & a_{2n} \\
\vdots & \vdots & \vdots & \ddots & \vdots & \vdots \\
a_{n-1,1} & a_{n-1,2} & a_{n-1,3} & \cdots & a_{n-1,n-1} & a_{n-1,n} \\
a_{n1} & a_{n2} & a_{n3} & \cdots & a_{n-1,n} & a_{nn}
\end{bmatrix}
\begin{bmatrix}
x_1 \\
x_2 \\
\vdots \\
x_{n-1} \\
x_n
\end{bmatrix}
\quad (2)
$$

We may write the product of A with the vector $\mathbf{x}$ as the following sum of vectors:

$$
\begin{matrix}
A_{-n+1} & & A_{-n+2} & & A_{-1} & & A_0 \\
\end{matrix}
$$

$$
\begin{bmatrix}
0 \\
0 \\
0 \\
\vdots \\
0 \\
a_{n1}x_1
\end{bmatrix}
+
\begin{bmatrix}
0 \\
0 \\
0 \\
\vdots \\
a_{n-1,1}x_1 \\
a_{n2}x_2
\end{bmatrix}
+ \cdots +
\begin{bmatrix}
0 \\
a_{21}x_1 \\
a_{32}x_2 \\
\vdots \\
a_{n-1,n-2}x_{n-2} \\
a_{n,n-1}x_{n-1}
\end{bmatrix}
+
\begin{bmatrix}
a_{11}x_1 \\
a_{22}x_2 \\
a_{33}x_3 \\
\vdots \\
a_{n-1,n-1}x_{n-1} \\
a_{nn}x_n
\end{bmatrix}
$$

$$
\begin{matrix}
A_1 & & A_2 & & A_{n-1} \\
\end{matrix}
$$

$$
+
\begin{bmatrix}
a_{12}x_2 \\
a_{23}x_3 \\
a_{34}x_4 \\
\vdots \\
a_{n-1,n}x_n \\
0
\end{bmatrix}
+
\begin{bmatrix}
a_{13}x_3 \\
a_{24}x_4 \\
a_{35}x_5 \\
\vdots \\
0 \\
0
\end{bmatrix}
+ \cdots +
\begin{bmatrix}
a_{1n}x_n \\
0 \\
0 \\
\vdots \\
0 \\
0
\end{bmatrix}
$$

Write the middle vector in this sum as $A_0 \times \mathbf{x}$,

$$
\begin{bmatrix}
a_{11}x_1 \\
a_{22}x_2 \\
a_{33}x_3 \\
\vdots \\
a_{n-1,n-1}x_{n-1} \\
a_{nn}x_n
\end{bmatrix}
= A_0 \times \mathbf{x}
$$

where this product $\times$ means component by component multiplication just as $+$ for vectors means component by component sum. This is called the *Hadamard product* of these vectors. In similar fashion

$$
\begin{bmatrix}
a_{12}x_2 \\
a_{23}x_3 \\
a_{34}x_4 \\
\vdots \\
a_{n-1,n}x_n \\
0
\end{bmatrix}
=
\begin{bmatrix}
a_{12} \\
a_{23} \\
a_{34} \\
\vdots \\
a_{n-1,n} \\
0
\end{bmatrix}
\times
\begin{bmatrix}
x_2 \\
x_3 \\
x_4 \\
\vdots \\
x_n \\
0
\end{bmatrix}
= A_1 \times \hat{\mathbf{x}}^1.
$$

In this we have used the notation $\hat{\mathbf{x}}^1$ to mean "push up once," giving the required part of the $\mathbf{x}$ vector. Continuing, we write the contribution of the A_{-1} diagonal as

$$
\begin{bmatrix}
0 \\
a_{21} \\
a_{32} \\
\vdots \\
a_{n-1,n-2} \\
a_{n,n-1}
\end{bmatrix}
\times
\begin{bmatrix}
0 \\
x_1 \\
x_2 \\
\vdots \\
x_{n-1}
\end{bmatrix}
= A_{-1} \times \hat{\mathbf{x}}^{-1}
$$

where the notation $\hat{\mathbf{x}}^{-1}$ means "push down once." In a similar fashion all the contributions may be written as vector products of the diagonals $A_{\pm k}$ of A times the corresponding pushed up or down version of $\mathbf{x}$, namely $\hat{\mathbf{x}}^{\pm k}$.

Tridiagonal Matrix–Matrix Product

Let C be the product of the two tridiagonal matrices A and B. The three nonzero diagonals of A and B are, respectively, A_{-1}, A_0, A_1, B_{-1}, B_0, and B_1. The resultant diagonals of C are C_{-2}, C_{-1}, C_0, C_1, and C_2. These are given by

$$
C_0 = \begin{bmatrix} c_{11} \\ c_{22} \\ c_{33} \\ \vdots \\ c_{nn} \end{bmatrix} = \begin{bmatrix} 0 & + & a_{11}b_{11} & + & a_{12}b_{21} \\ a_{21}b_{12} & + & a_{22}b_{22} & + & a_{23}b_{32} \\ a_{32}b_{23} & + & a_{33}b_{33} & + & a_{34}b_{43} \\ \vdots & & \vdots & & \vdots \\ a_{n,n-1}b_{n-1,n} & + & a_{nn}b_{nn} & + & 0 \end{bmatrix}
$$

$$
= \begin{bmatrix} 0 \\ a_{21}b_{12} \\ a_{32}b_{23} \\ \vdots \\ a_{n,n-1}b_{n-1,n} \end{bmatrix} + \begin{bmatrix} a_{11}b_{11} \\ a_{22}b_{22} \\ a_{33}b_{33} \\ \vdots \\ a_{nn}b_{nn} \end{bmatrix} + \begin{bmatrix} a_{12}b_{21} \\ a_{23}b_{32} \\ a_{34}b_{43} \\ \vdots \\ 0 \end{bmatrix}
$$

$$
= \begin{bmatrix} 0 \\ \uparrow \\ A_{-1} \\ | \\ \downarrow \end{bmatrix} \times \begin{bmatrix} 0 \\ \uparrow \\ B_1 \\ | \\ \downarrow \end{bmatrix} + A_0 \times B_0 + \begin{bmatrix} \uparrow \\ A_1 \\ | \\ \downarrow \\ 0 \end{bmatrix} \times \begin{bmatrix} \uparrow \\ B_{-1} \\ | \\ \downarrow \\ 0 \end{bmatrix}.
$$

Similarly

$$
C_1 = \begin{bmatrix} c_{12} \\ c_{23} \\ c_{34} \\ \vdots \\ c_{n-1,n} \end{bmatrix} = \begin{bmatrix} a_{11}b_{12} & + & a_{12}b_{22} \\ a_{22}b_{23} & + & a_{23}b_{33} \\ a_{33}b_{34} & + & a_{34}b_{44} \\ \vdots & & \vdots \\ a_{n-1,n-1}b_{n-1,n} & + & a_{n-1,n}b_{nn} \end{bmatrix}
$$

$$
= \begin{bmatrix} a_{11} \\ a_{22} \\ a_{33} \\ \vdots \\ a_{n-1,n-1} \end{bmatrix} \times \begin{bmatrix} b_{12} \\ b_{23} \\ b_{34} \\ \vdots \\ b_{n-1,n} \end{bmatrix} + \begin{bmatrix} a_{12} \\ a_{23} \\ a_{34} \\ \vdots \\ a_{n-1,n} \end{bmatrix} \times \begin{bmatrix} b_{22} \\ b_{33} \\ b_{44} \\ \vdots \\ b_{nn} \end{bmatrix}.
$$

We may write this as

$$
C_1 = A_0^{-1} \times B_1 + A_1 \times B_0^1
$$

where the superscript 1 means discard the first element and the superscript -1 means discard the last. Similarly

$$
C_{-1} = A_0^1 \times B_{-1} + A_{-1} \times B_0,
$$
$$
C_2 = A_1 \times B_1^1, \quad \text{and} \quad C_{-2} = A_{-1}^1 \times B_{-1}.
$$

Again, the superscript 1 means discard the first element.

Obviously Hadamard products have exactly the same time complexity and parallelization and vectorization properties as vector addition does.

Exercises

1. (5) Assume floating point numbers use 16 bits allocated as (11,5) meaning 11 bits for manissa and sign and 5 bits for exponent. Assume a bias of 15. (a) What is the largest positive number representable? The smallest negative number (largest in absolute value)? (b) What is the smallest positive number? The largest negative number? (c) Represent in this system the numbers 78.25, 0.2. (d) If the machine representation is (01000110100_11011), what decimal number does it represent?

2. (4) Assume a (11,5) floating point system as in Exercise 1 above. (a) How many numbers can be exactly represented? (b) How many numbers in the range $[1, 2)$ can be exactly represented? (c) Same question for the ranges $[2, 4)$ and $[1/32, 1/16)$?

3. (3) If $x_0 = 0.6$, $x_1 = 1.0$, $x_2 = 1.2$, and $f(x_0) = 4.0$, $f(x_1) = 5.3$, and $f(x_2) = 2.3$, find the condition of the calculation of $f[x_0, x_1, x_2]$, which is defined as

$$f[x_0, x_1, x_2] = \frac{f[x_0, x_1] - f[x_1, x_2]}{x_0 - x_2} = \frac{\frac{f(x_0)-f(x_1)}{x_0-x_1} - \frac{f(x_1)-f(x_2)}{x_1-x_2}}{x_0 - x_2}.$$

4. (3) Using the Vector Timing Data Table (p. 11), time an n-dimensional matrix vector product according to both the inner-product model and the linear combination of columns model. (Assume a single vector processor, not multiple parallel vector processors.)

5. (5) Using the Vector Timing Data Table (p. 11), time the ijk-forms for the $m \times n$ by $n \times q$ matrix product $C = AB$. Are there choices of m, n, and q for which the inner-product model is faster than the outer-product model?

6. (4) Use the Vector Timing Data Table (p. 11) to time (a) Row-oriented Back Substitution, (b) Column-oriented Back Substitiution. (See p. 132.)

7. (2) Show that a dot product can be done in $2 + \lceil(\log n)\rceil$ time, using $n/2$ processors.

8. (3) Let the matrices A, B, C, have orders $m \times n, n \times p$, and $p \times q$, respectively. How many operations are required to compute $A(BC)$? How many for $(AB)C$? Give an example where the first is preferred and an example where the second is preferred.

9. (3) Let A be an $m \times n$ matrix and B an $n \times q$ matrix. Assume there are $p = nmq$ distributed memory processors. Give a storage distribution of A and B across the processors so that all mnq multiplications needed to form AB can be done in parallel. Show that the time complexity is $1 + O(\log n)$.

10. (3) Let A and B be matrices with semibandwidths of α and β, respectively. Show that AB has semibandwidth $\alpha + \beta$.

11. (3) Show that if the nonsingular tridiagonal matrix A can be factored as $A = LU$, where L is lower triangular (p. 127) and U is upper triangular (p. 131), then both L and U are also tridiagonal.

12. (6) Let A be an $n \times n$ tridiagonal matrix. We want to calculate A^2 on a distributed memory parallel computer system having p processors, where p evenly divides n (approximately). Assume a multiplication or addition requires $t_a = t$ ns of time while a data movement between processors requires $t_c = ct$ ns, $c > 1$. As usual, processing is concurrent across processors, and assume that, within a processor, communication is concurrent with arithmetic calculation. Furthermore, assume that communication is sequential between processors (a LAN or bus-type system). Invent and compare the calculation time of two different ways of distributing the elements of A; the idea being to minimize this time. Specifically, do this for $n = 9, p = 3$. Note that, after the product $M = A^2$ is computed, the elements of M must be distributed in the same pattern as those of A, that is, if distribution is by the rows of A then it must be for M as well.

13. (5) Let A be a symmetric $n \times n$ tridiagonal matrix. Let $p_k(\lambda) = \det(\lambda I - A_k)$, where A_k is the $k \times k$ submatrix of A consisting of its first k rows and columns. (a) Show that

$$p_k(\lambda) = (\lambda - a_{kk})p_{k-1}(\lambda) - a_{k-1,k}^2 p_{k-2}(\lambda)$$

where $p_0(\lambda) = 1$ and $p_1(\lambda) = \lambda - a_{11}$. (b) Deduce an $O(\log^2 n)$ algorithm to compute all the $p_i(\lambda)$ using $O(n \log n)$ processors.

Programming Exercises

14. (6) Make up a timing table (or graph) similar to Table 1, p. 11, giving times for length m vectors to perform (a) vector addition and multiplication, (b) vector division, (c) a saxpy, (d) a dot product, and (e) an all powers multiply ($A^2, A^3, \ldots, A^n$). Do this using one of the programming models: DOACROSS, threads, or distributed memory.

15. (6) Same as above for some other programming model.

5

Direct Methods for Linear Systems and LU Decomposition

The problem of solving linear systems of equations is central in scientific computation. Systems of linear equations arise in many areas of science, engineering, finance, commerce, and other disciplines. They emerge directly through mathematical models in these areas or indirectly in the numerical solution of mathematical models as for example in the solution of partial differential equations. Because of the importance of linear systems, a great deal of work has gone into methods for their solution.

A system of m equations in n unknowns may be written in matrix form as $A\mathbf{x} = \mathbf{b}$ in which the coefficient matrix A is $m \times n$, while the unknown vector $\mathbf{x}$ and the right-hand side $\mathbf{b}$ are n-dimensional. The most important case is when the coefficient matix is square, corresponding to the same number of unknowns as equations. The more general $m \times n$ case can be reduced to this.

There are two main methods for solving these systems, *direct* and *iterative*. If arithmetic were exact, a direct algorithm would solve the system exactly in a predetermined finite number of steps. In the reality of inexact computation, a direct method still stops in the same number of steps but accepts some level of numerical error. A major consideration with respect to direct methods is mitigating this error. Direct methods are typically used on moderately sized systems in which the coefficient matrix is *dense*, meaning most of its elements are nonzero. By contrast, iterative methods are typically used on very large, sparse systems. Iterative methods asymptotically converge to the solution and so run until the approximation is deemed acceptable.

We take up direct methods in the present chapter and defer iterative methods to Chapter 8.

5.1 Triangular Systems

Often matrices that arise in scientific calculations will have special structure. Algorithms for taking advantage of that special structure are preferrable to

126

generalized algorithms because storage requirements can be reduced, the number of floating point operations can be reduced, and more stable algorithms can be obtained.

The general linear system of *order n* has the form

$$
\begin{array}{ccccccc}
a_{11}x_1 & + & a_{12}x_2 & + & \cdots & + & a_{1n}x_n & = & b_1 \\
a_{21}x_1 & + & a_{22}x_2 & + & \cdots & + & a_{2n}x_n & = & b_2 \\
\vdots & & \vdots & & & & \vdots & = & \vdots \\
a_{n1}x_1 & + & a_{n2}x_2 & + & \cdots & + & a_{nn}x_n & = & b_n
\end{array}
$$

In matrix notation this is written as $A\mathbf{x} = \mathbf{b}$. Some important special cases are lower triangular and upper triangular systems, tridiagonal, and symmetric systems. We examine triangular systems here and defer the other two to a later section.

Lower Triangular Systems – Forward Substitution

We first consider the special case in which the coefficient matrix A is *lower triangular*; this means $a_{ij} = 0$ if $j > i$. The system then takes the form

$$
\begin{array}{ccccccccc}
a_{11}x_1 & & & & & & & = & b_1 \\
a_{21}x_1 & + & a_{22}x_2 & & & & & = & b_2 \\
a_{31}x_1 & + & a_{32}x_2 & + & a_{33}x_3 & & & = & b_3 \\
\vdots & & \vdots & & \vdots & & & & \vdots \\
a_{n1}x_1 & + & a_{n2}x_2 & + & a_{n3}x_3 & + & \cdots & + & a_{nn}x_n & = & b_n
\end{array}
$$

If the diagonal elements are nonzero, $a_{ii} \neq 0$, $i = 1, \ldots, n$, then the system will have a unique solution. It is easy to see that

$$
\det A = \prod_{i=1}^{n} a_{ii},
$$

for example, by expanding the determinant by minors recursively choosing the first row for the expansion. Therefore, if $\det A \neq 0$, the system has a unique solution.

In this event, the solution of the lower triangular system is straightforward to compute. Solve the first equation for x_1 and, with this value in hand, eliminate x_1 from the remaining equations. This results in a lower triangular system of order $n - 1$, which may be similarly treated. In n such *stages* the system will be solved. This method is called *forward substitution*.

Formally we derive the algorithm by the use of *partition matrices* in which the arguments of a matrix equation are partitioned into two or more submatrices. So long as this is done in a consistent way, meaning the induced matrix products are legal, then the partitioning is valid. Thus we partition A into 4 submatrices of sizes 1×1, $1 \times n - 1$, $n - 1 \times 1$, and $n - 1 \times n - 1$. The compatible partitioning of $\mathbf{x}$ and $\mathbf{b}$ is into submatrices of sizes 1×1 and $n - 1 \times 1$. This gives

$$\begin{bmatrix} a_{11} & 0 & \dots & 0 \\ a_{21} & & & \\ \vdots & & A_2 & \\ a_{n1} & & & \end{bmatrix} \begin{bmatrix} x_1 \\ \mathbf{x}_2 \end{bmatrix} = \begin{bmatrix} b_1 \\ \mathbf{b}' \end{bmatrix}.$$

The submatrix products are $a_{11}x_1 = b_1$ and

$$x_1 \begin{bmatrix} a_{21} \\ \vdots \\ a_{n1} \end{bmatrix} + A_2\mathbf{x}_2 = \mathbf{b}'.$$

The first equation calculates the first unknown x_1

$$x_1 = b_1/a_{11}.$$

The matrix equation determines the reduced system, which is $A_2\mathbf{x}_2$ equal to the reduced right-hand side. Hence

$$A_2\mathbf{x}_2 = \mathbf{b}' - x_1 \begin{bmatrix} a_{21} \\ \vdots \\ a_{n1} \end{bmatrix}.$$

Therefore the updated right-hand side $\mathbf{b}_2$ is given in components by

$$b_i^{(2)} = b_i - x_1 a_{i1}, \quad i = 2, \dots, n.$$

The reduced system is now worked in the same way. After $n - 1$ such stages, a 1×1 system of the form $ax = b$ remains for the final unknown x_n. Let the stages be indexed by $j = 1, \dots, n - 1$, then, algorithmically,

Forward Substitution, column-oriented

```
loop  j=1 upto n-1
    x_j ← b_j/a_jj
    loop  i=j+1 upto n (in parallel)
        b_i ← b_i - a_ij * x_j;  // right-hand side update
    end loop
    barrier
end loop
x_n ← b_n/a_nn
```

The directed acyclic graph for this calculation is shown in Fig. 22 (shown left to right). We see that calculating the right-hand side updates can go in parallel,

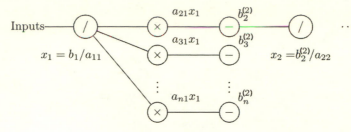

Fig. 22. DAG for column-oriented forward substitution.

but processing should not proceed until these calculations are done. We indicate this in the pseudocode given above by the use of a barrier.

Alternatively, the system may be treated from another point of view leading to a different algorithm. We will see that different algorithms entail substantially different parallelization consequences and so we pursue this development. Mathematically, the solution for each x_{ii} may be written directly from its equation in terms of earlier unknowns,

$$x_i = \frac{1}{a_{ii}} \left[b_i - \sum_{j=1}^{i-1} a_{ij} x_j \right], \quad i = 1, \ldots, n.$$

The expression translates directly into the following algorithm:

```
loop  i=1 upto n
    loop  j=1 upto i-1
        bᵢ ← bᵢ- aᵢⱼ * xⱼ; // right-hand side update
    end loop
    xᵢ ← bᵢ/aᵢᵢ
end loop
```

In the algorithm, as in the expression, the inner loop is vacuous when $i = 1$. This can be avoided by predefining x_1 and starting with $i = 2$ or by the following modification, which brings this algorithm close to the first one in appearance.

Forward substitution, row-oriented

```
loop  i=2 upto n
    xᵢ₋₁ ← bᵢ₋₁/aᵢ₋₁,ᵢ₋₁
    loop  j=1 upto i-1
        bᵢ ← bᵢ - aᵢⱼ * xⱼ;  // right-hand side update
    end loop
end loop
xₙ ← bₙ/aₙₙ
```

The directed acyclic graph for this calculation is shown in Fig. 23 (again left to right). We see that the right-hand side update is a fan-in calculation.

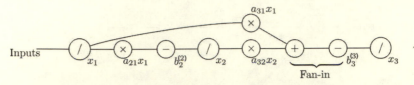

Fig. 23. DAG for row-oriented forward substitution.

Storage Considerations

As it now stands, both of the algorithms require storage for A, numbering $n(n + 1)/2$ elements, **b**, numbering n elements, and for **x**, another n elements. But the b_i are being modified during the course of the algorithm and when the ith unknown is calculated, b_i is no longer needed. So it is natural to store the x_i in the **b** array. Thus, over the course of the algorithm, the b_i are converted to the solutions; so we designate this as a *data conversion algorithm*.

Forward substitution, column-oriented data conversion

```
loop  j=1 upto n-1
   bⱼ ← bⱼ/aⱼⱼ
   loop  i=j+1 upto n (in parallel)
      bᵢ ← bᵢ - aᵢⱼ * bⱼ;  // right-hand side update
   end loop
   barrier
end loop
bₙ ← bₙ/aₙₙ
```

Forward substitution, row-oriented data conversion

```
loop  i=2 upto n
   bᵢ₋₁ ← bᵢ₋₁/aᵢ₋₁,ᵢ₋₁
   loop  j=1 upto i-1
      bᵢ ← bᵢ - aᵢⱼ * bⱼ;  // right-hand side update
   end loop
end loop
bₙ ← bₙ/aₙₙ
```

Comparing the column-oriented algorithms versus the row-oriented algorithms, we see that their principal point of difference is the order of the loops, i being the inner loop index in the former while j the inner loop index in the latter. As this is similar to interchanging the order of summation in mathematical equations, we introduce a formal notation for it.

Looping Notation

To facilitate interchanging the order of the loops in the algorithms of this chapter, we introduce a mathematical like "looping notation" and the notion of a "looping region" (see Fig. 24).

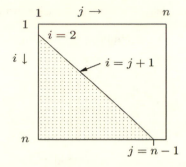

Fig. 24. "Looping Region" for forward substitution.

In each of the forward substitution algorithms above, the update equation must be carried out for all integral values of the indices i and j lying in the triangular region bounded by the lines $j = 1, i = n$, and $i = j + 1$ (see Fig. 24). By interchanging the order of the loops, we can bring one algorithm to the other, at least with respect to the updating. The conversion proceeds exactly as in interchanging the order of a double integral. Using the notation $\mathcal{L}^{b}_{i=a}$ to signify the loop,

$$\mathcal{L}^{b}_{i=a} \equiv \texttt{loop } i = a \ldots b,$$

the algorithms can be written, respectively,

$$\mathcal{L}^{n}_{j=1}\left\{x_j = b_j/a_{jj};\ \mathcal{L}^{n}_{i=j+1}\left\{b_i \leftarrow b_i - a_{ij} * x_j\right\}\right\},$$

and

$$\mathcal{L}^{n}_{i=1}\left\{\mathcal{L}^{i-1}_{j=1}\left\{b_i \leftarrow b_i - a_{ij} * x_j\right\};\ x_i = b_i/a_{ii}\right\}.$$

Upper-Triangular Systems – Back Substitution

Now consider the case in which the coefficient matrix A is *upper triangular*, that is, $a_{ij} = 0, j < i,$

$$
\begin{array}{ccccccccc}
a_{11}x_1 & + & a_{12}x_2 & + & \cdots & + & a_{1,n-1}x_{n-1} & + & a_{1n}x_n & = & b_1 \\
 & & a_{22}x_2 & + & \cdots & + & a_{2,n-1}x_{n-1} & + & a_{2n}x_n & = & b_2 \\
 & & & \ddots & & & \vdots & & \vdots & = & \vdots \\
 & & & & & & a_{n-1,n-1}x_{n-1} & + & a_{n-1,n}x_n & = & b_{n-1} \\
 & & & & & & & & a_{nn}x_n & = & b_n
\end{array}
$$

Again, if $\det A \neq 0$, then the system has a unique solution computed exactly as in forward substitution except now one works from the last unknown x_n to the first x_1. The pseudocode for row-oriented back substitution is

Back substitution, row-oriented

```
loop   i=n downto 1
    loop   j=n downto i+1
        bᵢ ← bᵢ - aᵢⱼ * xⱼ;
    end loop
    xᵢ ← bᵢ/aᵢᵢ
end loop
```

Alternatively, the order of looping may be interchanged leading to

Back substitution, column-oriented

```
loop   j=n downto 1
    xⱼ ← bⱼ/aⱼⱼ
    loop   i=j-1 downto 1 (in parallel)
        bᵢ ← bᵢ - aᵢⱼ * xⱼ;
    end loop
    barrier
end loop
```

This method of solution is column-oriented back substitution, or *column sweep*. As soon as a new value is determined, x_n, for example in the first step, that value is applied to each remaining equation and the product is subtracted from the right-hand side. Thus, immediately after x_n is determined, the right-hand side, b_i, of each equation $i = 1, \ldots, n - 1$, is updated to

$$b_i \leftarrow b_i - a_{in} * x_n.$$

This is saxpy operation and can be performed efficiently. However, as before, the vector lengths vary, this time from $n - 1$ down to 1.

Parallel Considerations for Triangular Systems

From the row-oriented forward substitution algorithm we see that there is 1 multiplication and 1 subtraction per innermost loop iteration. This loop is executed $i - 1$ times for $i = 2, \ldots, n$. Thus there are altogether

$$1 + 2 + \cdots + n - 1 = \frac{1}{2}(n - 1)n$$

multiplications and the same number of subtractions. From the algorithm it is seen that there are n divisions. Therefore, the operation count and hence also the single processor calculation time T_1 is

$$T_1 = (n - 1)n + n = O(n^2).$$

With respect to parallelization (or vectorization) the two algorithms entail distinct consequences. The innermost loop of the column-oriented algorithm is a scalar–vector multiply together with a vector–vector add (a so-called saxpy operation for scalar a x plus y)

$$\begin{bmatrix} b_{j+1} \\ \vdots \\ b_n \end{bmatrix} \leftarrow \begin{bmatrix} b_{j+1} \\ \vdots \\ b_n \end{bmatrix} - b_j \begin{bmatrix} a_{j+1,j} \\ \vdots \\ a_{nj} \end{bmatrix}.$$

The vector length is $n - j$, $j \geq 1$, and the loop completely parallelizes (and vectorizes). Therefore this loop can be done in $O(2)$ time, using at most $n - 1$ processors. The innermost loop is done $n - 1$ times and therefore the time is

$$T_n = O(2n).$$

Under the row-oriented version, the innermost loop is the innerproduct $\sum_{j=1}^{i-1} a_{ij} b_j$ (accumulated in b_i) of length up to $n - 1$. This will require $O(\log n)$ time using $O(\frac{1}{2}n)$ processors. Since the loop is executed $n - 1$ times,

$$T_{n/2} = O(n \log n).$$

A Surprising Matrix Solution

The algorithms forged above are not best possible given massive parallelism. Let U be the matrix of the negatives of the values of the strictly upper-triangular terms of A,

$$u_{ij} = -a_{ij}, \quad j > i.$$

Then A can be written as

$$A = D - U,$$

where D is the diagonal matrix consisting of the diagonal elements of A, $d_{ii} = a_{ii}$. The solution we are seeking is given in matrix terms as

$$\mathbf{x} = \mathbf{A}^{-1}\mathbf{b} = (\mathbf{D} - \mathbf{U})^{-1}\mathbf{b}.$$

Assume first that $D = I$, that is the diagonal terms of A are all 1. By direct calculation, one sees that the first superdiagonal of U^2 is zero. In the same way, the first and second superdiagonals of U^3 are seen to be zero. Continuing, the matrix U^{n-1} consists of only one nonzero term at most in the upper right-hand corner and finally U^n is the zero matrix (see the Exercises). Hence, multiplying the matrix sum $I + U + \cdots + U^{n-1}$ by $I - U$ gives the identity matrix, that is,

$$(I - U)^{-1} = I + U + U^2 + \cdots + U^{n-1}.$$

We know that all the products U^2 through U^{n-1} of $n \times n$ matrices can be calculated by the Russian Peasant Algorithm using $O(n^4)$ processors in $O(\log^2 n)$ time. Then the sum of n square matrices each $n \times n$ can be done also in $O(\log n)$ time using $O(n^3)$ processors. Likewise the matrix vector product is an $O(\log n)$ time calculation. Altogether, then $\mathbf{x}$ can be calculated in

$$O(\log^2 n + \log n + \log n) = O(\log^2 n)$$

time using $O(n^4)$ processors.

If one or more diagonal elements of A is different from 1, then each row of A can be divided by its diagonal element. In matrix terms this is the product $D^{-1}A$. The result is an upper-triangular matrix with unit diagonal elements as required. This multiplication can be done in unit time using $O(n^2)$ processors and hence does not change the complexity result.

If it is necessary to premultiply by D^{-1} then the inverse calculated above is $\left(D^{-1}A\right)^{-1}$. Hence the inverse of A itself is

$$A^{-1} = (D^{-1}A)^{-1}D^{-1}$$

since

$$(D^{-1}A)^{-1} = A^{-1}D,$$

again a unit time calculation.

5.2 Gaussian Elimination

Gaussian elimination is the most widely used method for solving a linear system when the coefficient matrix is dense. The idea is to successively modify the rows of the coefficient matrix so as to bring it to upper-triangular form while at the same time maintaining the solution of the original system in the new one. The resulting upper-triangular system $U\mathbf{x} = \mathbf{b}'$ is then solved by back substitution, $\mathbf{b}'$ being the correspondingly modified right-hand side. Each modification is equivalent to the multiplication of A on the left by an invertible matrix E. Normally these are simple lower triangular matrices. The cumulative effect $M = E_m \ldots E_2 E_1$ of them all is encapsulated in the matrix equation $MA = U$ in which M is lower triangular. This leads to the factorization $A = LU$ of A into the product of a lower-triangular matrix with an upper-triangular one. Such a factorization provides an efficient method for solving $A\mathbf{x} = \mathbf{b}$ when the system must be solved for more than one right-hand side.

Numerical stability of Gaussian elimination is an important issue. For those problems that require it, instability can be greatly reduced by partial or total *pivoting*, which amounts to reordering the system of equations. When such a permutation of the system must be done, it too can be represented as the matrix product on the left. The matrix P, which results from permuting the rows of I in some given way, is called a *permutation matrix*. And, as above, multiplying a matrix A by P on the left results in the same permutations to the rows of A. Note that a permutation matrix will not be lower triangluar (except for the identity permutation of course). With such a reordering the LU decomposition takes the form $PA = LU$.

Gaussian elimination can be parallelized and vectorized to some extent.

Elementary Row Operations

We will refer to any of the following three operations on the rows of a matrix as an *elementary row operation*,

(1) interchanging two rows,
(2) replacing a row by a nonzero scalar multiple of itself, or
(3) replacing a row by its sum with a scalar multiple of another.

An *elementary matrix E* is a matrix which results by performing an elementary row operation on the identity matrix I.

Consider the 3×3 linear system

$$\begin{bmatrix} 2 & -2 & -1 \\ 3 & -2 & 2 \\ 1 & -1 & 5 \end{bmatrix} \begin{bmatrix} x \\ y \\ z \end{bmatrix} = \begin{bmatrix} 3 \\ 7 \\ 7 \end{bmatrix}.$$

The *augmented matrix* is the coefficient marix together with the right-hand side column vector adjoined; although the unknowns themselves are omitted, their identity is maintained by the position of the columns of the matrix. For this system the augmented matrix is

$$\begin{bmatrix} 2 & -2 & -1 & \bigm| & 3 \\ 3 & -2 & 2 & \bigm| & 7 \\ 1 & -1 & 5 & \bigm| & 7 \end{bmatrix}.$$

Now carry out elementary row operation (3) on this matrix and replace the second row by its sum with $-3/2$ times the first,

$$\begin{bmatrix} 2 & -2 & -1 & \bigm| & 3 \\ 0 & 1 & 7/2 & \bigm| & 5/2 \\ 1 & -1 & 5 & \bigm| & 7 \end{bmatrix}.$$

Note that the same effect can be achieved by multiplying the first row by $3/2$ and *subtracting* from the second; henceforth we prefer this nuance of operation (3). Furthermore, we wish to save the multipliers in a matrix, say L, for subsequent use, so $\ell_{21} = 3/2$.

Similarly, multiplying the first row by $\ell_{31} = 1/2$ and subtracting from row 3 gives

$$\begin{bmatrix} 2 & -2 & -1 & 3 \\ 0 & 1 & 7/2 & 5/2 \\ 0 & 0 & 11/2 & 11/2 \end{bmatrix}.$$

This system is now upper triangular and can be solved by back substitution.

Our example illustrates that through the use of the elementary row operations, a general coefficient matrix can be converted to one in which its lower-triangular elements are annihilated.

In general, elementary row operations may be used, step by step, to bring a matrix A into *row echelon* form. This means the first nonzero element of any row is to the right of the first nonzero element of the previous row, that is, if $a_{i,f(i)}$ is the first nonzero element of row i, $a_{ij} = 0$, for $j < f(i)$, then $f(i) > f(i-1), i \neq 1$.

Note that we have used the a_{11} element, 2 in this example, to annihilate the other entries a_{21} and a_{31}. We refer to an entry used in this way as the *pivot* for the annihilation.

The following theorem asserts that each elementary row operation on A can be realized as the multiplication of A on the left by a matrix obtained from the identity by the same operation.

Theorem 1. *Let B be the matrix which results from performing an elementary row operation on A. Then $B = EA$, where E is the corresponding elementary matrix.*

In the example above, let E_1 be the elementary matrix for the annihilation of a_{21} and E_2 be the same for the a_{31} element. Put $M = E_2E_1$, then M is lower-triangular (see the Exercises) and

$$MA = \begin{bmatrix} 2 & -2 & -1 \\ 0 & 1 & 7/2 \\ 0 & 0 & 11/2 \end{bmatrix}, \quad \text{where } M = \begin{bmatrix} 1 & 0 & 0 \\ -3/2 & 1 & 0 \\ -1/2 & 0 & 1 \end{bmatrix}.$$

Gaussian Elimination – LU Decomposition

By saving the multipliers ℓ_{ij} formed during the elimination process, we arrive at a useful extension of Gaussian elimination. Denote this matrix of multipliers by L. Since the ℓ_{ij} are calculated only for $i > j$, this defines the strict lower-triangular part of L. In addition, set the diagonal of L to 1's and the strict upper-triangular part to 0's. Thus L is a *unit lower-triangular matrix*. As before, let U denote the upper-triangular result of Gaussian elimination.

If no row permutations are performed during the elimination process, then

$$A = LU.$$

We show this to be so by a recursive argument, which at the same time leads to an algorithm for computing L and U. We assume in what follows that the diagonal element at the kth stage, $a_{kk}^{(k)}$, as it comes up during the recursion, is not 0. If instead a zero should occur, row interchanges must be done and we consider this in the next section when we take up pivoting.

Set $A_1 = A$ and write $A_1 = LU$ in partitioned form

$$\begin{bmatrix} a_{11} & a_{12} & a_{13} & \cdots & a_{1n} \\ a_{21} & & & & \\ a_{31} & & A' & & \\ \vdots & & & & \\ a_{n1} & & & & \end{bmatrix}$$

$$= \begin{bmatrix} 1 & 0 & 0 & \cdots & 0 \\ \ell_{21} & & & & \\ \ell_{31} & & L_2 & & \\ \vdots & & & & \\ \ell_{n1} & & & & \end{bmatrix} \cdot \begin{bmatrix} u_{11} & u_{12} & u_{13} & \cdots & u_{1n} \\ 0 & & & & \\ 0 & & U_2 & & \\ \vdots & & & & \\ 0 & & & & \end{bmatrix} \quad (3)$$

In this, A' is the $n - 1 \times n - 1$ matrix that remains when the first row and column of A_1 are deleted. By multiplying out the right-hand side and equating like submatrices, we obtain

$$a_{11} = u_{11}$$

$$[a_{12} \quad a_{13} \quad \cdots \quad a_{1n}] = [u_{12} \quad u_{13} \quad \cdots \quad u_{1n}]$$

$$[a_{21} \quad a_{31} \quad \cdots \quad a_{n1}]^T = u_{11}[\ell_{21} \quad \ell_{31} \quad \cdots \quad \ell_{n1}]^T$$

$$A' = \begin{bmatrix} \ell_{21} \\ \ell_{31} \\ \vdots \\ \ell_{n1} \end{bmatrix} [u_{12} \quad u_{13} \quad \cdots \quad u_{1n}] + L_2 U_2.$$

Solving, we find that $u_{11} = a_{11}$ and

$$\ell_{i1} = a_{i1}/u_{11}, \quad i = 2, \ldots, n$$
$$u_{1j} = a_{1j}, \quad j = 2, \ldots, n.$$

To allow for recursion, the reduced version A_2 of A must be computed. When the decomposition is complete, the reduced matrix will be the product $L_2 U_2$;

hence, this defines A_2,

$$A_2 = L_2 U_2 = A' - \begin{bmatrix} \ell_{21} \\ \ell_{31} \\ \vdots \\ \ell_{n1} \end{bmatrix} [\, u_{12} \quad u_{13} \quad \ldots \quad u_{1n} \,].$$

In element form,

$$a_{ij}^{(2)} = a_{ij}^{(1)} - \ell_{i1} u_{1j}, \quad i, j = 2, \ldots, n.$$

This completes one stage of the recursion; the calculations are now repeated on A_2. Letting k index the recursion stages, $k = 1, 2, \ldots, n-1$, the algorithm may be written in *loop form* as follows:

$$
\mathcal{L}_{k=1}^{n-1} \Bigg\{
\begin{aligned}
& u_{kk} \leftarrow a_{kk} \\
& \mathcal{L}_{i=k+1}^{n} \Big\{ \ell_{ik} \leftarrow a_{ik}/u_{kk} \Big\} \\
& \mathcal{L}_{j=k+1}^{n} \Big\{ u_{kj} \leftarrow a_{kj} \Big\} \\
& \mathcal{L}_{i,j=k+1}^{n} \Big\{ a_{ij} \leftarrow a_{ij} - \ell_{ik} u_{kj} \Big\}
\end{aligned}
\Bigg\}
$$

We make several observations. First, rather than using storage for three matrices, only one is necessary; the same array can hold A, L, and U at the same time. Obviously after the kth stage, a_{pq} and u_{pq} are the same for $p = 1, \ldots, k$, $q = k, \ldots, n$. So we simply use the upper-triangular part of A to store U. This also obviates the first j-loop in the algorithm.

Then too, after ℓ_{ik} is calculated in the second loop, a_{ik} is no longer needed. In fact, these are precisely the elements annihilated in Gaussian elimination. So we store ℓ_{ik} simply by renaming it as a_{ik}. Upon completion of the algorithm then, the strictly lower-triangular part of A is the strictly lower-triangular part of L. Since the diagonal elements of L are 1, there is no need to store them. Finally, by looping over i before j, the first loop over i can be combined with the second.

With these modifications, the algorithm becomes

```
loop  k= 1 upto n-1
  loop  i = k+1 upto n (in parallel)
     aik ← aik/akk;  // save the multipliers
     loop  j= k+1 upto n
        aij ← aij - aik * akj; // update A
     end  loop
     barrier
  end  loop
end  loop
```

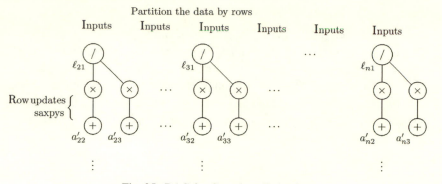

Fig. 25. DAG for Gaussian elimination.

In Fig. 25 we show the directed acyclic graph for Gaussian elimination. The calculation can be parallelized by rows, first computing the row multipliers ℓ_{i1}, $i = 2, \ldots, n$, in parallel. Then the row updates may be computed in parallel,

$$a'_{ij} = a_{ij} - \ell_{i1}a_{1j},$$

these are saxpy operations.

From the example above the product of the unit diagonal lower-triangular matrix of multipliers with the upper-triangular resultant matrix is A

$$LU = \begin{bmatrix} 1 & 0 & 0 \\ 3/2 & 1 & 0 \\ 1/2 & 0 & 1 \end{bmatrix} \begin{bmatrix} 2 & -2 & -1 \\ 0 & 1 & 7/2 \\ 0 & 0 & 11/2 \end{bmatrix} = \begin{bmatrix} 2 & -2 & -1 \\ 3 & -2 & 2 \\ 1 & -1 & 5 \end{bmatrix}.$$

The solution of the original system can be achieved by back substitution as mentioned in the previous section if the right-hand side is updated during the elimination process. Alternatively, the solution may be calculated directly from the LU decomposition as follows. In place of $\mathbf{b} = A\mathbf{x}$, we write

$$\mathbf{b} = LU\mathbf{x} = L\mathbf{y}, \quad \text{where} \quad \mathbf{y} = U\mathbf{x}.$$

Now solve the unit lower-triangular system $L\mathbf{y} = \mathbf{b}$ for $\mathbf{y}$ by forward substitution. Then find $\mathbf{x}$ from

$$U\mathbf{x} = \mathbf{y},$$

by back substitution.

When there is more than one right-hand side to solve with the same coefficient matrix, this is the most efficient method from the standpoint of operation count.

Operation Count

Both Gaussian elimination and LU decomposition require $O(n^3)$ operations. This is seen as follows. In the first step there are $n - 1$ rows to reduce, each row requires one division and $n - 1$ multiplications and subtractions for a total of $n - 1$ divisions and $(n - 1)^2$ multiplications or subtractions. In the second step there is one less row and one less column to do; therefore, there are $n - 2$ divisions and $(n - 2)^2$ multiplications and subtractions. Continue this way to arrive at

$$1 + 2 + \cdots + n - 1 = \frac{(n - 1)n}{2}$$

divisions and

$$1^2 + 2^2 + \cdots + (n - 1)^2 = \frac{(n - 1)n(2n - 1)}{6}$$

multiplications and subtractions, thus $O(n^3)$ operations. (This last identity is easily proved by induction.)

Row Interchanges

It is possible for a matrix A to be nonsingular but not have an LU decompositon. For example,

$$\begin{bmatrix} 0 & -1 \\ 1 & 1 \end{bmatrix}$$

is such a matrix. Its determinant is 1, but if $LU = A$, then $\ell_{11}u_{11} = a_{11} = 0$. Since $\ell_{11} = 1$, it must be that $u_{11} = 0$. But then $\det(U) = 0$ and so cannot equal $\det(A)$.

But we do have the following.

Theorem 2. *If A is nonsingular, then for some permutation matrix P, PA has an LU decomposition.*

Proof. Let P_{ij} be the permutation matrix that results by interchanging the ith and jth rows (and hence also the ith and jth columns) of the identity matrix. Also let E_k denote the elementary matrix that results from multiplying the first row of the identity by ℓ and adding to the kth row. Then by direct calculation

$$P_{ij}E_i = E_jP_{ij} = \begin{bmatrix} 1 & 0 & \cdots & 0 & \cdots & 0 & \cdots & 0 \\ 0 & 1 & \cdots & 0 & \cdots & 0 & \cdots & 0 \\ \vdots & \vdots & \vdots & \vdots & \vdots & \vdots & \vdots & \vdots \\ 0 & 0 & \cdots & 0 & \cdots & 1 & \cdots & 0 \\ \vdots & \vdots & \vdots & \vdots & \vdots & \vdots & \vdots & \vdots \\ \ell & 0 & \cdots & 1 & \cdots & 0 & \cdots & 0 \\ \vdots & \vdots & \vdots & \vdots & \vdots & \vdots & \vdots & \vdots \\ 0 & 0 & \cdots & 0 & \cdots & 0 & \cdots & 1 \end{bmatrix}.$$

This is the identity matrix with the ith and jth rows interchanged and an ℓ in the jth row, 1st column. If $k \neq i$ and $k \neq j$, then $P_{ij}E_k = E_kP_{ij}$ being the identity matrix with the ith and jth rows interchanged and an ℓ in the kth row, 1st column.

Suppose, without loss of generality, that after performing the reduction of the first column using a_{11} as a pivot, the second diagonal element becomes 0,

$$E_{n1}\ldots E_{31}E_{21}A = \begin{bmatrix} a_{11} & a_{12} & \cdots & a_{1n} \\ 0 & 0 & \cdots & a'_{2n} \\ 0 & a'_{32} & \cdots & a'_{3n} \\ \vdots & \vdots & \cdots & \vdots \\ 0 & a'_{n2} & \cdots & a'_{nn} \end{bmatrix}.$$

In this expression the first two elementary matrices are

$$E_{21} = \begin{bmatrix} 1 & 0 & 0 & \cdots & 0 \\ -\frac{a_{21}}{a_{11}} & 1 & 0 & \cdots & 0 \\ 0 & 0 & 1 & \cdots & 0 \\ \vdots & \vdots & \vdots & \cdots & \vdots \end{bmatrix} \quad E_{31} = \begin{bmatrix} 1 & 0 & 0 & \cdots & 0 \\ 0 & 1 & 0 & \cdots & 0 \\ -\frac{a_{31}}{a_{11}} & 0 & 1 & \cdots & 0 \\ \vdots & \vdots & \vdots & \cdots & \vdots \end{bmatrix}.$$

Now we interchange the second and third rows, assuming $a'_{32} \neq 0$, and continue. This is equivalent to multiplying by the permutation matrix P_{23}, which is I with the second and third rows interchanged. But instead, we can achieve the same thing by interchanging the second and third rows of the original matrix. Exactly the same computations are performed to each row. The difference is that now the E_{21} and E_{31} matrices become

$$E'_{21} = \begin{bmatrix} 1 & 0 & 0 & \cdots & 0 \\ -\frac{a_{31}}{a_{11}} & 1 & 0 & \cdots & 0 \\ 0 & 0 & 1 & \cdots & 0 \\ \vdots & \vdots & \vdots & \cdots & \vdots \end{bmatrix} \quad E'_{31} = \begin{bmatrix} 1 & 0 & 0 & \cdots & 0 \\ 0 & 1 & 0 & \cdots & 0 \\ -\frac{a_{21}}{a_{11}} & 0 & 1 & \cdots & 0 \\ \vdots & \vdots & \vdots & \cdots & \vdots \end{bmatrix}.$$

As shown above, $P_{23}E_{31} = E'_{21}P_{23}$ and $P_{23}E_{21} = E'_{31}P_{23}$. Furthermore, P_{23} commutes with all the other elementary matrices. Thus, noting that E'_{31} and E'_{21} commute, we have

$$P_{23}E_{n1} \ldots E_{31}E_{21}A = E_{n1} \ldots E'_{21}E'_{31}P_{23}A.$$

In a similar way, every permutation encountered during the reduction process can be moved up to be the first set of operations on A. With respect to each row, the operations performed on it are exactly the same. Finally note that a product of permutation matrices is also a permutation matrix.   ∎

Let P denote the permutation matrix, which is the product of all the permutations performed during the reduction. Then we have $PA = LU$. To solve $Ax = b$, multiply both sides of this matrix equation by P to get

$$LUx = PAx = Pb.$$

This shows we can still use the forward substitution followed by back substitution method for solving the system with the LU decomposition in hand by simply permuting the elements of b in the same way as the rows of A have been permuted. Of course, using the augmented form of Gaussian elimination, that is with b adjoined to the coefficient matrix, then any row interchanges on A will automatically be performed on b.

Rather than maintaining a permutation matrix, one just maintains a permutation vector, r. Start by initializing $r = (1, 2, 3, \ldots, n)$ to the identity permutation. Now as row swaps become necessary during reduction, do the same row swaps on the components of r. Then permute the rows of A and the elements of b in the same way as recorded by r.

Determinant

The *determinant* of an $n \times n$ square matrix $\det(A)$ can be regarded as a function of its n column vectors. We use the *dot notation* $a_{.j}$ to denote the jth column of A as if the dot stands for the various possibilities of the first index. Similarly $a_{i.}$ denotes the row vector consisting of the ith row of A. In this notation the column vectors of A are $a_{.1}, a_{.2}, \ldots, a_{.n}$. Alternatively, we may regard the determinant as a function of its n row vectors, $a_{1.}, a_{2.}, \ldots, a_{n.}$. In the following let us agree to use the rows and write

$$\det(a_{1.}, a_{2.}, \ldots, a_{n.})$$

signifying det is a function of its n rows. With respect to the rows then the determinant satisfies (in fact is defined by)

multilinearity
skew-symmetry, and
unity on the standard basis.

Multilinearity means that the determinant is linear in each row, for example, in the first row,

$$\det(\alpha\mathbf{x} + \beta\mathbf{y}, \mathbf{a}_{2.}, \ldots, \mathbf{a}_{n.}) = \alpha\det(\mathbf{x}, \mathbf{a}_{2.}, \ldots, \mathbf{a}_{n.}) + \beta\det(\mathbf{y}, \mathbf{a}_{2.}, \ldots, \mathbf{a}_{n.}).$$

Skew-symmetry means if any two arguments (rows) are interchanged, then the determinant changes sign, for example,

$$\det(\mathbf{x}, \mathbf{y}, \ldots, \mathbf{a}_{n.}) = -\det(\mathbf{y}, \mathbf{x}, \ldots, \mathbf{a}_{n.}).$$

The last condition means the determinant of the identity matrix I is 1.

It is easy to see that by skew-symmetry, if any two rows of a matrix are the same, then its determinant is 0. Furthermore, it follows that if a multiple of any row is added to another row, then the determinant is unchanged. For example, add α times the second row to the first and calculate,

$$\det(\alpha\mathbf{a}_{2.} + \mathbf{a}_{1.}, \mathbf{a}_{2.}, \ldots, \mathbf{a}_{n.}) = \alpha\det(\mathbf{a}_{2.}, \mathbf{a}_{2.}, \ldots, \mathbf{a}_{n.}) + \det(\mathbf{a}_{1.}, \mathbf{a}_{2.}, \ldots, \mathbf{a}_{n.})$$
$$= \det(\mathbf{a}_{1.}, \mathbf{a}_{2.}, \ldots, \mathbf{a}_{n.}).$$

Consider using elementary row operations to evaluate a determinant. We have shown above that in multiplying a row of the matrix by a scalar and adding to another row, the resultant matrix has the same determinant. If two rows must be interchanged, then the resultant matrix has determinant equal to -1 times the original. Upon reaching upper-triangular form, the determinant is just the product of the diagonal terms.

Thus the detminant of the original matrix, A, becomes available, essentially for free, as we do its LU decomposition. To carry out the calculation, initialize a variable, say det, to 1. With every row interchange, multiply det by -1. Upon reaching the reduced state, multiply det by the product of the main diagonal of U; this will be $\det(A)$.

Finding the Rank of A

The *row rank* of A is the number of rows of A, which are linearly independent. It is easy to see that the elementary row operations preserve row rank. Thus, upon reaching row echelon form, the row rank of A is equal to the number of remaining nonzero rows.

The *column rank* of A is the number of columns of A, which are linearly independent. And the *rank* of A is the dimension of its image space,

$$\text{rank}(A) = \dim\{\mathbf{y} \, : \, \mathbf{y} = A\mathbf{x}, \text{ all } \mathbf{x}\}.$$

As we have seen, the matrix vector product can be written as

$$\mathbf{y} = x_1\mathbf{a}_{.1} + x_2\mathbf{a}_{.2} + \cdots + x_n\mathbf{a}_{.n},$$

and therefore the column rank and rank are the same thing.

It is not so obvious that the elementary row operations also preserve column rank. Consider the linear combination

$$x_1\mathbf{a}_{.1} + x_2\mathbf{a}_{.2} + \cdots + x_n\mathbf{a}_{.n} = 0,$$

where $\mathbf{a}_{.i}$ denotes the ith column of A. If the only solution of this is the trivial solution ($x_1 = x_2 = \ldots = x_n = 0$), then all columns are linearly independent and the column rank of A is n.

But suppose that there is some nontrivial solution. By interchanging columns of A if necessary, we can assume that $x_n \neq 0$ in such a solution. In this case the (new) last column of A is a linear combination of the others and so we may discard it and ask again if there is a nontrivial solution for the first $n - 1$ columns.

By repeatedly interchanging columns of A and solving the reduced set of columns, eventually we reach the point where the only solution is the trivial one. If r columns remain and $n - r$ columns have been discarded, when that point is reached, then the column rank of A is equal to r.

Now consider the effect of performing column swaps on A. Given a linear system, $A\mathbf{x} = \mathbf{b}$, a column swap exchanges the position of the unknowns.

$$\begin{array}{cccc} x_1 & x_2 & \ldots & x_n \end{array}$$
$$\begin{bmatrix} a_{11} & a_{12} & \cdots & a_{1n} \\ \vdots & \vdots & \cdots & \vdots \end{bmatrix}.$$

If columns one and two of A are interchanged, then the "first" unknown now corresponds to x_2,

$$\begin{array}{cccc} x_2 & x_1 & \ldots & x_n \end{array}$$
$$\begin{bmatrix} a_{12} & a_{11} & \cdots & a_{1n} \\ \vdots & \vdots & \cdots & \vdots \end{bmatrix}.$$

Column interchanges can be kept track of in the same way as row interchanges, by initializing and maintaining a column permutation vector $\mathbf{c} = (1, 2, 3, \ldots, n)$.

By perfoming both row and column interchanges during Gaussian elimination, A can be brought to the form

$$
\begin{bmatrix}
u_{11} & u_{12} & \cdots & u_{1r} & \cdots & u_{1n} \\
0 & u_{22} & \cdots & u_{2r} & \cdots & u_{2n} \\
\vdots & \vdots & \cdots & \vdots & \cdots & \vdots \\
0 & 0 & \cdots & u_{rr} & \cdots & u_{rn} \\
0 & 0 & \cdots & 0 & \cdots & 0 \\
\vdots & \vdots & \cdots & \vdots & \cdots & \vdots \\
0 & 0 & \cdots & 0 & \cdots & 0
\end{bmatrix},
\tag{4}
$$

where u_{11} through u_{rr} are not zero. In this form it is clear that no column, say the ith, $1 \le i \le r$, can be written as a linear combination of columns coming before it because $u_{ii} \ne 0$. Hence the rank of A is r, the number of nonzero diagonal terms.

Hence we have demonstrated the following theorem.

Theorem 3. *The row rank of A equals the column rank of A equals the rank of A.*

Now assume that the row reduction leading to Eq. (4) is applied to the augmented matrix, that is to say, to the RHS as well. Then we have arrived at the following system:

$$
\left[
\begin{array}{cccccc|c}
u_{11} & u_{12} & \cdots & u_{1r} & \cdots & u_{1n} & b_1' \\
0 & u_{22} & \cdots & u_{2r} & \cdots & u_{2n} & b_2' \\
\vdots & \vdots & \cdots & \vdots & \cdots & \vdots & \vdots \\
0 & 0 & \cdots & u_{rr} & \cdots & u_{rn} & b_r' \\
0 & 0 & \cdots & 0 & \cdots & 0 & b_{r+1}' \\
\vdots & \vdots & \cdots & \vdots & \cdots & \vdots & \vdots \\
0 & 0 & \cdots & 0 & \cdots & 0 & b_n'
\end{array}
\right],
$$

where b_i', $i = 1, \ldots, n$, is the resulting RHS. Clearly if $A\mathbf{x} = \mathbf{b}$ is to have a solution, we must have

$$
b_{r+1}' = b_{r+2}' = \ldots = b_n' = 0.
$$

Furthermore, if this is the case, then the unknowns $x_{r+1}, x_{r+2}, \ldots, x_n$, can take arbitrary values. Assume that these unknowns are given values and consider the partition matrix formulation of the system partitioned between the first r and last $n - r$ unknowns

$$\begin{bmatrix} u_{11} & u_{12} & \cdots & u_{1r} \\ 0 & u_{22} & \cdots & u_{2r} \\ \vdots & \vdots & \cdots & \vdots \\ 0 & 0 & \cdots & u_{rr} \end{bmatrix} \begin{bmatrix} x_1 \\ x_2 \\ \vdots \\ x_r \end{bmatrix} + \begin{bmatrix} u_{1,r+1} & \cdots & u_{1n} \\ u_{2,r+1} & \cdots & u_{2n} \\ \vdots & \cdots & \vdots \\ u_{r,r+1} & \cdots & u_{rn} \end{bmatrix} \begin{bmatrix} x_{r+1} \\ x_{r+2} \\ \vdots \\ x_n \end{bmatrix} = \begin{bmatrix} b'_1 \\ b'_2 \\ \vdots \\ b'_r \end{bmatrix}.$$

Subtract the second term from both sides and define the b'' as their difference

$$\begin{bmatrix} b''_1 \\ b''_2 \\ \vdots \\ b''_r \end{bmatrix} = \begin{bmatrix} b'_1 \\ b'_2 \\ \vdots \\ b'_r \end{bmatrix} - x_{r+1} \begin{bmatrix} u_{1,r+1} \\ u_{2,r+1} \\ \vdots \\ u_{r,r+1} \end{bmatrix} - x_{r+2} \begin{bmatrix} u_{1,r+2} \\ u_{2,r+2} \\ \vdots \\ u_{r,r+2} \end{bmatrix} - \cdots - x_n \begin{bmatrix} u_{1n} \\ u_{2n} \\ \vdots \\ u_{rn} \end{bmatrix}.$$

Now solve the triangular system

$$\begin{bmatrix} u_{11} & u_{12} & \cdots & u_{1r} & | & b''_1 \\ 0 & u_{22} & \cdots & u_{2r} & | & b''_2 \\ \vdots & \vdots & \cdots & \vdots & | & \vdots \\ 0 & 0 & \cdots & u_{rr} & | & b''_r \end{bmatrix}.$$

Therefore we see that there is a solution for every choice of values for $x_{r+1}, \ldots, x_n$, and that the solutions $x_1, x_2, \ldots, x_r$, are given as linear functions of these $n - r$ unknowns. Thus the infinity of solutions is organized as a *solution space* of dimension $n - r$.

Theorem 4 (Rank Theorem). *For an $m \times n$ linear system $\mathbf{A}x = \mathbf{b}$*

$$\mathrm{rank}(A) + \dim(solution\ space) = n.$$

Pivoting

Some linear systems prove to be numerically unstable when solved as discussed above. The culprit is the matrix of coefficients. The solution calculated for such a problem depends wildly on small errors such as round-off error and on other factors such as the order of the equations. A coefficient matrix leading to numerical instability is said to be *ill-conditioned*. Fortunately the problem of numerical stability can be greatly reduced by partial or total *pivoting* which is effectively an optimal reordering of the equations or of the unknowns.

Consider the following system

$$\epsilon x + by = e$$
$$cx - dy = f.$$

In this, all coefficients are positive and ϵ is meant to be much smaller than the other numbers. Gaussian elimination gives

$$\epsilon x + by = e$$

$$-\left(d + \frac{cb}{\epsilon}\right)y = f - \frac{ce}{\epsilon}.$$

Hence

$$y = -\frac{f - \frac{ce}{\epsilon}}{d + \frac{cb}{\epsilon}},$$

and, using this in the first equation,

$$x = \frac{1}{\epsilon}\left(e - b\left(\frac{f - \frac{ce}{\epsilon}}{-d - \frac{cb}{\epsilon}}\right)\right).$$

The expression for x entails the difference of numbers that could be the same size, with the danger of significant loss of precision, followed by the multiplication by a very large factor. In fact, using 4-place decimal precision and taking the values $\epsilon = 0.0003$, $b = 1.566$, $c = 0.3454$, $d = 2.436$, $e = 1.569$, and $f = 1.018$ as suggested by Conte and deBoor, the numerical solution comes out $y = 1.001$ and $x = 3.333$. The actual solution is $y = 1$ and $x = 10$.

How can this be ameliorated? Recall that one of the allowable operations is the interchange of equations. We do just that to use c as the pivot. Then this elimination process gives

$$0.3454x - 2.436y = 1.018$$

$$\left(1.566 - (-2.436) * \frac{0.0003}{.3454}\right)y = 1.569 - (1.018) * \left(\frac{0.0003}{.3454}\right).$$

The second equation becomes $1.568y = 1.568$ and hence $y = 1$. Turning to x,

$$x = \frac{1.018 + 2.436y}{0.3454} = 10.01.$$

Much better!

How can it be predicted that using c as a pivot is much better than ϵ? It is not just that ϵ is small because one could divide the first equation through by ϵ to start with and then the coefficient of x is 1. It is that ϵ is small relative to the other coefficients of the row (that is b).

Scaled partial pivoting is the technique to handle this. Let us pick up the solution, in matrix form, at the kth stage; we have

$$
\begin{bmatrix}
a_{11} & \cdots & a_{1,k-1} & a_{1k} & \cdots & a_{1n} \\
\vdots & \cdots & a_{k-1,k-1} & a_{k-1,k} & \cdots & a_{k-1,n} \\
0 & \cdots & 0 & a_{kk} & \cdots & a_{kn} \\
0 & \cdots & 0 & a_{k+1,k} & \cdots & a_{k+1,n} \\
\vdots & \cdots & \vdots & \vdots & \cdots & \vdots \\
0 & \cdots & 0 & a_{nk} & \cdots & a_{nn}
\end{bmatrix}.
$$

Among the possibilities $a_{kk}, a_{k+1,k}, \ldots, a_{nk}$, which should be used as the pivot? To decide, let the *size* of each row, d_i, be the largest in absolute value of the remaining row elements,

$$
d_i = \max\{|a_{ik}|, |a_{i,k+1}|, \ldots, |a_{in}|\}, \quad k \le i \le n.
$$

Then the *relative size*, r_i, of a pivot candidate is its absolute value divided by the row size for its row,

$$
r_i = |a_{ik}|/d_i.
$$

Exchange rows in such a way as to pivot on the row with the largest relative pivot.

In the example above, the size of the first row is $b = 1.566$ and the size of the second is $d = 2.436$. The relative size of the pivot candidate ϵ is $0.0003/1.566 = 0.00019$ while the relative size of the candidate c is $0.3454/2.436 = 0.1417$; thus, choose c as the pivot.

Keeping track of exchanged rows gives rise to a permutation matrix P as we discussed above; hence,

$$
LU = PA.
$$

Gaussian elimination itself, without pivoting, can be parallelized stage by stage, that is, at the kth stage when annihilating the elements i, k for $i = k + 1, \ldots, n$, these updates may be done in parallel. Unfortunately pivoting entails an additional complication to the parallelization of Gaussian elimination (or LU decomposition). This is explored in the Exercises.

Total Pivoting

Total pivoting means that column interchanges are allowed as well as row interchanges. Figuring the optimal pivot is easier under total pivoting, just use the remaining coefficient which is largest in absolute value. Thus, at the kth stage (with primes denoting the matrix elements at this stage), if for some p and q, both in the range k to n,

$$|a'_{pq}| \geq |a'_{ij}|, \quad k \leq i, j \leq n,$$

then a'_{pq} is an optimal pivot and can be brought to the k, k position by interchanging rows k and p and columns k and q.

An Example Putting It All Together

Consider the 3×3 system

$$\begin{bmatrix} 1 & -1 & 5 \\ 2 & -2 & -1 \\ 3 & -2 & 2 \end{bmatrix} \begin{bmatrix} x \\ y \\ z \end{bmatrix} = \begin{bmatrix} 7 \\ 3 \\ 7 \end{bmatrix}.$$

Working on the coefficient matrix

$$\begin{bmatrix} 1 & -1 & 5 \\ 2 & -2 & -1 \\ 3 & -2 & 2 \end{bmatrix},$$

we interchange the first and third columns so as to pivot on the 5, which is the largest in magnitude remaining element of the coefficient matrix

$$\begin{bmatrix} 5 & -1 & 1 \\ -1 & -2 & 2 \\ 2 & -2 & 3 \end{bmatrix}.$$

Annihilating a_{21} and a_{31}, and storing the multipliers as described gives

$$\begin{bmatrix} 5 & -1 & 1 \\ -1/5 & -11/5 & 11/5 \\ 2/5 & -8/5 & 13/5 \end{bmatrix}.$$

To get the $13/5$ into the pivot position, interchange the second and third rows and then the second and third columns

$$\begin{bmatrix} 5 & 1 & -1 \\ 2/5 & 13/5 & -8/5 \\ -1/5 & 11/5 & -11/5 \end{bmatrix}.$$

Note that we have interchanged the entire rows including the stored elements of L. The column permutation vector is now $\mathbf{c} = [\,3 \quad 1 \quad 2\,]$ and the row permutation vector is $\mathbf{r} = [\,1 \quad 3 \quad 2\,]$. Finally, using $13/5$ to annihilate $11/5$, and again storing the multiplier, gives

$$\begin{bmatrix} 5 & 1 & -1 \\ 2/5 & 13/5 & -8/5 \\ -1/5 & 11/13 & -11/13 \end{bmatrix}.$$

So the L and U matrices are

$$\begin{bmatrix} 1 & 0 & 0 \\ 2/5 & 1 & 0 \\ -1/5 & 11/13 & 1 \end{bmatrix} \begin{bmatrix} 5 & 1 & -1 \\ 0 & 13/5 & -8/5 \\ 0 & 0 & -11/13 \end{bmatrix}.$$

Letting P_L be the elementary matrix obtained by performing the row interchanges on the identity I, and letting P_R be the elementary matrix obtained by performing the column permutations on the identity, we have

$$LU = P_L A P_R$$

$$\begin{bmatrix} 5 & 1 & -1 \\ 2 & 3 & -2 \\ -1 & 2 & -2 \end{bmatrix} = \begin{bmatrix} 1 & 0 & 0 \\ 0 & 0 & 1 \\ 0 & 1 & 0 \end{bmatrix} \begin{bmatrix} 1 & -1 & 5 \\ 2 & -2 & -1 \\ 3 & -2 & 2 \end{bmatrix} \begin{bmatrix} 0 & 1 & 0 \\ 0 & 0 & 1 \\ 1 & 0 & 0 \end{bmatrix}.$$

To solve the given system, permute the RHS as given by the row permutation vector and solve the lower triangular system

$$\begin{bmatrix} 1 & 0 & 0 \\ 2/5 & 1 & 0 \\ -1/5 & 11/13 & 1 \end{bmatrix} \begin{bmatrix} u \\ v \\ w \end{bmatrix} = \begin{bmatrix} 7 \\ 7 \\ 3 \end{bmatrix}.$$

This gives $u = 7$, $v = 21/5$ and $w = 11/13$. Then solving the upper-triangular system,

$$\begin{bmatrix} 5 & 1 & -1 \\ 0 & 13/5 & -8/5 \\ 0 & 0 & -11/13 \end{bmatrix} \begin{bmatrix} x_1 \\ x_2 \\ x_3 \end{bmatrix} = \begin{bmatrix} 7 \\ 21/5 \\ 11/13 \end{bmatrix}.$$

We get $x_1 = 1$, $x_2 = 1$, and $x_3 = -1$. Remembering the column permutation vector $c = [3 \quad 1 \quad 2]$, we restore the original order, $z = 1, x = 1$, and $y = -1$.

5.3 ijk-Forms for LU Decomposition

Just as there are several ways to perform a matrix–matrix multiply owing to the possibility of rearranging the order of summation, the same holds for LU decomposition. Since there are again three indices, i, j, and k, there are correspondingly $3!=6$ possibilities. They organize themselves into three pairs, depending on the location of the summation over k.

As before, the calculation performed within the innermost loop is the same, namely the row element update

$$a_{ij} = a_{ij} - \ell_{ik} * a_{kj}.$$

Depending on the form, this can be a saxpy operation or a dot product. Hence the parallelization prospects and speed of the decomposition vary over the different forms.

kij-Form

As given on p. 138, the algorithm is, in looping notation,

kij-form (ignoring ℓ_{ik} updates)

$$\mathcal{L}_{k=1}^{n-1}\mathcal{L}_{i=k+1}^{n}\mathcal{L}_{j=k+1}^{n}(a_{ij} \leftarrow a_{ij} - \ell_{ik}a_{kj}).$$

From this basic algorithm we get the looping region for LU decomposition (see Fig. 26). Note that for fixed k the region is a square from $k+1$ to n in both i and j; the region is precisely the remaining matrix to process and k is like a time slice of the progress.

Now add the multiplier calculations.

kji-form coded with ℓ_{ik} updates:

```
loop  k= 1 to n-1
  loop  i = k+1 to n
  ℓik ← aik/akk;
    loop  j= k+1 to n
      aij ← aij - ℓik * akj;
    end  loop
  end  loop
end  loop
```

Since the innermost loop index is j, the row element update is a saxpy operation (i.e., a vector calculation). Furthermore, the elements of the matrix, a_{ij}, are updated once and for all, so this is called an *immediate update* method.

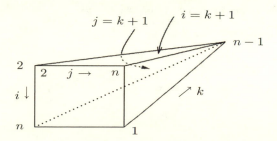

Fig. 26. "Looping Region" for LU decomposition k is like a "time slice" of the matrix during the decomposition.

kji-Form

Since the looping region for fixed k is a square, we may simply interchange the i and j loops to get the kji-form.

kji-form (ignoring ℓ_{ik} updates)

$$\mathcal{L}_{k=1}^{n-1}\mathcal{L}_{j=k+1}^{n}\mathcal{L}_{i=k+1}^{n}(a_{ij} \leftarrow a_{ij} - \ell_{ik}a_{kj}).$$

To add the multiplier calculation, note that a different multiplier ℓ_{ik} is needed for each different i in the innermost loop. Therefore, these must be calculated separately in advance.

The kji-form coded with ℓ_{ik} updates:

```
loop  k= 1 to n-1
   loop  s = k+1 to n
      ℓsk ← ask/akk;
   end  loop
   loop  j= k+1 to n
      loop  i = k+1 to n
         aij ← aij - ℓik * akj;
      end  loop
   end  loop
end  loop
```

Here again the innermost loop is a saxpy operation but in this case the matrix elements are updated in stages. We refer to this as a *delayed update* method.

jki-Form

This time a slice through the looping region for a fixed j cuts the "back wall" $j = k + 1$; hence, k depends on j.

jki-Form (ignoring ℓ_{ik} updates)

$$\mathcal{L}_{j=2}^{n}\mathcal{L}_{k=1}^{j-1}\mathcal{L}_{i=k+1}^{n}(a_{ij} \leftarrow a_{ij} - \ell_{ik}a_{kj}).$$

As above, the multipliers must be precalculated.

jki-form coded with ℓ_{ik} updates:

```
loop  j= 2 to n
   loop  s = j to n
      ℓs,j-1 ← as,j−1/aj-1, j-1;
   end  loop
   loop  k= 1 to j-1
      loop  i = k+1 to n
         aij ← aij - ℓik * akj;
      end  loop
   end  loop
end  loop
```

To illustrate how this algorithm works, we carry it out manually for the case where $n = 4$.

```
loop  j=2 to n; //so j = 2,3,4
j ← 2
   loop    s=j to n; //compute ℓs,j−1 for s = 2,3,4
   ℓ21 ← a21/a11
   ℓ31 ← a31/a11
   ℓ41 ← a41/a11

   k = 1
     i = 2,3,4
        a'22 ← a22 - ℓ21 * a12
        a'32 ← a32 - ℓ31 * a12
        a'42 ← a42 - ℓ41 * a12
```

Snapshot at this stage:

$$\begin{bmatrix} a_{11} & a_{12} & a_{13} & a_{14} \\ 0 & a'_{22} & a_{23} & a_{24} \\ 0 & a'_{32} & a_{33} & a_{34} \\ 0 & a'_{42} & a_{43} & a_{44} \end{bmatrix}.$$

```
//Back to the outer-loop
j ← 3
   s = 3,4
   ℓ32 ← a'32/a'22
   ℓ42 ← a'42/a'22
   k = 1,2
   k ← 1
     i = 2,3,4 //first update to the third column
        a'23 ← a23 - ℓ21 * a13
        a'33 ← a33 - ℓ31 * a13
        a'43 ← a43 - ℓ41 * a13
   k ← 2
     i = 3,4 //second update to the third column
        a''33 ← a'33 - ℓ32 * a23
        a''43 ← a'43 - ℓ42 * a23
```

Snapshot at this stage,

$$\begin{bmatrix} a_{11} & a_{12} & a_{13} & a_{14} \\ 0 & a'_{22} & a'_{23} & a_{24} \\ 0 & 0 & a''_{33} & a_{34} \\ 0 & 0 & a''_{43} & a_{44} \end{bmatrix}.$$

```
//Back to the outer-loop
j ← 4
  s ← 4
  ℓ₄₃ ← a″₄₃/a′₂₂
  k = 1,2,3
  k ← 1
    i = 2,3,4 //first update to the fourth column
      a′₂₄ ← a₂₄ - ℓ₂₁ * a₁₄
      a′₃₄ ← a₃₄ - ℓ₃₁ * a₁₄
      a′₄₄ ← a₄₄ - ℓ₄₁ * a₁₄
  k ← 2
    i = 3,4 //second update to the fourth column
      a″₃₄ ← a′₃₄ - ℓ₃₂ * a′₂₄
      a″₄₄ ← a′₄₄ - ℓ₄₂ * a′₂₄
  k ← 3 //third update to the fourth column
    i ← 4
      a‴₄₄ ← a″₄₄ - ℓ₄₂ * a′₂₄
```

Snapshot at the final stage.

$$\begin{bmatrix} a_{11} & a_{12} & a_{13} & a_{14} \\ 0 & a'_{22} & a'_{23} & a'_{24} \\ 0 & 0 & a''_{33} & a''_{34} \\ 0 & 0 & 0 & a'''_{44} \end{bmatrix}.$$

We leave it to the reader to do the ikj-form.

jik-Form

Once again for fixed j the slice through the looping region (Fig. 26) gives a trapezoidal region whose "back wall" is the plane $j = k+1$ and whose "ceiling" is the plane $i = k+1$. But now since i is summed in second place, there are two cases: whether i is at the level of the "ceiling" or at the level of the "back wall." Thus we have the following algorithm (with ℓ_{ik} multiplier updates ignored for now).

The jik-form

$$\mathcal{L}^n_{j=2}\mathcal{L}^n_{i=2}\mathcal{L}^{\min(i-1,j-1)}_{k=1}(a_{ij} \leftarrow a_{ij} - \ell_{ik}a_{kj}).$$

We see that the row element update

$$a_{ij} = a_{ij} - \ell_{ik} * a_{kj}$$

is not a vector operation here but instead a dot product since the left-hand side is not indexed by k.

We leave it to the reader to add the multiplier calculation as required for this form and the ijk form as well.

Summary

kji and kij: immediate update, saxpies;
jki and ikj: delayed update, saxpies/linear combinations; and
ijk and jik: delayed update, inner products.

5.4 Bordering Algorithm for LU Decomposition

In the previous sections we have partitioned the working submatrix of the decomposition, using 1×1 blocks (and whatever size for the rest of the matrix). But it is possible to use larger blocks. In this section the working submatrices are $1 \times j - 1$ for the unknown vector ℓ_j and $j - 1 \times 1$ for the unknown vector u_j. Of course, the current version of A must be compatibly partitioned. This gives

$$
\begin{array}{c}
\begin{array}{ccc} j-1 & 1 & n-j \end{array} \\
\begin{array}{c} j-1 \\ 1 \\ n-j \end{array}
\left[\begin{array}{c|c|c}
L_{j-1} & 0 & 0 \\ \hline
\ell_j & 1 & 0 \\ \hline
L' & \ell' & L''
\end{array}\right]
\end{array}
\begin{array}{c}
\begin{array}{ccc} j-1 & 1 & n-j \end{array} \\
\left[\begin{array}{c|c|c}
U_{j-1} & u_j & U' \\ \hline
0 & u_{jj} & u' \\ \hline
0 & 0 & U''
\end{array}\right]
\end{array}
$$

$$
= \begin{array}{c}
\begin{array}{ccc} j-1 & 1 & n-j \end{array} \\
\begin{array}{c} j-1 \\ 1 \\ n-j \end{array}
\left[\begin{array}{c|c|c}
A_{j-1} & a_j & A' \\ \hline
\hat{a}_j & a_{jj} & a' \\ \hline
A'' & a'' & A'''
\end{array}\right].
\end{array}
$$

The submatrices L_{j-1} and U_{j-1} are already solved for and known. At this stage, we solve for ℓ_j, u_j, and u_{jj}. As indicated, u_{jj} and a_{jj} are scalars.

By considering the partition matrix product of the first row of L with the second column of U, we get the system

$$L_{j-1}u_j = a_j.$$

This is a lower triangular system of size $j - 1$, which may be solved for u_j using forward substitution.

The partition matrix product of the second row of L with the first column of U gives the matrix equation

$$\ell_j U_{j-1} = \hat{a}_j;$$

both ℓ_j and $\hat{a}_j$ are $j-1$ row vectors, U_{j-1} is upper triangular. It may be solved as is (or equivalently, its transpose) by forward substitution to give ℓ_j.

Finally, the scalar u_{jj} is solved for from the equation

$$\ell_j u_j + u_{jj} = a_{jj};$$

the product of the row vector ℓ_j and the column vector u_j is a scalar.

So by this bordering method one solves two lower-triangular systems and then one scalar equation to complete one stage of the decomposition.

5.5 Algorithm for Matrix Inversion in $\log^2 n$ Time

In the Exercises there are two problems showing how to compute the inverse of a triangular matrix in $O(\log^2 n)$ time using $O(n^3)$ processors (an excessive number). Remarkably, it is possible to invert any nonsingular matrix in the same time. This outstanding fact was discovered in 1976 by Csanky. For completeness we reproduce his algorithm here.

The characteristic polynomial $\phi(\lambda)$ of the $n \times n$ matrix A is

$$\phi(\lambda) = \det(\lambda I - A) = \lambda^n + c_1 \lambda^{n-1} + \cdots + c_{n-1}\lambda + c_n$$
$$= \prod_{i=1}^{n}(\lambda - \lambda_i), \qquad (5)$$

where $\lambda_1, \ldots, \lambda_n$ are the eigenvalues of A and $c_1, \ldots, c_n$ are the coefficients of the characteristic polynomial. By the Cayley–Hamilton Theorem, that A satisfies its own characteristic polynomial, we have

$$A^n + c_1 A^{n-1} + \cdots + c_{n-1}A + c_n I = 0,$$

or equivalently

$$c_n I = -(A^n + c_1 A^{n-1} + \cdots + c_{n-1}A).$$

Multiply this on both sides by A^{-1} and divide by c_n to obtain

$$A^{-1} = -\frac{1}{c_n}\left(A^{n-1} + c_1 A^{n-2} + \cdots + c_{n-1}I\right).$$

If A is nonsingular, then $c_n \neq 0$ since, by Eq. (5), $c_n = (-1)^n \prod_{i=1}^{n} \lambda_i$.

We know that the matrix powers can be computed in time $O(\log^2 n)$ using n^4 processors, so it remains to compute the coefficients $c_1, \ldots, c_n$.

Let $t_k = \text{tr}(A^k)$ for $k = 1, \ldots, n$, where the trace $\text{tr}(B)$ of a matrix B is the sum of its diagonal elements. Given B, $\text{tr}(B)$ can be computed in order $O(\log n)$ time. It was discovered by Leverrier that the characteristic polynomial coefficients are related to the traces by the following lower-triangular linear system.

$$
\begin{bmatrix}
1 & 0 & \cdots & \cdots & \cdots & 0 \\
t_1 & 2 & 0 & \cdots & \cdots & 0 \\
\vdots & \ddots & \ddots & \ddots & \cdots & \vdots \\
t_{k-1} & \cdots & t_1 & k & \cdots & 0 \\
\vdots & \ddots & \ddots & \ddots & \ddots & \vdots \\
t_{n-1} & \cdots & t_{k-1} & \cdots & t_1 & n
\end{bmatrix}
\begin{bmatrix}
c_1 \\ \vdots \\ \vdots \\ \vdots \\ \vdots \\ c_n
\end{bmatrix}
= -
\begin{bmatrix}
t_1 \\ \vdots \\ \vdots \\ \vdots \\ \vdots \\ t_n
\end{bmatrix}.
\tag{6}
$$

This remarkable fact is derived by differentiating the characteristic polynomial in two different ways. On the one hand

$$
\frac{d\phi}{d\lambda} = n\lambda^{n-1} + c_1(n-1)\lambda^{n-2} + \cdots + c_{n-1}.
\tag{7}
$$

While, on the other, we differentiate the product of linear factors form,

$$
\frac{d\phi}{d\lambda} = \frac{d}{d\lambda}\left[\prod_{i=1}^{n}(\lambda - \lambda_i)\right] = \sum_{i=1}^{n}\prod_{j\neq i}(\lambda - \lambda_j) = \sum_{i=1}^{n}\frac{\phi(\lambda)}{\lambda - \lambda_i}.
$$

Next substitute the geometric series

$$
\frac{1}{\lambda - \lambda_i} = \frac{1}{\lambda(1 - \lambda_i/\lambda)} = \frac{1}{\lambda}\left(1 + \frac{\lambda_i}{\lambda} + \frac{\lambda_i^2}{\lambda^2} + \cdots\right),
$$

which is valid for $|\lambda| > |\lambda_i|$. We get

$$
\begin{aligned}
\frac{d\phi}{d\lambda} &= \frac{\phi(\lambda)}{\lambda}\sum_{i=1}^{n}\left(1 + \frac{\lambda_i}{\lambda} + \frac{\lambda_i^2}{\lambda^2} + \cdots\right) \\
&= \frac{\phi(\lambda)}{\lambda}\left(\sum_{1}^{n}1 + \frac{\sum_{1}^{n}\lambda_i}{\lambda} + \frac{\sum_{1}^{n}\lambda_i^2}{\lambda^2} + \cdots\right) \\
&= (\lambda^n + c_1\lambda^{n-1} + \cdots + c_n)\left(\frac{n}{\lambda} + \frac{t_1}{\lambda^2} + \frac{t_2}{\lambda^3} + \cdots\right).
\end{aligned}
\tag{8}
$$

This expression for $d\phi/d\lambda$ is valid for all $|\lambda| > |\lambda_i|$ for all $i = 1, \ldots, n$. Therefore we can equate the coefficients of like powers of λ between

Eqs. (7) and (8) to get

$$
\begin{aligned}
nc_1 + t_1 &= c_1(n-1) \\
nc_2 + c_1 t_1 + t_2 &= c_2(n-2) \\
nc_3 + c_2 t_1 + c_1 t_2 + t_3 &= c_3(n-3) \\
\vdots &= \vdots \\
nc_n + c_{n-1}t_1 + \cdots + c_1 t_{n-1} + t_n &= 0.
\end{aligned}
$$

This gives the system (6).

Exercises

1. (5) Show that a strictly upper-triangular matrix is nilpotent, that is, some power of a strictly upper-triangular matrix is the zero matrix.
2. (6) Show that the sum and product of two upper- (lower-) triangular matrices is upper (lower) triangular. Show that the inverse of an upper (lower) matrix is also upper (lower) triangular.
3. (3) Show that triangular factorization is unique as follows: If A is invertible and $L_1 U_1 = A = L_2 U_2$, where L_1 and L_2 are unit lower triangular and U_1 and U_2 are upper triangular, then $L_1 = L_2$ and $U_1 = U_2$. (Unit lower triangular means lower triangular with 1's on the main diagonal.)
4. (4) Show that the matrix

$$
A = \begin{bmatrix} 2 & 2 & 1 \\ 1 & 1 & 1 \\ 3 & 2 & 1 \end{bmatrix}
$$

   is invertible, but that A cannot be written as the product of a lower-triangular matrix with an upper-triangular matrix. Be sure your argument works independently of a decomposition method.
5. (5) (a) Show that the inverse E_{i1}^{-1} of the elementary matrix E_{i1} (multiply the first row by ℓ_{i1} and add to the ith row)

$$
E_{i1} = \begin{bmatrix} 1 & 0 & \cdots & 0 \\ \vdots & \vdots & \cdots & 0 \\ \ell_{i1} & 0 & \cdots & 0 \\ \vdots & \vdots & \cdots & 0 \\ 0 & 0 & \cdots & 1 \end{bmatrix} \quad \text{is} \quad E_{i1}^{-1} = \begin{bmatrix} 1 & 0 & \cdots & 0 \\ \vdots & \vdots & \cdots & 0 \\ -\ell_{i1} & 0 & \cdots & 0 \\ \vdots & \vdots & \cdots & 0 \\ 0 & 0 & \cdots & 1 \end{bmatrix}.
$$

(b) Show that the product of $E_{r1}E_{s1}$ is

$$E = \begin{bmatrix} 1 & 0 & \cdots & 0 \\ \vdots & \vdots & \cdots & 0 \\ \ell_{r1} & 0 & \cdots & 0 \\ \vdots & \vdots & \cdots & 0 \\ \ell_{s1} & 0 & \cdots & 0 \\ 0 & 0 & \cdots & 1 \end{bmatrix}.$$

(c) Deduce that $A = (E_{21}^{-1} \ldots E_{n1}^{-1})U_1 = L_1U_1$, where L_1 and U_1 are the LU decomposion matrices after the first step of Gaussian elimination.

6. (4) Find the number of operations, up to order of magnitude, required to calculate the determinant of an $n \times n$ matrix by (1) LU decomposition and (2) expansion by minors.

7. (4) (a) What is the number of arithmetic operations for multiplying an upper-triangular matrix by another upper-triangular matrix? (b) What is the number of arithmetic operations for multiplying an upper-triangular matrix by a full matrix?

8. (5) Show that if A is nonsingular, symmetric ($A^T = A$), and has a triangular factorization, $A = LU$, then $U = DL^T$, with D the diagonal matrix having the same diagonal entries as U.

9. (3) The Vandermonde matrix on $x_1, x_2, \ldots, x_n$, is

$$V = \begin{bmatrix} 1 & x_1 & x_1^2 & \cdots & x_1^{n-1} \\ 1 & x_2 & x_2^2 & \cdots & x_2^{n-1} \\ \vdots & \vdots & \vdots & \cdots & \vdots \\ 1 & x_n & x_n^2 & \cdots & x_n^{n-1} \end{bmatrix}.$$

It is known that $\det V = \prod_{1 \le j < i \le n}(x_i - x_j)$. Find an $O(\log n)$ algorithm for computing $\det V$. How many arithmetic operations are required? (The Vandermonde matrix results from the problem of interpolating an $n - 1$ degree polynomial $a_0 + a_1x + a_2x^2 + \cdots + a_{n-1}x^{n-1}$ through n points (x_1, y_1), $(x_2, y_2), \ldots, (x_n, y_n)$. The vector of coefficients $\mathbf{a} = (a_0, a_1, \ldots, a_{n-1})^T$ is the solution to $V\mathbf{a} = \mathbf{y}$.)

10. (4) Suppose the $n \times n$ matrix A can be represented as $A = I - L$, where I is the $n \times n$ identity matrix as usual and L is strictly lower triangular. (a) Show that A inverse is given by

$$A^{-1} = (I + L^{2^{\lceil \log n \rceil - 1}})(I + L^{2^{\lceil \log n \rceil - 2}}) \ldots (I + L^8)(I + L^4)(I + L^2)(I + L).$$

(b) Deduce an $O(\log^2 n)$ algorithm using n^3 processors as an alternative to back substitution.

11. (4) Derive an algorithm to decompose $A = L'U'$ into the product of a lower-triangular matrix L' and a *unit* upper-triangular matrix U'.

12. (4) Show how to use elementary matrices $E_1, E_2, \ldots, E_r$, to obtain a UL decomposition of A with U unit upper triangular and L lower triangular,

$$E_r \ldots E_2 E_1 A = L, \qquad A = E_1^{-1} \ldots E_r^{-1} L,$$

provided no zero pivots arise in the decomposition. (An alternate method, which uses column permutations as well as the elementary row operations, permutes the rows in reverse order and then the columns too, does an LU on that, and then reverse permutes back.)

13. (8) Let F be the matrix that results by performing an elementary column operation on the identity I. (a) Show that AF is the matrix that results by performing the same elementary column operation on A. (b) Show that A has a decomposition $A = MR$, where M is lower triangular and R is unit upper triangular obtained by performing a sequence of elementary column operations provided no zero pivots arise in the decomposition. (c) Using part (b) and the results of the previous problem, show that $\det(AB) = \det(A)\det(B)$.

14. (6) Let A be an $n \times n$ unit lower-triangular matrix defined by

$$\begin{bmatrix} 1 & 0 & 0 & \cdots & 0 \\ a_{21} & 1 & 0 & \cdots & 0 \\ a_{31} & a_{32} & 1 & \cdots & 0 \\ \vdots & & & \ddots & \vdots \\ a_{n1} & a_{n2} & \cdots & & 1 \end{bmatrix}.$$

Define the matrix E_i, $1 \le i \le n$, as follows:

$$\begin{bmatrix} 1 & 0 & \cdots & & & & 0 \\ 0 & 1 & \cdots & & & & 0 \\ \vdots & & \ddots & & & & 0 \\ 0 & 0 & \cdots & 1 & & & 0 \\ 0 & 0 & \cdots & a_{i+1,i} & 1 & & 0 \\ \vdots & & & \cdots & & \ddots & \vdots \\ 0 & 0 & \cdots & a_{n,i} & 0 & \cdots & 1 \end{bmatrix}.$$

(a) Show that $A = E_1 E_2 \ldots E_{n-1}$. (b) Find the inverse of E_i. (c) Deduce an $O(\log^2 n)$ algorithm for computing A^{-1}. What is the total number of operations needed?

15. (5) Write a DAG for LU decomposition with partial pivoting.

16. (3) Write out the correct coding for an LU decomposition using the jik-form; include the ℓ_{ik} updates.

Programming Exercises

17. (8) Code and execute the three LU-decomposition forms $kij, ikj,$ and jik. Obtain a table or graph of times as a function of n. (One can use the Hilbert matrix H_n (p. 177) for the tests.)

18. (6) Assume $\sum_{k=1}^{n} k^5$ is given in closed form by some 6th degree polynomial,

$$\sum_{k=1}^{n} k^5 = a_0 + a_1 n + a_2 n^2 + \cdots + a_6 n^6.$$

(a) Using the specific values of the sum for $n = 0, 1, \ldots, 6$ (e.g., for $n = 0$ the sum is 0 (hence $a_0 = 0$), for $n = 1$ the sum is 1, for $n = 2$ the sum is $1^5 + 2^5 = 33$, and so on), write the solution for the polynomial coefficients as a linear system of equations. (b) Write a program and solve this system of equations, without pivoting, under four different rearrangements: first, with the equations written in order of small to large n and the unknowns in the order of small to large subscript, in this arrangement the first equation is $1 = a_1 + a_2 + \cdots + a_6$. Second, with the equations written in order of large to small n and the same order of the unknowns, in this arrangement the first equation is $12201 = 6a_1 + 36a_2 + 216a_3 + 1296a_4 + 7776a_5 + 46656a_6$. Third, with the equations in order of small to large n and the unknowns in order of large to small subscript, thus the first equation is $1 = a_6 + a_5 + a_4 + a_3 + a_2 + a_1$. And finally, with the equations in order of large to small n and unknowns in order of large to small subscript, thus the first equation is $12201 = 46656a_6 + 7776a_5 + 1296a_4 + 216a_3 + 36a_2 + 6a_1$. (The problems with numerical accuracy you should see in this exercise are examined in the chapter on Error Analysis.)

6

Direct Methods for Systems
with Special Structure

6.1 Tridiagonal Systems – Thompson's Algorithm

The system to be solved takes the form

$$
\begin{array}{llllll}
d_1x_1 & + & e_1x_2 & & & = & b_1 \\
f_2x_1 & + & d_2x_2 & + & e_2x_3 & & & = & b_2 \\
& & f_3x_2 & + & d_3x_3 & + & e_3x_4 & & = & b_3 \\
& & & \ddots & & \ddots & & \ddots & & \vdots \\
& & & & f_{n-1}x_{n-2} & + & d_{n-1}x_{n-1} & + & e_{n-1}x_n & = & b_{n-1} \\
& & & & & & f_nx_{n-1} & + & d_nx_n & = & b_n
\end{array}
$$

where we use the notation $d_k = a_{kk}$, $k = 1, \ldots, n$, for the diagonal elements, $e_k = a_{k,k+1}$, $k = 1, \ldots, n-1$, for the superdiagonal elements, and $f_k = a_{k,k-1}$, $k = 2, \ldots, n$, for the subdiagonal elements. All other coefficients are 0. Following the development on p. 137, Eqs. (3) become

$$u_{11} = d_1$$
$$[\, u_{12} \quad u_{13} \quad \ldots \quad u_{1n} \,] = [\, e_1 \quad 0 \quad \ldots \quad 0 \,]$$
$$u_{11} [\, \ell_{21} \quad \ell_{31} \quad \ldots \quad \ell_{n1} \,]^T = [\, f_2 \quad 0 \quad \ldots \quad 0 \,]^T$$
$$A_2 = L_2 U_2 = [a_{ij}] - [\ell_{i1}u_{1j}] \quad 2 \leq i, j \leq n.$$

So we see that

$$
\begin{array}{lll}
u_{11} = d_1, & u_{12} = e_1, & \ell_{21} = f_2/u_{11}, \quad \text{and} \\
u_{1j} = 0, & j = 3, \ldots, n & \ell_{i1} = 0, \quad i = 3, \ldots, n.
\end{array}
$$

Therefore only the element d_2 is updated, it becomes

$$d_2^{(2)} = d_2 - \ell_{21}u_{12}.$$

It follows that the update matrix A_2 is also tridiagonal and so recursion can proceed just as above. We have also shown that L and U are themselves tridiagonal, as well as triangular. Hence we have the theorem

162

Theorem 1. *If the kth update $d_k^{(k)} \neq 0, k = 1, \ldots, n-1, (d_1^{(1)} = d_1)$, then $A = LU$, where L is unit lower triangular and tridiagonal and U is upper triangular and tridiagonal.*

We have demonstrated the algorithm

$$\mathcal{L}_{k=1}^{n-1} \left\{ \begin{array}{l} \end{array} \right.$$

$$u_{kk} \leftarrow d_k$$

$$u_{k,k+1} \leftarrow e_k$$

$$\ell_{k+1,k} \leftarrow f_{k+1}/u_{kk}$$

$$d_{k+1} \leftarrow d_{k+1} - \ell_{k+1,k} * u_{k,k+1}$$

$$\left. \begin{array}{l} \end{array} \right\}.$$

By utilizing the storage of the input data to double as the storage for the outputs, over the course of the algorithm the vector $\mathbf{f}$ becomes the vector $[\ell_{k+1,k}]$, $k = 1, \ldots, n-1$, the vector $\mathbf{e}$ becomes the vector $[u_{k,k+1}]$, $k = 1, \ldots, n-1$, and the vector $\mathbf{d}$ becomes the vector $[u_{kk}]$, $k = 1, \ldots, n$.

Thompson Algorithm

```
loop  k= 1 upto n-1
        f_{k+1} ← f_{k+1}/d_k;
        d_{k+1} ← d_{k+1} - f_{k+1} * e_k;
end  loop
```

6.2 Tridiagonal Systems – Odd–Even Reduction

Unfortunately Thompson's algorithm does not parallelize. In this section we examine a method that does. We write again the tridiagonal system,

$$
\begin{array}{rcl}
d_1 x_1 + e_1 x_2 & = & b_1 \\
f_2 x_1 + d_2 x_2 + e_2 x_3 & = & b_2 \\
f_3 x_2 + d_3 x_3 + e_3 x_4 & = & b_3 \\
\ddots \qquad \ddots \qquad \ddots & & \vdots \\
f_{n-1} x_{n-2} + d_{n-1} x_{n-1} + e_{n-1} x_n & = & b_{n-1} \\
f_n x_{n-1} + d_n x_n & = & b_n
\end{array}
$$

Consider solving the system as follows, for every odd integer i, if $d_i \neq 0$, solve $f_i x_{i-1} + d_i x_i + e_i x_{i+1} = b_i$ for the odd variable x_i in terms of the even variables x_{i-1} and x_{i+1},

$$x_i = \frac{1}{d_i}(b_i - f_i x_{i-1} - e_i x_{i+1}), \quad \text{provided } d_i \neq 0. \tag{9}$$

The first equation is slightly different and, if n is odd, so is the last,

$$x_1 = \frac{1}{d_1}(b_1 - e_1 x_2)$$

$$x_n = \frac{1}{d_n}(b_n - f_n x_{n-1}), \quad \text{if } n \text{ is odd.}$$

However, by defining $f_1 = 0$ and $e_n = 0$, then equation (9) holds in all cases.

Substitute these x_i's into the even equations to arrive at a new tridiagonal system of size $n' = \lfloor n/2 \rfloor$, about half that of the original. Thus for k even, $k = 2, 4, \ldots, n'$,

$$\frac{-f_{k-1}f_k}{d_{k-1}}x_{k-2} + \left(\frac{-e_{k-1}f_k}{d_{k-1}} + d_k + \frac{-e_k f_{k+1}}{d_{k+1}}\right)x_k + \frac{-e_k e_{k+1}}{d_{k+1}}x_{k+2}$$
$$= b_k - \frac{f_k b_{k-1}}{d_{k-1}} - \frac{e_k b_{k+1}}{d_{k+1}}.$$

So the recursion equations for the constants are, for $k = 2i, i = 1, 2, \ldots, \lfloor n/2 \rfloor$,

$$f_k = \frac{-f_{k-1}f_k}{d_{k-1}}$$

$$d_k = \frac{-e_{k-1}f_k}{d_{k-1}} + d_k + \frac{-e_k f_{k+1}}{d_{k+1}}$$

$$e_k = \frac{-e_k e_{k+1}}{d_{k+1}}$$

$$b_k = b_k - \frac{f_k b_{k-1}}{d_{k-1}} - \frac{e_k b_{k+1}}{d_{k+1}},$$

recall, $f_1 = e_n = 0$.

Continue this until reaching a single equation which may be solved for its single unknown. The final reduction will either be from three equations and three unknowns to a single equation, or from two equations in two unknowns to a single equation. Then backsubstitute using Eq. (9), reversing the reductions, to obtain the other unknowns.

We can illustrate this schmatically with the help of the notation $n(p, q)$ meaning the diagonal unknown for an equation is x_n and the equation also depends on x_p and x_q. For $n = 4$ the diagram is as follows.

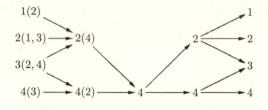

It shows that x_1 is eliminated from the second equation using the first and similarly, x_3 is eliminated from the second equation using the third. But this also introduces x_4 into the new second equation. In the same way, eliminating x_3 from the equation for x_4 introduces x_2. This is indicated at the second stage, of the diagram. Upon determining x_4, it is backsubstituted into the 2(4) equation and x_2 is computed. From there, both x_1 and x_3 can be solved.

The algorithm fails if $d_i = 0$ at some stage, and this can happen even if the system is not singular. For example, this occurs when $n = 4$ and all tridiagonal coefficients equal to 1. However, this combination of coefficients is quite special and does not occur under normal circumstances. When it does, some other method must be used.

Parallel Considerations

One stage of the algorithm is depicted in Fig. 27. Thus 4 steps are required per stage and 6 processors per overlapping series of 3 indices. (Although the divisions are shared between these banks, the multiplications at the second step are not.)

There is an entirely different way to parallelize the algorithm which is explored in the problems.

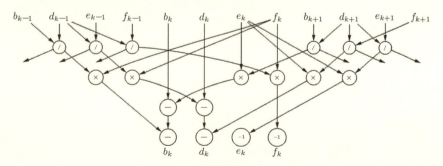

Fig. 27. DAG for one stage of odd-even reduction.

6.3 Symmetric Systems – Cholesky Decomposition

In this section we assume that A is a symmetric matrix, $A^T = A$, and we seek
a decomposition of the form $A = LDU$ with L and U unit triangular matrices
and D diagonal.

Set $A_1 = A$ and write $A_1 = LDU$ in partitioned form

$$
\begin{bmatrix} a_{11} & a_{12} & \cdots & a_{1n} \\ \hline a_{21} & & & \\ \vdots & & A' & \\ a_{n1} & & & \end{bmatrix}
$$

$$
= \begin{bmatrix} 1 & 0 & \cdots & 0 \\ \hline \ell_{21} & & & \\ \vdots & & L_2 & \\ \ell_{n1} & & & \end{bmatrix} \begin{bmatrix} d_{11} & 0 & \cdots & 0 \\ \hline 0 & & & \\ \vdots & & I & \\ 0 & & & \end{bmatrix} \begin{bmatrix} 1 & u_{12} & \cdots & u_{1n} \\ \hline 0 & & & \\ \vdots & & U_2 & \\ 0 & & & \end{bmatrix}.
$$

In this, A' is the $n-1 \times n-1$ matrix that remains when the first row and
column of A_1 are deleted. By multiplying out the right-hand side and equating
like submatrices we obtain

$$a_{11} = d_{11}$$

$$
\begin{bmatrix} a_{21} \\ \vdots \\ a_{n1} \end{bmatrix} = d_{11} \begin{bmatrix} \ell_{21} \\ \vdots \\ \ell_{n1} \end{bmatrix}
$$

$$
[a_{12} \quad \cdots \quad a_{1n}] = d_{11}[u_{12} \quad \cdots \quad u_{1n}]
$$

$$
A' = d_{11} \begin{bmatrix} \ell_{21} \\ \vdots \\ \ell_{n1} \end{bmatrix} [u_{12} \quad \cdots \quad u_{1n}] + L_2 U_2.
$$

Thus $d_{11} = a_{11}$ and

$$\ell_{i1} = a_{i1}/d_{11}, \quad i = 2, \ldots, n$$
$$u_{1j} = a_{1j}/d_{11}, \quad j = 2, \ldots, n.$$

To allow for recursion, the reduced version A_2 of A must be computed. When
the decomposition is complete, the reduced matrix will be the product $L_2 U_2$;
hence, this defines A_2,

$$
A_2 = L_2 U_2 = A' - d_{11} \begin{bmatrix} \ell_{21} \\ \vdots \\ \ell_{n1} \end{bmatrix} [u_{12} \quad \cdots \quad u_{1n}].
$$

In element form, this is

$$a_{ij}^{(2)} = a_{ij}^{(1)} - d_{11}\ell_{i1}u_{1j}, \quad i, j = 2, \ldots, n.$$

This completes one stage of the recursion; the calculations are now repeated on A_2.

Some observations are in order. Since A is symmetric, $a_{ij} = a_{ji}$ for all i and j, which allows for some simplifications. First, the equation for u_{1j} can be taken as

$$u_{1j} = a_{j1}/d_{11} \quad j = 2, \ldots, n.$$

From this we see that $u_{1j} = \ell_{j1}$, $j = 2, \ldots, n$. But then the update equation for a_{ij} becomes

$$a_{ij}^{(2)} = a_{ij}^{(1)} - d_{11}\ell_{i1}\ell_{1j}, \quad i, j = 2, \ldots, n.$$

And from this it follows that

$$a_{ij}^{(2)} = a_{ji}^{(2)}, \quad i, j = 2, \ldots, n.$$

Thus A_2 is also symmetric. By recursion, it follows that $u_{kj} = \ell_{jk}, k = 1, \ldots, n$, $j = k + 1, \ldots, n$, and so $U^T = L$. In particular, there is no need to store or compute U. In addition, since A_2 is symmetric, the update loop need only take place over the lower-triangular part (or upper-triangular part). We have proved the following.

Theorem 1. *If A is symmetric, then A can be written in the form*

$$A = LDL^T$$

where L is unit lower triangular and D is diagonal.

With these modifications we present the algorithm. Letting k index the recursion stages, $k = 1, 2, \ldots, n - 1$, the algorithm may be written in loop form as follows.

$$\mathcal{L}_{k=1}^{n-1}\Big\{$$
$$d_{kk} \leftarrow a_{kk}$$
$$\mathcal{L}_{i=k+1}^{n}\Big\{$$
$$\ell_{ik} \leftarrow a_{ik}/d_{kk}$$
$$\mathcal{L}_{j=k+1}^{i}\big\{a_{ij} \leftarrow a_{ij} - d_{kk}\ell_{ik}\ell_{jk}\big\}$$
$$\Big\}$$
$$\Big\}$$
$$d_{nn} \leftarrow a_{nn}$$

The last statement is required so that d_{nn} is given a value.

Now consider storage requirements. Since A is symmetric, only the lower triangular elements of A must be stored, there are $n(n + 1)/2$ in number. Upon completion of the algorithm, we would like these to consist of D on the diagonal and L on the strict lower-triangular part. In the algorithm above, once an ℓ_{ij} is calculated, the corresponding matrix element a_{ij} is not needed; therefore, we may replace the latter by the former. The same goes for the diagonal elements. The algorithm becomes this.

Symmetric Gaussian Elimination

```
loop  k= 1 upto n-1
    loop  i = k+1 upto n
        aik ← aik/akk;
        loop  j= k+1 upto i
            aij ← aij - akkaik * ajk;
        end  loop
    end  loop
end  loop
```

Upon completion D is the diagonal of (the resulting) A, $d_{kk} = a_{kk}$, $k = 1, \ldots, n$, and the strict lower-triangular part of A is the corresponding part of L. Since L is unit triangular, the diagonal elements of L are all 1.

A matrix A is *positive definite* if for all $\mathbf{x} \neq 0$, the dot product of $A\mathbf{x}$ with $\mathbf{x}$ is positive, (use $< \cdot, \cdot >$ to indicate the dot product)

$$\langle A\mathbf{x}, \mathbf{x} \rangle = \langle \mathbf{x}, A\mathbf{x} \rangle > 0.$$

In the construction above, if A is also positive definite, then so is D since for all $\mathbf{y}$, taken as $\mathbf{y} = L^T \mathbf{x}$,

$$0 \leq \langle \mathbf{x}, A\mathbf{x} \rangle = \langle \mathbf{x}, LDL^T \mathbf{x} \rangle$$
$$= \langle L^T \mathbf{x}, DL^T \mathbf{x} \rangle = \langle \mathbf{y}, D\mathbf{y} \rangle.$$

Therefore, the diagonal elements d_{kk} are positive and we may define

$$D^{1/2} = \begin{bmatrix} \sqrt{d_{11}} & 0 & \cdots & 0 \\ 0 & \sqrt{d_{22}} & \cdots & 0 \\ \vdots & \vdots & \ddots & \vdots \\ 0 & 0 & \cdots & \sqrt{d_{nn}} \end{bmatrix}.$$

Then $D^{1/2}D^{1/2} = D$ and so we may write LDL^T as

$$A = \left(LD^{1/2}\right)\left(LD^{1/2}\right)^T = CC^T,$$

where $C = LD^{1/2}$. This is Cholesky's decomposition of a positive definite symmetric matrix.

Of course, we can use the algorithm above to find L and D and compute C from them, but we prefer an algorithm to compute C directly. From a partition matrix decomposition as above, we obtain the recursion equations,

$$c_{11} = \sqrt{a_{11}}$$
$$c_{i1} = a_{i1}/c_{11}, \quad i = 2, \ldots, n$$
$$a_{ij}^{(2)} = a_{ij}^{(1)} - c_{i1}c_{j1}, \quad 2 \le i, j \le n.$$

Again, by symmetry, the update need only take place over the lower-triangular part, that is, for $j = k + 1, \ldots, i$. These considerations lead to the following algorithm in loop form.

$$\mathcal{L}_{k=1}^{n-1}\Bigg\{$$

$$c_{kk} \leftarrow \sqrt{a_{kk}}$$
$$\mathcal{L}_{i=k+1}^{n}\Bigg\{$$

$$c_{ik} \leftarrow a_{ik}/c_{kk}$$
$$\mathcal{L}_{j=k+1}^{i}\Big\{ a_{ij} \leftarrow a_{ij} - c_{ik}c_{jk} \Big\}$$

$$\Bigg\}$$

$$\Bigg\}$$

$$c_{nn} \leftarrow \sqrt{a_{nn}}$$

Again, the last statement is required to write c_{nn}. As noted above, if A is positive definite, then the diagonal elements $c_{kk} = \sqrt{d_{kk}}$ are positive for all $k = 1, \ldots, n$.

As before, we may store the elements of C in A as they are computed thereby converting the lower-triangular part of A to the output over the course of the run.

Cholesky Decomposition Algorithm

```
loop  k= 1 upto n-1
     akk ← √akk
     loop  j= k+1 upto n
          aik ← aik/akk;
          loop  j= k+1 upto i
                aij ← aij-aik * ajk;
          end  loop
     end  loop
end  loop
ann ← √ann
```

Some ijk-Forms for Cholesky

The algorithm above is the kij form for the triple loop. We derive the ijk-form. From the looping region figure below, i must run from 2 to n to encompass the region. Next, a given value of i corresponds to intersecting the region with a horizontal plane at that value of i; this gives a triangular subregion as shown. To encompass this subregion in turn, j must run from 2 to i. Finally, fixing both i and j corresponds to a line on the triangular subregion showing that k runs from 1 to the back surface $j = k + 1$ or $k = j - 1$. Therefore, we have

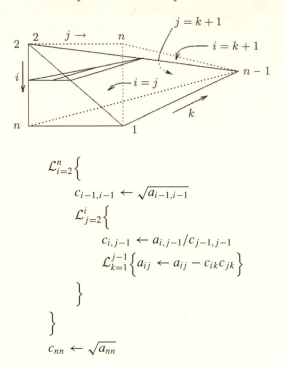

$$\mathcal{L}_{i=2}^{n}\Big\{$$

$$c_{i-1,i-1} \leftarrow \sqrt{a_{i-1,i-1}}$$

$$\mathcal{L}_{j=2}^{i}\Big\{$$

$$c_{i,j-1} \leftarrow a_{i,j-1}/c_{j-1,j-1}$$

$$\mathcal{L}_{k=1}^{j-1}\Big\{a_{ij} \leftarrow a_{ij} - c_{ik}c_{jk}\Big\}$$

$$\Big\}$$

$$\Big\}$$

$$c_{nn} \leftarrow \sqrt{a_{nn}}$$

Exercises

1. (3) Make a DAG for Thompson's Algorithm.
2. (5) Analyze the ijk-forms for the Cholesky algorithm.
3. (6) Let A be a tridiagonal matrix. (a) Show that the solution of the system $A\mathbf{x} = \mathbf{b}$ can be expressed as a linear recurrence. (b) Develop an $O(\log n)$ algorithm to determine $\mathbf{x}$, using $O(n)$ operations.
4. (4) Show that it is possible to apply odd–even reduction when A is *block tridiagonal*. That is, suppose that A can be partitioned into $k \times k$ blocks such that the resulting matrix of blocks is nonzero at most on the main diagonal

and the first super- and subdiagonals. Explain how to carry out the solution of $A\mathbf{x} = \mathbf{b}$.

5. (5) (a) In odd–even reduction, the first phase is combining equations so as to reduce the number of unknown down to one. Show how to modify odd–even reduction as explained above so that any desired unknown can be found at the end of this reduction phase. (b) Show that, with enough processors, all unknowns may be solved in parallel by the technique of part (a). Show that the complexity of odd–even reduction is $O(\log n)$ using $O(n)$ processors.

6. (7) Let A be a nonsingular $n \times n$ lower-triangular matrix such that $n = 2^k$ for some k. Partition A into blocks of size $\frac{n}{2} \times \frac{n}{2}$ according as

$$A = \begin{bmatrix} A_{11} & 0 \\ A_{21} & A_{22} \end{bmatrix}.$$

(a) Show that A^{-1} is given by

$$A^{-1} = \begin{bmatrix} A_{11}^{-1} & 0 \\ -A_{22}^{-1} A_{21} A_{11}^{-1} & A_{22}^{-1} \end{bmatrix}.$$

(b) Use this to devise an $O(\log^2 n)$ algorithm for computing A^{-1}. How many operations will be required?

7. (8) Any symmetric postive definite matrix A can be expressed in the form $A = LDL^T$, where L is a lower-triangular matrix, and D is a diagonal matrix with positive diagonal entries. Devise a parallel algorithm that computes L and D in time $O(\log^3 n)$, where n is the size of matrix A. Hint: Compute a square matrix X, of approximately half the size of A, such that

$$\begin{bmatrix} I & 0 \\ X & I \end{bmatrix} A \begin{bmatrix} I & X^T \\ 0 & I \end{bmatrix} = \begin{bmatrix} B_1 & 0 \\ 0 & B_2 \end{bmatrix},$$

where B_1 and B_2 are some matrices, and proceed recursively.

Programming Exercises

8. (6) In view of problem 5 above, write a program to solve a tridiagonal system for any given unknown. Test it on some example problems. Parallelize your solution to solve for all unknowns at once and test it as well. Present timing results of your runs.

9. (5) Write a Cholesky algorithm and use it to find the eigenvalues of the negative of the matrix on p. 197.

7

Error Analysis and QR Decomposition

7.1 Error and Residual – Matrix Norms

As we have seen, in computing the solution of a linear system, the number of floating point operations carried out is on the order of n^3 for additions and multiplications and n^2 for divisions. They will number in the millions for even moderately sized problems. Each such operation is subject to roundoff error. Moreover, even the original elements of A and $\mathbf{b}$ may not be known exactly. As a result, any computed solution $\hat{\mathbf{x}}$ will be only an approximation to the exact solution $\mathbf{x}$.

A numerical error made in operating on one of the system's equations is equivalent to transacting the operation on a slightly different equation. Thus, surrounding each equation is an *error envelope* within which lies the equation actually manipulated. Figure 28 illustrates (exaggeratedly) error envelopes for an $n = 2$ system and the consequent effect on the computed solution. As the figure shows, the computed solution lies in the *uncertainty region*, which is the intersection of the error envelopes for each equation. Projecting this region onto each coordinate axis gives the *uncertainty interval* containing the computed solution for that variable.

When the lines are nearly parallel, the uncertainty region can be extensive. This is associated with approximate singularity of the system. As the figure shows, the instability in some variables can be much greater than in others depending on the orientation of the lines. This observation might help decide which *norm* to use in sizing vectors.

If $\hat{\mathbf{x}}$ is the computed solution for $A\mathbf{x} = \mathbf{b}$, then its *error vector* is the difference

$$\mathbf{e} = \hat{\mathbf{x}} - \mathbf{x},$$

which we cannot know (without having the exact solution already). But we can attempt to infer $\mathbf{e}$ by comparing $A\hat{\mathbf{x}}$ with $\mathbf{b}$. The *residual* $\mathbf{r}$ is defined as

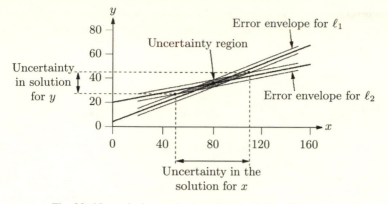

Fig. 28. Numerical error in the solution of a 2×2 system.

this difference

$$\mathbf{r} = A\hat{\mathbf{x}} - \mathbf{b}.$$

Thus $\hat{\mathbf{x}}$ is the exact solution of the system $A\hat{\mathbf{x}} = \mathbf{b} + \mathbf{r}$.

The vectors $\mathbf{e}$ and $\mathbf{r}$ may be visualized with respect to Fig. 28. The first component of $\mathbf{e}$, $\hat{x} - x$, can be as large as one half the uncertainty interval for x and likewise for $\hat{y} - y$. The point $(\hat{x}, \hat{y})$ lies in the uncertainty region surrounding the point of intersection of the lines; $\mathbf{e}$ is the vector between these two points and it could be a large vector. The computed value $\hat{b}_1 = a_{11}\hat{x} + a_{12}\hat{y}$ defines a line parallel to ℓ_1 through $(\hat{x}, \hat{y})$, thus a line lying within the error envelope of ℓ_1. Therefore, $|r_1|$ is the distance between these two lines. Similarly, $|r_2|$ is the distance between ℓ_2 and a line lying within its error envelope. These values are on the order of roundoff error and so are small.

Consider the following example due to W. Kahan,

$$A = \begin{bmatrix} 1.2969 & 0.8648 \\ 0.2161 & 0.1441 \end{bmatrix}, \qquad \mathbf{b} = \begin{bmatrix} 0.8642 \\ 0.1440 \end{bmatrix}. \qquad (10)$$

An approximate solution is $\hat{\mathbf{x}} = (\,0.9911 \quad -0.4870\,)^T$, and the corresponding residual is exactly equal to

$$\mathbf{r} = [\,-10^{-8} \quad 10^{-8}\,]^T.$$

It would seem the approximate solution is good. However, not a single digit is meaningful, the exact solution is

$$\mathbf{x} = [\,2 \quad -2\,]^T.$$

It is easy to understand the source of difficulty in this example. Using a_{11} as a pivot (the pivot of choice under either total or partial pivoting), the reduced second equation is

$$a'_{22} = a_{22} - \frac{a_{12}a_{21}}{a_{11}} = \frac{1}{a_{11}}\det A$$

$$= 0.1441 - \frac{0.2161}{1.2969}0.8648 = 0.1441 - 0.144099923 \approx 10^{-8}.$$

Thus, a small error in a'_{22} leads to a very big error in x_2. In terms of **e** and **r**, a perturbation in one or both of these equations on the order of 10^{-8} leads to a perturbation in x_2 on the order of 1.

The Size of Vectors and Matrices

A natural measure of the magnitude of a vector is its length or *norm*. The three most used norms are the *Euclidean* or ℓ_2 norm, $\| \cdot \|_2$, the Manhattan or ℓ_1 norm, $\| \cdot \|_1$, and the sup norm or ℓ_∞ norm, $\| \cdot \|_\infty$. These are defined as follows:

$$\|(x_1, x_2, \ldots, x_n)^T\|_2 = \left[\sum_1^n x_i^2\right]^{1/2},$$

$$\|(x_1, x_2, \ldots, x_n)^T\|_1 = \sum_1^n |x_i|,$$

$$\|(x_1, x_2, \ldots, x_n)^T\|_\infty = \max_{1 \le i \le n} \{|x_i|\}.$$

These are called the *p-norms* with $p = 2$ for the Euclidean norm, $p = 1$, for the Manhattan norm, and $p = \infty$ for the sup norm. A useful generalization of the sup norm is the weighted sup norm. Let w be a vector of positive components, $w > 0$, the *w-weighted sup norm*, $\| \cdot \|_\infty^w$, is defined as

$$\|x\|_\infty^w = \max_i \left|\frac{x_i}{w_i}\right|.$$

Let A be the matrix of a linear function mapping n-dimensional space to itself; thus, A is an $n \times n$ matrix. Given a norm $\| \cdot \|$ on the space, the *operator norm* for A is defined as

$$\|A\| = \max_{\|x\|=1} \|Ax\|.$$

In particular

$$\|A\|_\infty^w = \max_{\|x\|_\infty^w=1} \|Ax\|_\infty^w.$$

Theorem 1. $\|Ax\| \le \|A\|\|x\|$.

Proof. This is immediate from the definition of $\|A\|$ if $\|x\| = 1$. If $\|x\| = 0$, then $x = 0$ and also $Ax = 0$ so it holds in this case too. Otherwise, put $u = x/\|x\|$, then $\|u\| = 1$ and we have

$$\left\| A\left(\frac{x}{\|x\|}\right) \right\| \le \|A\|.$$

Multiply through by $\|x\|$ and get the stated result. ∎

Theorem 2. $\|A\|_\infty$ *is the maximum of the row sums of the matrix of absolute values of* A, *in particular*

$$\|A\|_\infty^w = \max_i \frac{1}{w_i} \sum_{j=1}^n |a_{ij} w_j|. \tag{11}$$

Proof. How big can

$$\|Ax\|_\infty^w = \max_i \frac{1}{w_i} |a_{i1}x_1 + a_{i2}x_2 + \cdots + a_{in}x_n| \tag{12}$$

be subject to $|x_k|/w_k \le 1$ for $k = 1, 2, \ldots, n$? For a moment, fix i and choose the sign of x_k equal to that of a_{ik} (unless $a_{ik} = 0$ in which case take $x_k = 0$). Then all terms add in (12), so the maximum is achieved by maximizing each term, that is, by taking $x_k/w_k = \pm 1$ (with the sign as specified above). With these choices we have

$$|a_{i1}x_1 + a_{i2}x_2 + \cdots + a_{in}x_n| = a_{i1}w_1 \frac{x_1}{w_1} + a_{i2}w_2 \frac{x_2}{w_2} + \cdots + a_{in}w_n \frac{x_n}{w_n}$$

$$= |a_{i1}|w_1 + |a_{i2}|w_2 + \cdots + |a_{in}|w_n.$$

Hence the right-hand side of (12) becomes

$$\max_i \left\{ \frac{1}{w_i} (|a_{i1}|w_1 + |a_{i2}|w_2 + \cdots + |a_{in}|w_n) \right\},$$

which was to be shown. ∎

The *spectral radius* $\rho(M)$ of a matrix M is

$$\rho(M) = \max\{|\lambda| \ : \ \lambda \text{ is an eigenvalue of } M\}.$$

Theorem 3.
(a) $\rho(A) \le \|A\|$ *for every operator norm.*
(b) *Given* $\epsilon > 0$, *there is an operator norm,* $\| \cdot \|_\epsilon$ *say, such that* $\|A\|_\epsilon \le \rho(A) + \epsilon$.

Proof. (a) Let λ be an eigenvalue such that $|\lambda| = \rho(A)$ and let x be an eigenvector for λ; we may assume without loss of generality that $\|x\| = 1$. Then $Ax = \lambda x$ so $\|Ax\| = |\lambda|$. This shows $\rho(A) \leq \|A\|$.

(b) To see this, we use the *Jordan Canonical Form* Theorem, whose proof is beyond the scope of the present book. We will need Jordan Canonical Form later on anyhow and using it here makes the proof of (b) quite simple. For a complete statement of the theorem, see p. 211; briefly, there is a basis of the space in which matrix J of the linear transformation defined by A is (i) upper triangular, (ii) tridiagonal, (iii) the diagonal consists of the eigenvalues repeated according to their multiplicities, and (iv) the superdiagonal consists of either 1's or 0's. A column of J with 0 on the superdiagonal corresponds to an eigenvector **e** of A while a column with a superdiagonal 1 corresponds to a pseudoeigenvector **f**. Of course, an eigenvector satisfies $(A - \lambda I)\mathbf{e} = 0$ for its eigenvalue λ. A pseudoeigenvector for λ, **f**, satisfies $(A - \lambda I)\mathbf{f} = \mathbf{g}$, where **g** is either an eigenvector for λ or another pseudoeigenvector for λ. By replacing each pseudoeigenvector by a suitable multiple of $\epsilon/2$, the Jordan matrix becomes one with an $\epsilon/2$ replacing each 1 on the superdiagonal. (This is further elaborated in the Exercises.) Now the present result follows from Theorem 2 above. For the norm to use, by writing a vector x in terms of the Jordan basis, say $\mathbf{g}_1, \mathbf{g}_2, \ldots, \mathbf{g}_n$ (consisting of eigenvectors and pseudoeigenvectors),

$$x = \alpha_1 \mathbf{g}_1 + \alpha_2 \mathbf{g}_2 + \cdots + \alpha_n \mathbf{g}_n$$

then define

$$\|x\| = \max_i \{|\alpha_i|\}.$$

This is easily shown to be a norm.   ∎

A *positive matrix* is one all of whose elements are positive; we indicate this by writing $A > 0$, thus $a_{ij} > 0$ for all i and j. Similarly, if it is only known that $a_{ij} \geq 0$ for all i and j, then A is a *nonnegative matrix* and we write $A \geq 0$. If for two matrices A and B, their difference $B - A > 0$ is positive, we may write $B > A$.

Theorem 4. *If $B \geq A \geq 0$ then $\|B\|_\infty^w \geq \|A\|_\infty^w$.*

Proof. This is an immediate consequence of Eq. (11).   ∎

Condition Number

As above let $\mathbf{e} = \hat{\mathbf{x}} - \mathbf{x}$ be the error vector and $\mathbf{r} = A\hat{\mathbf{x}} - \mathbf{b}$ be the residual. Then

$$\mathbf{r} = A\hat{\mathbf{x}} - A\mathbf{x} = A\mathbf{e} \quad \text{hence} \quad \mathbf{e} = A^{-1}\mathbf{r}.$$

Applying the operator norm inequality to these, Theorem 1, we have

$$\|\mathbf{r}\| \leq \|A\|\|\mathbf{e}\| \quad \text{and} \quad \|\mathbf{e}\| \leq \|A^{-1}\|\|\mathbf{r}\|.$$

Or solving for $\|\mathbf{e}\|$,

$$\frac{\|\mathbf{r}\|}{\|A\|} \leq \|\mathbf{e}\| \leq \|A^{-1}\|\|\mathbf{r}\|. \tag{13}$$

Similarly from $\mathbf{b} = A\mathbf{x}$ and $\mathbf{x} = A^{-1}\mathbf{b}$ we get

$$\frac{\|\mathbf{b}\|}{\|A\|} \leq \|\mathbf{x}\| \leq \|A^{-1}\|\|\mathbf{b}\|.$$

Reciprocating the members gives

$$\frac{1}{\|A^{-1}\|\|\mathbf{b}\|} \leq \frac{1}{\|\mathbf{x}\|} \leq \frac{\|A\|}{\|\mathbf{b}\|}. \tag{14}$$

We can now derive upper and lower bounds for the relative error in the solution $\mathbf{x}$; from above

$$\frac{\|\mathbf{e}\|}{\|\mathbf{x}\|} \leq \frac{\|A\|\|\mathbf{e}\|}{\|\mathbf{b}\|} \leq \frac{\|A^{-1}\|\|A\|\|\mathbf{r}\|}{\|\mathbf{b}\|}. \tag{15}$$

And from below

$$\frac{\|\mathbf{e}\|}{\|\mathbf{x}\|} \geq \frac{\|\mathbf{r}\|}{\|A\|}\frac{1}{\|\mathbf{x}\|} \geq \frac{\|\mathbf{r}\|}{\|A\|}\frac{1}{\|A^{-1}\|\|\mathbf{b}\|}. \tag{16}$$

Evidently the product $\|A\|\|A^{-1}\|$ is central to the computational error inherent in solving a linear system. This key number is called the *condition number of A* (with respect to the norm $\|\cdot\|$),

$$\text{cond}(A) = \|A\|\|A^{-1}\|.$$

If the p-norm is used for vectors, $p = 1,2,\infty$, then we write $\text{cond}_p(A)$. Summarizing Eqs. (15) and (16), we have

$$\text{cond}^{-1}(A)\frac{\|\mathbf{r}\|}{\|\mathbf{b}\|} \leq \frac{\|\mathbf{e}\|}{\|\mathbf{x}\|} \leq \text{cond}(A)\frac{\|\mathbf{r}\|}{\|\mathbf{b}\|}. \tag{17}$$

Example. *A matrix well-known for having bad condition number is the Hilbert Matrix, which, for order n, is defined as*

$$H_n = \begin{bmatrix} 1 & 1/2 & 1/3 & \cdots & 1/n \\ 1/2 & 1/3 & 1/4 & \cdots & 1/(n+1) \\ 1/3 & 1/4 & 1/5 & \cdots & 1/(n+2) \\ \vdots & \vdots & \vdots & \ddots & \vdots \\ 1/n & 1/(n+1) & 1/(n+2) & \cdots & 1/(2n-1) \end{bmatrix}.$$

The Hilbert Matrix is symmetric. The reader is invited to calculate the condition number of H_n in the Exercises.

In the previous section we saw that $\hat{x}$ can be interpreted as the exact solution of the perturbed system $A\hat{x} = b + r$, where r is the perturbation, $r = \Delta b$, of b. But now we wish to allow the possibility that A may be perturbed as well, say by ΔA. Hence, let $\hat{x}$ be the exact solution of the perturbed system

$$(A + \Delta A)\hat{x} = b + \Delta b.$$

With e the error vector as above, this equation expands to

$$A(x + e) + \Delta A\hat{x} = Ax + \Delta b.$$

Subtract Ax and $\Delta A\hat{x}$ to get

$$Ae = \Delta b - \Delta A\hat{x}$$

$$\|e\| = \|A^{-1}\Delta b - A^{-1}\Delta A\hat{x}\|$$

$$\leq \|A^{-1}\|\|\Delta b\| + \|A^{-1}\|\|\Delta A\|\|\hat{x}\|.$$

The last line follows from the triangle inequality and the operator norm inequality for A^{-1}. Dividing by $\|x\|$ gives

$$\frac{\|e\|}{\|x\|} \leq \|A^{-1}\| \left(\frac{\|\Delta b\|}{\|x\|} + \|\Delta A\| \frac{\|\hat{x}\|}{\|x\|} \right). \tag{18}$$

Using (14) as an estimate for the first term on the right in (18) gives

$$\frac{\|e\|}{\|x\|} \leq \|A^{-1}\| \left(\|A\| \frac{\|\Delta b\|}{\|b\|} + \|\Delta A\| \frac{\|\hat{x}\|}{\|x\|} \right),$$

or, factoring out $\|A\|$,

$$\frac{\|e\|}{\|x\|} \leq \|A^{-1}\|\|A\| \left(\frac{\|\Delta b\|}{\|b\|} + \frac{\|\Delta A\|}{\|A\|} \frac{\|\hat{x}\|}{\|x\|} \right). \tag{19}$$

This shows that the relative error in x is bounded by the roundoff errors in A and b with the bound on the order of the product $\|A\|\|A^{-1}\|$.

If there is no error in A, then $\Delta b = r$ and (19) gives

$$\frac{\|e\|}{\|x\|} \leq \text{cond}(A) \frac{\|r\|}{\|b\|}$$

as before.

If there is no error in b, then we obtain

$$\|e\| \leq \text{cond}(A)\|\hat{x}\| \frac{\|\Delta A\|}{\|A\|} \tag{20}$$

which shows how large the absolute error may be. Both of these inequalities are sharp meaning that equality can be achieved for the right choices of A and $\mathbf{b}$ (see [10]).

Part (b) of the following is a consequence of part (a) of Theorem 3 above.

Theorem 5.

(a) $\mathrm{cond}(A) \geq 1$ *(since* $1 = \|I\| = \|AA^{-1}\| \leq \|A\|\|A^{-1}\|$*).*

(b) $\mathrm{cond}(A) \geq \rho(A)\rho(A^{-1}) = |\lambda_{\max}|/|\lambda_{\min}|,$ *where* $\lambda_{\max}$ *is the largest and* $\lambda_{\min}$ *is the smallest eigenvalue of* A *in modulus.*

From the theorem we can see that matrices with both very large and very small eigenvalues have bad condition.

Return to the example at the beginning of the section.

$$A = \begin{bmatrix} 1.2969 & 0.8648 \\ 0.2161 & 0.1441 \end{bmatrix}, \qquad \mathbf{b} = \begin{bmatrix} 0.8642 \\ 0.1440 \end{bmatrix}$$

with exact solution $\mathbf{x} = (2 \ {-2})^T$. The vector $\hat{\mathbf{x}} = (0.9911 \ {-0.4870})^T$ solves the system with right-hand side equal to the residual $\mathbf{r} = (-10^{-8} \ 10^{-8})^T$. The eigenvalues of A are $\lambda_2 = 1.441$ and $\lambda_1 = .69 \times 10^{-8}$. Therefore $\mathrm{cond}(A) \approx \lambda_2/\lambda_1 = 2.05857 \times 10^8$. Since

$$\|\mathbf{e}\|_2 = \left\| \begin{bmatrix} .9911 - 2 \\ -.487 + 2 \end{bmatrix} \right\|_2 = 2.6838$$

and here,

$$\|\Delta\mathbf{b}\|_2 = \|\mathbf{r}\|_2 = 10^{-8}\sqrt{2}$$

the estimate of Eq. (20) gives $2.6838 \leq \mathrm{cond}(A)\|\Delta\mathbf{b}\| = 2.91125$.

Step-by-Step Error in the Elimination Process

At some stage of a decomposition process, suppose the computed intermediate at this point is $\hat{A}^{(k)}$ while an exactly calculated intermediate would be $A^{(k)}$. Their difference, E, is the (matrix) error of the process so far,

$$\hat{A}^{(k)} = A^{(k)} + E.$$

Now suppose that the next step of the decomposition is the multiplication by the elementary matrix M. Then the new error will be given by the equation

$$M\hat{A}^{(k)} = MA^{(k)} + ME,$$

and the new error is ME. If M is a matrix of norm 1, then the error gets no worse by this step (with respect to this norm),

$$\|ME\| \le \|M\|\|E\| = \|E\|, \quad \text{if} \quad \|M\| = 1.$$

7.2 Givens Rotations

A *plane rotation matrix* is a matrix having the form

$$M = \begin{bmatrix} 1 & 0 & \cdots & 0 & \cdots & 0 & \cdots & 0 \\ 0 & 1 & \cdots & 0 & \cdots & 0 & \cdots & 0 \\ \vdots & \vdots & \vdots & \vdots & \vdots & \vdots & \vdots & \vdots \\ 0 & 0 & \cdots & \cos\theta & \cdots & \sin\theta & \cdots & 0 \\ \vdots & \vdots & \vdots & \vdots & \vdots & \vdots & \vdots & \vdots \\ 0 & 0 & \cdots & -\sin\theta & \cdots & \cos\theta & \cdots & 0 \\ \vdots & \vdots & \vdots & \vdots & \vdots & \vdots & \vdots & \vdots \\ 0 & 0 & \cdots & 0 & \cdots & 0 & \cdots & 1 \end{bmatrix}, \tag{21}$$

where $m_{ii} = m_{jj} = \cos\theta$ and $m_{ij} = -m_{ji} = \sin\theta$. This matrix represents a clockwise rotation by angle θ in the 2-dimensional subspace of the ith and jth components.

A plane rotation matrix is an example of an *orthogonal matrix*. A matrix $Q = [\, \mathbf{q}_{.1} \quad \mathbf{q}_{.2} \quad \cdots \quad \mathbf{q}_{.n} \,]$ is orthogonal if its columns are orthonormal, that is,

$$\mathbf{q}_{.i}{}^T \mathbf{q}_{.j} = \begin{cases} 0 & \text{if } i \ne j, \\ 1 & \text{if } i = j. \end{cases}$$

Theorem 1.
(a) A plane rotation matrix is an orthogonal matrix.
(b) Q is orthogonal if and only if $Q^{-1} = Q^T$.
(c) The product of a finite number of orthogonal matrices is also orthogonal.
(d) Every orthogonal matrix Q has an ℓ_2-norm of 1.
(e) $\mathrm{cond}_2(Q) = 1$ for Q orthogonal.

Proof. Part (a) follows from the fact that the columns of a rotation matrix are orthonormal. Let $\mathbf{x} = (x_1, x_2, \ldots, x_n)^T$ be an ℓ_2 unit vector, $\sum_i x_i^2 = 1$. Let $\mathbf{q}_{.j}$ of Q denote the columns of Q. Then (b) follows since QQ^T is the matrix $C = [c_{ij}]$, where c_{ij} is the dot product $\mathbf{q}_{.i} \cdot \mathbf{q}_{.j}$. For (c), if Q_1 and Q_2 are orthogonal, then $(Q_1 Q_2)^{-1} = Q_2^{-1} Q_1^{-1} = Q_2^T Q_1^T = (Q_1 Q_2)^T$. For (d), note that since the columns $\mathbf{q}_{.j}$ of Q are orthonormal, then the norm of

$$Q\mathbf{x} = x_1 \mathbf{q}_{.1} + x_2 \mathbf{q}_{.2} + \cdots + x_n \mathbf{q}_{.n}$$

is exactly $\sum_i x_i^2 = 1$ again. This proves (d). Since Q^{-1} is also orthogonal when Q is, part (e) follows. ∎

Returning to a plane rotation matrix M, note that the product MA differs from A only in the ith and jth rows. The new ith row will be

$$a'_{ik} = a_{ik} \cos\theta + a_{jk} \sin\theta, \quad k = 1, \ldots, n \tag{22}$$

and the new jth row will be

$$a'_{jk} = a_{ik} \sin\theta - a_{jk} \cos\theta, \quad k = 1, \ldots, n. \tag{23}$$

The idea is to make the new jith entry zero, $a'_{ji} = 0$. For this we solve

$$0 = a_{ii} \sin\theta - a_{ji} \cos\theta$$

for $\sin\theta$ and get $\sin\theta = (a_{ji}/a_{ii}) \cos\theta$. Substituting this into $\cos^2\theta + \sin^2\theta = 1$ gives

$$\left(1 + \frac{a_{ji}^2}{a_{ii}^2}\right) \cos^2\theta = 1$$

or

$$\cos\theta = \frac{a_{ii}}{\sqrt{a_{ii}^2 + a_{ji}^2}}. \tag{24}$$

Similarly

$$\sin\theta = \frac{a_{ji}}{\sqrt{a_{ii}^2 + a_{ji}^2}}. \tag{25}$$

The angle θ is never computed, only the combinations $\cos\theta$ and $\sin\theta$. Since M is the matrix of a plane rotation, it is an orthogonal matrix and $\|M\|_2 = 1$. Hence M neither increases nor decreases the numerical error. This means that pivoting is not required with Givens Rotations.

In a way similar to Gaussian elimination, successive application of rotations can bring about the reduction of A to upper-triangular or "right-triangular" form. To see this, suppose the initial segments of the ith and jth rows have already been nulled, that is $j > i$, and $a_{ik} = a_{jk} = 0$ for $k = 1, \ldots, i - 1$,

$$\begin{bmatrix} * & \cdots & * & * & \cdots & * & \cdots & * \\ \vdots & \vdots & \vdots & \vdots & \vdots & \vdots & \vdots & \vdots \\ 0 & \cdots & 0 & a_{ii} & \cdots & * & \cdots & * \\ \vdots & \vdots & \vdots & \vdots & \vdots & \vdots & \vdots & \vdots \\ 0 & \cdots & 0 & a_{ji} & \cdots & * & \cdots & * \\ \vdots & \vdots & \vdots & \vdots & \vdots & \vdots & \vdots & \vdots \\ * & \cdots & * & * & \cdots & * & \cdots & * \end{bmatrix}.$$

Then from Eq. (22)

$$a'_{ik} = a_{ik} \cos \theta + a_{jk} \sin \theta = 0, \quad \text{for} \quad k = 1, \ldots, i - 1,$$

and from Eq. (23)

$$a'_{jk} = a_{ik} \sin \theta - a_{jk} \cos \theta = 0, \quad \text{for} \quad k = 1, \ldots, i - 1,$$

so the initial segments remain nulled. But now $a'_{ji} = 0$ as well.

Notice that even if $a_{ii} = 0$, the rotation can still be performed to annihilate a_{ji} since the denominators of (24) and (25) are not zero. (If $a_{ji} = 0$ there is no need to perform the rotation, or equivalently, use the rotation angle $\theta = 0$ with the result that the rotation matrix is the identity I.) This proves the following.

Theorem 2. *Every square matrix can be right triangularized by a sequence of Givens rotations.*

Parallel Implementation

Since a Givens rotation affects only 2 rows, several such rotations can be performed simultaneously; approximately $n/2$ simultaneous rotations can be done. However, to reduce a matrix to upper-triangular form, the rotations must be carried out in a systematic way. A schedule for carrying out the rotations may be defined with the help of 2 functions $T(j, k)$ and $S(j, k)$ defined for $1 \le k < j \le n$. In this, the jkth entry is zeroed at stage $T(j, k)$ by a Givens rotation on rows j and $S(j, k)$. Of course, such a schedule must satisfy certain consistency conditions see pp. 31.

One possible schedule is

$$T(j, k) = n - j + 2k - 1$$
$$S(j, k) = j - 1.$$

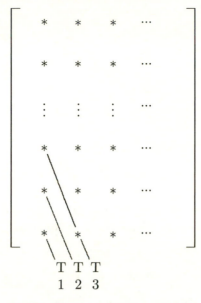

Fig. 29. Givens annihilation schedule.

To understand this schedule, rewrite it as

$$j - 2k = n - 1 - T.$$

When $T = 1$, the element $j = n$ and $k = 1$ is annihilated using rows $j = n$ and $S = n - 1$. When $T = 2$, the element $(n - 1, 1)$ is annihilated. And, at time $T = 3$, two elements, $(n, 2)$ and $(n - 1, 1)$ are annihilated; and so on (see Fig. 29).

According to this schedule, the last entry to be zeroed is $j = n, k = n - 1$. Hence the time required is $T(n, n - 1) = 2n - 3$.

A Given's rotation can be done in $O(1)$ time using n processors. Only 2 rows are affected by each rotation so the new values are computed with a constant number of operations. Hence $n/2$ such rotations can be carried out in parallel in $O(1)$ time, using $n^2/2$ processors. Thus the whole algorithm is $O(n)$ time using $n^2/2$ processors. The efficiency is on the order of 1 since the single processor time is $O(n^3)$.

Orthogonal Basis

Suppose that a sequence of Givens rotations is carried out using the rotation matrices M_k, $k = 2, \ldots, n$, reducing the $n \times n$ matrix A to right-triangular form, R,

$$R = M_n M_{n-1} \ldots M_2 A.$$

Let Q transpose be the product of these rotation matrices

$$Q^T = M_n M_{n-1} \ldots M_2, \quad \text{hence} \quad R = Q^T A. \tag{26}$$

Then

$$Q = M_2^T \ldots M_{n-1}^T M_N^T, \tag{27}$$

and we can write A as the product

$$A = QR. \tag{28}$$

This decomposition of A into the product of an orthogonal times an upper-triangular matrix is called a *QR decomposition* of A.

If $\mathbf{y} = A\mathbf{x}$ for some $\mathbf{x}$, then by (28), $\mathbf{y} = Q\mathbf{z}$ for $\mathbf{z} = R\mathbf{x}$ so the image of A is contained in the image of Q. Conversely, if A is full rank, then the images are equal

$$\text{Img}(A) = \text{Img}(Q)$$

since then both have the same dimension. In this case, the columns of Q, $\mathbf{q}_{\cdot 1}$, $\mathbf{q}_{\cdot 2}, \ldots, \mathbf{q}_{\cdot n}$, form an orthonormalization of the columns of A. Furthermore, no diagonal element of R is zero since $\det(A) \neq 0$. We have proved the following.

Theorem 3. *Consider the QR decomposition of the $n \times n$ matrix A. If A has full rank, then the columns of Q form an orthonormalization of the columns of A and rank$(R) =$ rank(A).*

By (26), the elements of R are given by

$$R_{ij} = \mathbf{q}_{\cdot i}^T \mathbf{a}_{\cdot j},$$

where $\mathbf{q}_{\cdot i}$ is the ith column of Q and $\mathbf{a}_{\cdot j}$ is the jth column of A.

Exercises

1. (5) Show that $\|A\|_1$ is the maximum of the column sums of the matrix of absolute values of A.
2. (5) Let E_{i1} for $i = 2, \ldots, n$, denote the simple matrix for annihilating the element a_{i1} of A. (a) What is cond(E_{i1})? (b) If $E_1 = E_{n1} E_{n-1,1} \ldots E_{21}$, what is cond$(E_1)$? (c) If E_j is the product of simple matrices used in the jth stage of Gaussian Elimination, $j = 1, \ldots, n - 1$, what is cond$(E_{n-1} E_{n-2} \ldots E_1)$?
3. (4) What is the operation count of a triangularization by Givens rotations?
4. (4) Find a schedule for implementing Givens rotations for the case of an 8×8 matrix that needs fewer than 13 parallel stages.

5. (3) Suppose triangularization has proceeded to the point that a_{ii} is being "used" to annihilate a_{ji}, $j > i$, but $a_{ii} = 0$. How should one continue? What happens if A is singular?

6. (3) Show how to use Givens rotations in a "nondiagonal annihilator" way by using element i, k to annihilate element j, k, where $k \neq i$. Find $\cos \theta$ and $\sin \theta$. What is the rotation matrix M? Observe that if the initial parts of the ith and jth rows, $a_{im} = a_{jm} = 0$, $1 \leq m < k$, are zero, then they will also be zero afterwards.

7. (4) Explain how to apply Givens rotations on the right (instead of on the left) so as to decompose A into the form LQ, where L is lower triangular and Q is orthogonal.

Programming Exercises

8. (4) Calculate the condition number of the 6-dimensional Hilbert matrix $H_6 = (1/(i + j - 1))$, $i, j = 1, \ldots, 6$.

9. (6) Write a Givens Rotation algorithm to produce a QR decomposition.

10. (5) (a) Use your Givens Rotation algorithm to solve the $\sum_{k=1}^{n} k^5$ problem (see p. 161). (b) Compare the results with a Gaussian elimination solver that does not use pivoting.

8

Iterative Methods for Linear Systems

In this chapter we study iterative methods for solving linear systems. One reason for using iterative methods is that some linear systems are problematic for the direct methods we studied in the previous chapters. Very large systems fall into this category. Such systems arise in the numerical solution of partial differential equations where there can be many unknowns, 10^5 or more! One such class of problems is the numerical solution to Poisson's equation, which we present below to illustrate the ideas of the chapter. Moreover, very large systems are usually *sparse* which is to say most of the elements of the coefficient matrix are zero. It is generally the case that the nonzero elements lie in a regular pattern, making it possible to generate them as needed rather than storing them at all.

Another reason to study iterative methods is that some linear systems arise naturally in iterative form, that is, in the form $\mathbf{x} = \mathbf{b} + G\mathbf{x}$. This is true for Poisson's equation mentioned above.

To deal with problems such as these, iterative methods have been developed and are widely used. Moreover, some of these methods parallelize easily and effectively.

8.1 Jacobi Iteration or the Method of Simultaneous Displacements

Write the system $A\mathbf{x} = \mathbf{b}$ in equation form and solve for each diagonal unknown; that is, use the ith equation to solve for x_i. Thus

$$x_1 = \frac{1}{a_{11}} \left[b_1 - \sum_{j=2}^{n} a_{1j} x_j \right]$$

$$x_2 = \frac{1}{a_{22}} \left[b_2 - \left(a_{21} x_1 + \sum_{j=3}^{n} a_{2j} x_j \right) \right]$$

$$\vdots$$

$$x_n = \frac{1}{a_{nn}} \left[b_n - \sum_{j<n} a_{nj} x_j \right].$$

In general

$$x_i = \frac{1}{a_{ii}} \left[b_i - \left(\sum_{j<i} a_{ij} x_j + \sum_{j>i} a_{ij} x_j \right) \right]. \tag{29}$$

We might try to solve the system as follows. Initially guess values $x_1^0, x_2^0, \ldots,$ x_n^0. Throughout this chapter we will use superscripts to denote the iteration index of $\mathbf{x}$ (and subscripts for the component scalars), thus

$$\mathbf{x}^0 = \begin{bmatrix} x_1^0 & x_2^0 & \cdots & x_n^0 \end{bmatrix}^T.$$

Using these in the right-hand side of (29), calculate new, possibly better, values of the $x's$. Denote these by $x_1^1, x_2^1, \ldots, x_n^1$. Now continue the procedure obtaining the sequence of solutions $\mathbf{x}^2, \mathbf{x}^3, \ldots$, which hopefully converges.

If only old values, x_i^m, are used in the calculation of the new ones, x_i^{m+1}, $i = 1, 2, \ldots, n$, then the process is called *Jacobi iteration*. It is evident that the calculation of each component is independent of the other components; hence, Jacobi iteration parallelizes by component with no problem. On the other hand, Jacobi iteration requires that two sets of components be kept in memory all the time.

In Fig. 30 we illustrate Jacobi iteration for the simple system

$$3x_1 - x_2 = 0$$
$$-x_1 + 2x_2 = 0$$

Given starting values x_1^0 and x_2^0, we use the first equation with the given x_2 to find the updated value of x_1,

$$x_1^1 = \frac{1}{3} x_2^0$$

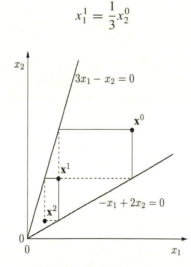

Fig. 30. Jacobi iteration.

and the second equation with the given x_1 to find the updated x_2,

$$x_2^1 = \frac{1}{2}x_1^0.$$

Hence the next approximation to the solution is $\mathbf{x}^1 = (x_1^1, x_2^1)$. Continuing in this way, the iterates converge to $(0, 0)$, which is the solution of the system. Note that if the equations are reversed, then iteration proceeds the opposite way, from $\mathbf{x}^2$ to $\mathbf{x}^1$ to $\mathbf{x}^0$ and so on.

Let $e_i^m = x_i^m - x_i$ be the difference between the ith component of the exact solution and the ith component of the mth iterate, $m \geq 0$. And let $\mathbf{e} = [e_1 \quad e_2 \quad \cdots \quad e_n]^T$ denote the error vector. Then using (29), once for x_i and once for x_i^{m+1}, we can write

$$|e_i^{m+1}| = \left| -\sum_{j \neq i} \frac{a_{ij}}{a_{ii}}(x_j^m - x_j) \right| = \left| -\sum_{j \neq i} \frac{a_{ij}}{a_{ii}} e_j^m \right| \leq \sum_{j \neq i} \left| \frac{a_{ij}}{a_{ii}} \right| \|\mathbf{e}^m\|_\infty. \quad (30)$$

Let

$$K = \max_{1 \leq i \leq n} \sum_{j \neq i} \left| \frac{a_{ij}}{a_{ii}} \right|, \quad (31)$$

then from (30),

$$\|\mathbf{e}^{m+1}\|_\infty \leq K \|\mathbf{e}^m\|_\infty \leq \cdots \leq K^m \|\mathbf{e}^1\|_\infty.$$

Hence, if $K < 1$, $\mathbf{e}^m \to 0$ as $m \to \infty$.

The condition that $K < 1$ amounts to

$$\sum_{j \neq i} |a_{ij}| < |a_{ii}|, \quad \text{for all } i,$$

which is expressed by saying that A is *diagonally dominant* (by rows).

Let $D = \text{diag} A$ be the $n \times n$ diagonal matrix agreeing with the diagonal of A and let B be the difference $B = A - D$. In matrix form, Jacobi iteration can be written as

$$\mathbf{x}^{m+1} = -D^{-1} B \mathbf{x}^m + D^{-1} \mathbf{b}.$$

And the error vector satisfies

$$\mathbf{e}^{m+1} = M \mathbf{e}^m \quad \text{where} \quad M = D^{-1} B.$$

The condition that $K < 1$ is exactly the condition that $\|M\|_\infty < 1$.

Theorem 1. *If the spectral radius of the iteration matrix M is less than 1, $\rho(M) < 1$, then Jacobi iteration converges.*

Proof. This follows from Jordan Canonical Form (see p. 211). In particular, if $\lambda_1, \ldots, \lambda_n$ are the eigenvalues of M, then the eigenvalues of M^k are $\lambda_1^k, \ldots, \lambda_n^k$, which tend to 0 as $k \to \infty$. ∎ ∎

8.2 Gauss–Seidel Iteration or the Method of Successive Displacements

Alternatively, one might use new values of x_i as soon as they become available. For example, when calculating x_2^1, the new value x_1^1 is known and may be used instead of the old value x_1^0. Similarly, in calculating x_i^1, the new values x_j^1 for $j < i$ are known. If new values are used in every case, $i = 2, \ldots, n$, then the procedure is called *Gauss–Seidel iteration* and the update equation (29) becomes

$$x_i^{m+1} = \frac{1}{a_{ii}} \left[b_i - \left(\sum_{j<i} a_{ij} x_j^{m+1} + \sum_{j>i} a_{ij} x_j^m \right) \right]. \tag{32}$$

Figure 31 illustrates the convergence of the previous example,

$$3x_1 - x_2 = 0$$
$$-x_1 + 2x_2 = 0$$

As before the iterations converge to $(0, 0)$, but in different manner. The partial solutions proceed from hyperplane to hyperplane so at the end of an iteration the current iterate lies on the last hyperplane. As above, if the equations are reversed, iterations proceed away from the origin and hence diverge.

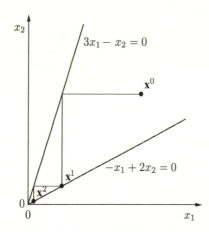

Fig. 31. Gauss–Seidel iteration.

To figure the error, let $e_i^{m+1} = x_i^{m+1} - x_i$ as before and use (32) and (29) to obtain

$$e_i^{m+1} = -\sum_{j=1}^{i-1} \frac{a_{ij}}{a_{ii}} e_j^{m+1} - \sum_{j=i+1}^{n} \frac{a_{ij}}{a_{ii}} e_j^m, \quad i = 1, 2, \ldots, n.$$

This leads to

$$|e_i^{m+1}| \le \sum_{j=1}^{i-1} \left| \frac{a_{ij}}{a_{ii}} \right| \|\mathbf{e}^{m+1}\|_\infty + \sum_{j=i+1}^{n} \left| \frac{a_{ij}}{a_{ii}} \right| \|\mathbf{e}^m\|_\infty, \quad i = 1, 2, \ldots, n.$$

Using the particular i in this inequality for which $|e_i^{m+1}| = \|\mathbf{e}^{m+1}\|_\infty$, we get

$$\|\mathbf{e}^{m+1}\|_\infty \le \sum_{j=1}^{i-1} \left| \frac{a_{ij}}{a_{ii}} \right| \|\mathbf{e}^{m+1}\|_\infty + \sum_{j=i+1}^{n} \left| \frac{a_{ij}}{a_{ii}} \right| \|\mathbf{e}^m\|_\infty.$$

And this becomes

$$\|\mathbf{e}^{m+1}\|_\infty \le \frac{\sum_{j=i+1}^{n} \left| \frac{a_{ij}}{a_{ii}} \right|}{1 - \sum_{j=1}^{i-1} \left| \frac{a_{ij}}{a_{ii}} \right|} \|\mathbf{e}^m\|_\infty \le K \|\mathbf{e}^m\|_\infty,$$

where

$$K = \max_{1 \le i \le n} \frac{\sum_{j=i+1}^{n} |a_{ij}/a_{ii}|}{1 - \sum_{j=1}^{i-1} |a_{ij}/a_{ii}|}. \tag{33}$$

Theorem 1. *Let K_J be the Jacobi contraction factor of Eq. (31) and let K_{GS} be the Gauss–Seidel contraction factor above, Eq. (33). If $K_J < 1$ then $K_{GS} < K_J$.*

Proof. For $i = 1, 2, \ldots, n$ put

$$r_i = \sum_{j=1}^{i-1} \left| \frac{a_{ij}}{a_{ii}} \right|, \qquad s_i = \sum_{j=i+1}^{n} \left| \frac{a_{ij}}{a_{ii}} \right|.$$

Then

$$K_J = \max_i (r_i + s_i), \qquad K_{GS} = \max_i \frac{s_i}{1 - r_i}.$$

If $K_J < 1$ then $1 - r_i > 0$ for all i and

$$r_i + s_i - \frac{s_i}{1 - r_i} = \frac{r_i(1 - (r_i + s_i))}{1 - r_i} \ge \frac{r_i}{1 - r_i} (1 - K_J) \ge 0.$$

Hence

$$r_i + s_i \ge \frac{s_i}{1 - r_i}$$

for all i from which the conclusion follows.   ∎

As above, we may treat this from a matrix point of view. Let L be the lower-triangular part of A and $-R$ the strict upper-triangular part. Then A can be decomposed as $A = L - R$ and Gauss–Seidel iteration is

$$L\mathbf{x}^{m+1} = R\mathbf{x}^m + \mathbf{b}.$$

or, solving for $\mathbf{x}^{m+1}$,

$$\mathbf{x}^{m+1} = \hat{M}\mathbf{x}^m + L^{-1}\mathbf{b},$$

where

$$\hat{M} = L^{-1}R.$$

A proof of the following may be found in [1].

Theorem 2. *Let M be the Jacobi update matrix and $\hat{M}$ the Gauss–Seidel update matrix for the system $A\mathbf{x} = \mathbf{b}$. If $\rho(|M|) < 1$ then $\rho(\hat{M}) < \rho(|M|)$. In particular, if $M \geq 0$ and Jacobi iteration converges, then so does Gauss–Seidel iteration.*

An advantage of Gauss–Seidel iteration is that only one set of components x_i need be stored. On the other hand, since a given component $\mathbf{x}_j$ must wait to be updated until all components $\mathbf{x}_i$ ahead of it, the issue of parallelization is more complicated and may not even be possible.

8.3 Fixed-Point Iteration

We pause in our study of iteration methods for linear systems to obtain some results about iteration methods generally. The method of *fixed-point iteration* is very powerful and may be used to solve both linear and nonlinear equations or systems of equations.

First let $g(\cdot)$ be a continuous real-valued function of a single real variable x. We seek an argument x^*, called a *fixed point* of g, so that $g(x^*) = x^*$. *Fixed point iteration* is the procedure for finding a fixed point just as in the Jacobi or Gauss–Seidel iteration. Let x_0 be an initial approximation to a fixed point. Since x is a scalar variable, we will indicate the iteration number by subscript. Then given an approximation x_m, construct, hopefully, a better approximation x_{m+1} as

$$x_{m+1} = g(x_m), \quad m = 0, 1, \ldots.$$

If the sequence $\{x_m\}_0^\infty$ converges, say to x^*, then its limit is a fixed point of g because

$$g(x^*) = g(\lim_{m\to\infty} x_m) = \lim_{m\to\infty} g(x_m) = \lim_{m\to\infty} x_{m+1} = x^*.$$

The technique of fixed-point iteration is quite general and may be used to find roots. For example, x^* is a root of $f(x)$ if and only if x^* is a fixed point of g, where

$$g(x) = x + cf(x)$$

and c is a constant or a function of x (provided that, as a function of x, $c(x^*) \neq 0$). Another possibility is

$$g(x) = (1 - \gamma)x + \gamma(x + cf(x)) \tag{34}$$

for a parameter $\gamma \neq 0$. Here, γ fraction of the full update is combined with $1 - \gamma$ fraction of the last iteration to give the new approximation.

In this regard recall Newton's method for roots. Assuming that we want the root x^* of the function f, we solve the linear model of f at x_0, namely

$$y - f(x_0) = f'(x_0)(x - x_0)$$

for its root; setting $y = 0$ and solving for x we get the new approximation

$$x_1 = x_0 - \frac{f(x_0)}{f'(x_0)}.$$

Therefore the iteration function here is

$$g(x) = x - \frac{f(x)}{f'(x)}.$$

The role of c is played by $1/f'(x)$.

In the following theorem, Ω is a subset of Euclidean space $\mathbb{R}^d$ of some dimension $d \geq 1$ and the x's and y's are d-vectors.

Theorem 1 (Fixed-Point Iteration). *Let g be a continuous map of the closed and bounded region Ω into itself. Then g has a fixed point x^* in Ω. Furthermore, if g is* contractive, *i.e., for some $K < 1$*

$$\|g(y) - g(x)\| \leq K\|y - x\|, \quad x, y \in \Omega,$$

then fixed-point iteration will converge for any starting point $x_0 \in \Omega$ and

$$\|x_m - x^*\| \leq \frac{K}{1 - K}\|x_m - x_{m-1}\|$$

$$\leq \frac{K^m}{1 - K}\|x_1 - x_0\|. \tag{35}$$

Proof. The first conclusion is known as Brouwer's Fixed-Point Theorem. For the second, note that, since x^* is a fixed point for g,

$$\|x_m - x^*\| = \|g(x_{m-1}) - g(x^*)\| \leq K\|x_{m-1} - x^*\|$$

$$\leq K(\|x_{m-1} - x_m\| + \|x_m - x^*\|).$$

Hence

$$(1 - K)\|x_m - x^*\| \leq K\|x_{m-1} - x_m\|$$

and the first inequality follows. Also

$$\|x_{m-1} - x_m\| = \|g(x_{m-2}) - g(x_{m-1})\| \leq K\|x_{m-2} - x_{m-1}\|$$
$$= K\|g(x_{m-3}) - g(x_{m-2})\| \leq K^2\|x_{m-3} - x_{m-2}\|$$
$$\ldots \leq K^{m-1}\|x_0 - x_1\|.$$

Combining this with the first inequality gives the second. ∎

We may apply the Fixed-Point Iteration theorem immediately to Jacobi and Gauss–Siedel Iteration with K estimated as in Eq. (31) or (33), respectively. Thus the error of the mth iterate is approximately $K/(1 - K)$ times the difference between successive iterations, Eq. (35). Or we may estimate the contraction factor K numerically as in the proof

$$\|x_{m+1} - x_m\| \approx K\|x_m - x_{m-1}\|$$

giving

$$K \approx \frac{\|x_{m+1} - x_m\|}{\|x_m - x_{m-1}\|}.$$

One also sees from (35) that convergence is *linear*. This is to say that the error decreases by a constant factor on each iteration. In general, we say an iteration process *converges order n* if the error on the mth iteration is less than a constant times the previous error to the nth power, that is,

$$e_{m+1} \leq Ce_m^n.$$

For example, Newton's method is quadratically convergent (see [11]).

8.4 Relaxation Methods

Relaxation methods are a slight modification of the Jacobi and Gauss–Seidel methods above along the lines of Eq. (34) in which a fraction of the newly computed update is mixed with the complimentary fraction of the old. The fraction γ of the full update used is the *relaxation parameter*.

Jacobi overrelaxation or JOR is this idea applied to the Jacobi method and gives the relaxation update as

$$x_i^{m+1} = (1 - \gamma)x_i^m - \frac{\gamma}{a_{ii}}\left[\sum_{j \neq i} a_{ij}x_j^m - b_i\right], \quad i = 1, \ldots, n.$$

In matrix notation this becomes

$$\mathbf{x}^{m+1} = (1 - \gamma)\mathbf{x}^m - \gamma(D^{-1}B\mathbf{x}^m - D^{-1}\mathbf{b})$$
$$= M_\gamma \mathbf{x}^m + \gamma D^{-1}\mathbf{b},$$

where D is the diagonal part of A and $B = A - D$ as before and

$$M_\gamma = (1 - \gamma)I - \gamma D^{-1}B.$$

Relaxation applied to Gauss–Seidel iteration, called successive overrelaxation or SOR, gives the update equations as

$$x_i^{m+1} = (1 - \gamma)x_i^m - \frac{\gamma}{a_{ii}}\left[\sum_{j<i} a_{ij}x_j^{m+1} + \sum_{j>i} a_{ij}x_j^m - b_i\right], \quad i = 1, \ldots, n.$$

$$(36)$$

For the matrix form of SOR, let $A = L + D + R$, where now L and R are the strict lower- and upper-triangular parts of A, respectively, and D is the diagonal. Then (36) becomes

$$\mathbf{x}^{m+1} = (1 - \gamma)\mathbf{x}^m - \gamma D^{-1}[L\mathbf{x}^{m+1} + R\mathbf{x}^m - \mathbf{b}].$$

Solve for $\mathbf{x}^{m+1}$,

$$\mathbf{x}^{m+1} = M_\gamma \mathbf{x}^m + C\mathbf{b},$$

where in this case

$$M_\gamma = (I + \gamma D^{-1}L)^{-1}[(1 - \gamma)I - \gamma D^{-1}R]$$

and

$$C = \gamma(I + \gamma D^{-1}L)^{-1}D^{-1}.$$

In each case, optimally choose γ to minimize the spectral radius of M_γ. This is usually done empirically as an *a priori* determination is difficult.

8.5 Application to Poisson's Equation

Consider Poisson's equation on the unit square

$$\frac{\partial^2 f}{\partial x^2}(x, y) + \frac{\partial^2 f}{\partial y^2}(x, y) = g(x, y), \quad (x, y) \in [0, 1]^2,$$

where g is a given real valued function. A solution is a function f defined on the square satisfying the partial differential equation and having prescribed values on the boundary of the unit square. To solve the problem numerically, a uniform grid is introduced over the unit square; let

$$f_{i,j} = f(i/N, j/N), \quad 0 \le i, j \le N,$$
$$g_{i,j} = g(i/N, j/N), \quad 0 \le i, j \le N,$$

for N a positive integer ≥ 2. Letting $\Delta = 1/N$, the partial derivatives can be numerically approximated by the central differences

$$\frac{\partial^2 f}{\partial x^2}(x, y) \approx \frac{1}{\Delta^2} [f(x + \Delta, y) - 2f(x, y) + f(x - \Delta, y)]$$

and

$$\frac{\partial^2 f}{\partial y^2}(x, y) \approx \frac{1}{\Delta^2} [f(x, y + \Delta) - 2f(x, y) + f(x, y - \Delta)].$$

This is called a *5-point stencil*. Now substitute this into Poisson's equation, thus for $x = i/N$ and $y = j/N$,

$$\frac{1}{\Delta^2}[f_{i+1,j} - 2f_{i,j} + f_{i-1,j}] + \frac{1}{\Delta^2}[f_{i,j+1} - 2f_{i,j} + f_{i,j-1}] = g_{i,j}.$$

Rearranging, we get

$$-4f_{i,j} + f_{i+1,j} + f_{i-1,j} + f_{i,j+1} + f_{i,j-1} = \Delta^2 g_{i,j}$$

from which follows

$$f_{i,j} = \frac{1}{4}(f_{i+1,j} + f_{i-1,j} + f_{i,j+1} + f_{i,j-1}) - \frac{1}{4N^2} g_{i,j}, \quad 0 < i, j < N.$$

This is a system of $(N - 1)^2$ equations in the same number of unknowns, namely, the values of f at the interior grid points.

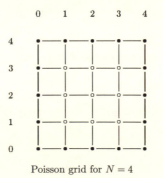

Poisson grid for $N = 4$

For example, take $N = 4$; the equations are

$$f_{1,1} = \frac{1}{4}(f_{2,1} + f_{0,1} + f_{1,2} + f_{1,0}) - \frac{1}{64}g_{1,1}$$

$$f_{2,1} = \frac{1}{4}(f_{3,1} + f_{1,1} + f_{2,2} + f_{2,0}) - \frac{1}{64}g_{2,1}$$

$$f_{3,1} = \frac{1}{4}(f_{4,1} + f_{2,1} + f_{3,2} + f_{3,0}) - \frac{1}{64}g_{3,1}$$

$$f_{1,2} = \frac{1}{4}(f_{2,2} + f_{0,2} + f_{1,3} + f_{1,1}) - \frac{1}{64}g_{1,2}$$

$$f_{2,2} = \frac{1}{4}(f_{3,2} + f_{1,2} + f_{2,3} + f_{2,1}) - \frac{1}{64}g_{2,2}$$

$$f_{3,2} = \frac{1}{4}(f_{4,2} + f_{2,2} + f_{3,3} + f_{3,1}) - \frac{1}{64}g_{3,2}$$

$$f_{1,3} = \frac{1}{4}(f_{2,3} + f_{0,3} + f_{1,4} + f_{1,2}) - \frac{1}{64}g_{1,3}$$

$$f_{2,3} = \frac{1}{4}(f_{3,3} + f_{1,3} + f_{2,4} + f_{2,2}) - \frac{1}{64}g_{2,3}$$

$$f_{3,3} = \frac{1}{4}(f_{4,3} + f_{2,3} + f_{3,4} + f_{3,2}) - \frac{1}{64}g_{3,3}.$$

The unknowns are the interior values of f, $f_{1,1}$, $f_{2,1}$, $f_{3,1}$, $f_{1,2}$, $f_{2,2}$, $f_{3,2}$, $f_{1,3}$, $f_{2,3}$, and $f_{3,3}$. As boundary points, the values of $f_{1,0}$, $f_{2,0}$, $f_{3,0}$, $f_{0,1}$, $f_{4,1}$, $f_{0,2}$, $f_{4,2}$, $f_{0,3}$, $f_{4,3}$, $f_{1,4}$, $f_{2,4}$, and $f_{3,4}$ are given.

Notice that, as written, the equations are already in the form for iteration. Usually relaxation methods are used; hence, the iteration equations become

$$f_{i,j}(t+1) = (1 - \gamma)f_{i,j}(t)$$
$$+ \frac{\gamma}{4}[f_{i+1,j}(t) + f_{i-1,j}(t) + f_{i,j+1}(t) + f_{i,j-1}(t)] - \frac{\gamma}{4N^2}g_{i,j}.$$

For comparison, we work out the standard $A\mathbf{x} = \mathbf{b}$ form of this iteration system. To write the system in matrix form, let the unknown vector $\mathbf{x}$ correspond to the unknowns organized by rows

$$\mathbf{x} = (f_{1,1} \quad f_{2,1} \quad f_{3,1} \quad f_{1,2} \quad \cdots \quad f_{3,3})^T.$$

Multiplying each row by -4 gives the system

$$
\begin{bmatrix}
-4 & 1 & 0 & 1 & 0 & 0 & 0 & 0 & 0 \\
1 & -4 & 1 & 0 & 1 & 0 & 0 & 0 & 0 \\
0 & 1 & -4 & 0 & 0 & 1 & 0 & 0 & 0 \\
\hline
1 & 0 & 0 & -4 & 1 & 0 & 1 & 0 & 0 \\
0 & 1 & 0 & 1 & -4 & 1 & 0 & 1 & 0 \\
0 & 0 & 1 & 0 & 1 & -4 & 0 & 0 & 1 \\
\hline
0 & 0 & 0 & 1 & 0 & 0 & -4 & 1 & 0 \\
0 & 0 & 0 & 0 & 1 & 0 & 1 & -4 & 1 \\
0 & 0 & 0 & 0 & 0 & 1 & 0 & 1 & -4
\end{bmatrix}
\begin{bmatrix}
f_{1,1} \\ f_{2,1} \\ f_{3,1} \\ f_{1,2} \\ f_{2,2} \\ f_{3,2} \\ f_{1,3} \\ f_{2,3} \\ f_{3,3}
\end{bmatrix}
$$

$$
=
\begin{bmatrix}
\frac{g_{1,1}}{16} - f_{1,0} - f_{0,1} \\
\frac{g_{2,1}}{16} - f_{2,0} \\
\frac{g_{3,1}}{16} - f_{3,0} - f_{4,1} \\
\frac{g_{1,2}}{16} - f_{0,2} \\
\frac{g_{2,2}}{16} \\
\frac{g_{3,2}}{16} - f_{4,2} \\
\frac{g_{1,3}}{16} - f_{0,3} - f_{1,4} \\
\frac{g_{2,3}}{16} - f_{2,4} \\
\frac{g_{3,3}}{16} - f_{4,3} - f_{3,4}
\end{bmatrix}.
$$

Thus the coefficient matrix is symmetric and block tridiagonal. By symmetry the eigenvalues are real.

In fact the eigenvalues are all strictly negative. To see this, let λ be an eigenvalue of A and let $\mathbf{x}$ be a corresponding eigenvector.[1] Let x_i be the component of $\mathbf{x}$ largest in absolute value; for the sharpest case, suppose this is x_5. By normalization we may assume $x_5 = 1$, then, in absolute value, the other components are less than, or equal to, 1. Now the fifth component of the eigenvalue equation $(A - \lambda I)\mathbf{x} = 0$ is is

$$x_2 + x_4 + (-4 - \lambda) + x_6 + x_8 = 0. \tag{37}$$

Take absolute values and get

$$|-4 - \lambda| = |-x_2 - x_4 - x_6 - x_8| \le |x_2| + |x_4| + |x_6| + |x_8| \le 4.$$

This shows that $-8 \le \lambda \le 0$. By Eq. (37) it is only possible for $\lambda = 0$ if $x_2 = x_4 = x_6 = x_8 = 1$. But then the fourth component of the eigenvalue equation is

$$x_1 - 4 + x_7 = 0,$$

---

[1] This arguement is essentially that of the *Gerschgorin Circle Theorem*.

which is impossible. This shows that A is negative definite or equivalently that $-A$ is positive definite. We state the following from [12].

Theorem 1. *Let A be Hermitian symmetric (A conjugate transpose equals A) with positive diagonal elements. Then the Gauss–Seidel method for solving $A\mathbf{x} = \mathbf{b}$ will converge, for any choice of starting vector, if and only if A is positive definite.*

8.6 Parallelizing Gauss–Seidel Iteration

As has already been pointed out, Gauss–Seidel updating is inherently sequential. But when the coefficient matrix is sparse, it may be possible to organize the updating in such a way as to allow some degree of parallelization.

By way of example, consider the problem

$$
\begin{aligned}
x_1 &= & a_{12}x_2 & & & + & a_{14}x_4 \\
x_2 &= a_{21}x_1 & & & & + & a_{24}x_4 \\
x_3 &= & a_{32}x_2 & & & & \\
x_4 &= & & a_{43}x_3 & & + & a_{45}x_5 \\
x_5 &= & a_{52}x_2 & + & a_{53}x_3. & &
\end{aligned}
$$

The Directed Acyclic Graph for Gauss–Seidel iteration is given in Fig. 32. One sees that 4 time steps are required per iteration.

To see how the components are interrelated, their dependencies expressed by means of a directed graph called a *component dependency graph* (CDG). An arc is drawn from vertex i to j, $(i, j) \in A$, if and only if the update of x_j depends on x_i. Thus the CDG for this problem is shown in Fig. 33.

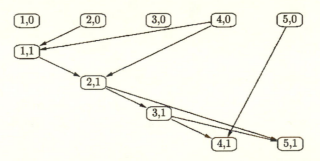

Fig. 32. DAG for the order $x_1, x_2, \dots, x_5$; $((i, k)$ indicates variable i at iteration k).

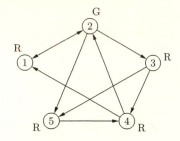

Fig. 33. Component Dependency Graph for a 5-variable problem.

Now consider reordering the variables as x_1, x_4, x_5, x_3, x_2. The update equations are then

$$
\begin{aligned}
x_1 &= & + \; a_{14}x_4 & & & + \; a_{12}x_2 \\
x_4 &= & & a_{45}x_5 \; + \; a_{43}x_3 & & \\
x_5 &= & & & a_{53}x_3 \; + \; a_{52}x_2 \\
x_3 &= & & & & a_{32}x_2 \\
x_2 &= a_{21}x_1 \; + \; a_{24}x_4.
\end{aligned}
$$

The directed acyclic graph for this order is given in Fig. 34, and it shows that all updates except for x_2 can proceed in one time. Hence, a total of 2 time steps are now required or a 50% savings in time.

Discovering an optimal ordering of the components of a Gauss–Seidel update is closely related to the problem of coloring the CDG. A *coloring* of a graph G using K colors is a function h assigning color $k = h(i)$ to node i for each node of G. In Fig. 33, we show a coloring, which assigns red (R) to nodes 1, 3, 4, and 5, and green (G) to node 2. This coloring satisfies the conditions of the following Theorem about reordering the components. (For a proof, see [1].)

Theorem 1. *There exists an ordering of the variables of Gauss–Seidel iteration so that a* sweep *(i.e., an update of the variables) can be done in K parallel steps if and only if there exists a coloring of the CDG using K colors with the property that no positive cycle has all nodes the same color.*

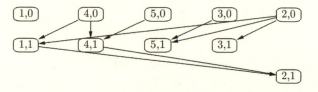

Fig. 34. DAG for the order x_1, x_4, x_5, x_3, x_2.

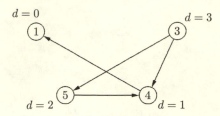

Fig. 35. The subgraph of "red" nodes and their path lengths.

In the application of this theorem to component updating there are two rules:

1. All components having the same color will be updated at the same time. The order of the colors is arbitrary.
2. The variables colored by the same color must be ordered as follows: the subgraph consisting of those nodes of a given color will be acyclic. For every node i of the color, let $d(i)$ denote the length of the *longest* directed path starting at i. The node at the end of the subgraph of like colored nodes will have $d = 0$. Order the variables in the order of increasing d; ties are broken arbitrarily.

In our example, the subgraph of red nodes along with their paths length $d(\cdot)$ is shown in Fig. 35. With deference to the rules above, the ordering for these nodes is 1, 4, 5, and 3. The "green" node, 2, can precede or follow these as desirable.

Of course, it must not be forgotten that any order of updating chosen must preserve convergence which is sensitive to the order of the variables.

Gauss–Seidel With Red–Black Coloring

Certain 2-dimensional field effect problems (heat flow, stress fields, etc.) lead to a 2-dimensional mesh of nodes and bidirectional edges (see Fig. 36). Such a dependency graph can be colored with two colors, red and black. If a processor is assigned to each node, then the efficency will be 50%. But by assigning both a red and a black node to a single processor, and banking the processors (i.e., first the bank of red processors, and then the black), the efficiency goes up to 100%.

8.7 Conjugate Gradient Method

Conjugate gradient is a special method that can be used when the matrix of coefficients is positive definite symmetric. Although we include it here as an iterative method, theoretically the exact solution is determined after n iterations.

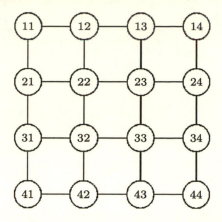

Fig. 36. A two-dimensional mesh which can be colored red–black.

Let A be a positive definite symmetric $n \times n$ matrix; then

$$\langle \mathbf{x}, \mathbf{y} \rangle = \mathbf{y}^T A \mathbf{x}$$

defines an inner product $\langle \cdot, \cdot \rangle$ on n-dimensional vector space. The vectors $\mathbf{e}_1$, $\mathbf{e}_2, \ldots, \mathbf{e}_n$ are A-*conjugate* if they are mutually orthogonal with respect to this inner-product which is to say

$$\mathbf{e}_j^T A \mathbf{e}_i = 0, \quad i \neq j.$$

Let $\mathbf{x}^*$ be a solution to $A\mathbf{x} = \mathbf{b}$ and write $\mathbf{x}^*$ in terms of the $\mathbf{e}$'s,

$$\mathbf{x}^* = \alpha_1 \mathbf{e}_1 + \alpha_2 \mathbf{e}_2 + \cdots + \alpha_n \mathbf{e}_n. \tag{38}$$

Apply A to both sides

$$\mathbf{b} = A\mathbf{x}^* = \alpha_1 A\mathbf{e}_1 + \alpha_2 A\mathbf{e}_2 + \cdots + \alpha_n A\mathbf{e}_n,$$

and, to solve for α_i, multiply both sides of this by $\mathbf{e}_i^T$ and invoke A-conjugacy to get

$$\alpha_i = \frac{\mathbf{e}_i^T \mathbf{b}}{\mathbf{e}_i^T A \mathbf{e}_i} \quad 1 \leq i \leq n. \tag{39}$$

We use this idea to generate successive approximations $\mathbf{x}_0, \mathbf{x}_1, \ldots, \mathbf{x}_n$, to the solution of the linear system $A\mathbf{x} = \mathbf{b}$. Essentially the method orthogonalizes the sequence of residuals

$$\mathbf{r}_k = \mathbf{b} - A\mathbf{x}_k, \quad k = 0, \ldots, n-1.$$

This constructs a sequence of A-conjugate vectors $\mathbf{e}_1, \mathbf{e}_2, \ldots, \mathbf{e}_n$, for use in (38). Moreover, the method simultanously constructs the α's as well.

Start with $\mathbf{x}_0 = 0$; hence, $\mathbf{r}_0 = \mathbf{b}$ and take $\mathbf{e}_1 = \mathbf{r}_0$. Next put

$$\mathbf{x}_1 = \alpha_1 \mathbf{e}_1, \qquad \alpha_1 = \frac{\mathbf{e}_1^T \mathbf{b}}{\mathbf{e}_1^T A \mathbf{e}_1},$$

choosing α_1 according to (39). The residual is

$$\mathbf{r}_1 = \mathbf{b} - A\mathbf{x}_1.$$

Then $\mathbf{e}_2$ is given by

$$\mathbf{e}_2 = \mathbf{r}_1 + \beta_2 \mathbf{e}_1, \qquad \beta_2 = -\frac{\mathbf{e}_1^T A \mathbf{r}_1}{\mathbf{e}_1^T A \mathbf{e}_1},$$

in which β_2, as specified, is chosen so that $\mathbf{e}_1$ and $\mathbf{e}_2$ are A-conjugate.
  In general, for $k = 1, 2, \ldots, n - 1$, put

$$\mathbf{x}_k = \mathbf{x}_{k-1} + \alpha_k \mathbf{e}_k, \qquad \alpha_k = \frac{\mathbf{e}_k^T \mathbf{b}}{\mathbf{e}_k^T A \mathbf{e}_k}. \tag{40}$$

And

$$\mathbf{r}_k = \mathbf{b} - A\mathbf{x}_k. \tag{41}$$

Then

$$\mathbf{e}_{k+1} = \mathbf{r}_k + \beta_{k+1} \mathbf{e}_k, \qquad \beta_{k+1} = -\frac{\mathbf{e}_k^T A \mathbf{r}_k}{\mathbf{e}_k^T A \mathbf{e}_k}. \tag{42}$$

Lastly,

$$\mathbf{x}_n = \mathbf{x}_{n-1} + \alpha_n \mathbf{e}_n, \qquad \alpha_n = \frac{\mathbf{e}_n^T \mathbf{b}}{\mathbf{e}_n^T A \mathbf{e}_n}$$

is the exact solution.
  We illustrate the method by solving the linear system having (positive definite) coefficient matrix

$$\begin{bmatrix} 3 & 1 & -2 \\ 1 & 2 & 1 \\ -2 & 1 & 4 \end{bmatrix}$$

and right-hand side $\mathbf{b} = [\,-1 \quad 8 \quad 12\,]^T$. Then $\mathbf{e}_1 = \mathbf{b} = [\,-1 \quad 8 \quad 12\,]^T$ and, from (40),

$$\mathbf{x}_1 = \frac{\mathbf{e}_1^T \mathbf{b}}{\mathbf{e}_1^T A \mathbf{e}_1} \mathbf{e}_1 = \begin{bmatrix} -0.22448979591836735 \\ 1.7959183673469388 \\ 2.693877551020408 \end{bmatrix}.$$

For the next iteration, the residual is

$$\mathbf{r}_1 = \mathbf{b} - A\mathbf{x}_1 = \begin{bmatrix} 3.2653061224489797 \\ 1.9387755102040813 \\ -1.020408163265305 \end{bmatrix}.$$

Subtract $\mathbf{r}_1$'s projection onto $\mathbf{e}_1$ to get $\mathbf{e}_2$,

$$\mathbf{e}_2 = \mathbf{r}_1 - \frac{\mathbf{e}_1^T A \mathbf{r}_1}{\mathbf{e}_1^T A \mathbf{e}_1} \mathbf{e}_1 = \begin{bmatrix} 3.1913237905258773 \\ 2.5306341655888986 \\ -0.1326201801880793 \end{bmatrix}.$$

This allows the calculation of the next approximation

$$\mathbf{x}_2 = \mathbf{x}_1 + \frac{\mathbf{e}_2^T \mathbf{b}}{\mathbf{e}_2^T A \mathbf{e}_2} \mathbf{e}_2 = \begin{bmatrix} 0.5897063749023108 \\ 2.441554091771798 \\ 2.6600424249190575 \end{bmatrix}.$$

Finally, the last iteration provides the ressidual

$$\mathbf{r}_2 = \mathbf{b} - A\mathbf{x}_2 = \begin{bmatrix} 0.1094116333593842 \\ -0.13285698336496488 \\ 0.09768895835659386 \end{bmatrix}$$

and the A-conjugate basis vector

$$\mathbf{e}_3 = \mathbf{r}_2 - \frac{\mathbf{e}_2^T A \mathbf{r}_2}{\mathbf{e}_2^T A \mathbf{e}_2} \mathbf{e}_2 = \begin{bmatrix} 0.1174950483840094 \\ -0.12644705207040943 \\ 0.09735304008960906 \end{bmatrix}.$$

Projecting gives the solution

$$\mathbf{x} = \mathbf{x}_2 + \frac{\mathbf{e}_3^T \mathbf{b}}{\mathbf{e}_3^T A \mathbf{e}_3} \mathbf{e}_3 = \begin{bmatrix} 1.0000000000002167 \\ 1.9999999999997684 \\ 3.000000000000184 \end{bmatrix}.$$

This gives a good numerical approximation to the exact solution $\mathbf{x} = \begin{bmatrix} 1 & 2 & 3 \end{bmatrix}^T$.

Remark. *The procedure indicated above is essentially the Gram-Schmidt process for orthogonalizing a sequence of vectors* $\mathbf{x}_1, \mathbf{x}_2, \ldots$. *To start, take* $\mathbf{y}_1 = \mathbf{x}_1$ *and* $\mathbf{u}_1 = \mathbf{y}_1 / \|\mathbf{y}_1\|$. *Next put* $\mathbf{y}_2 = \mathbf{x}_2 - \langle \mathbf{x}_2, \mathbf{u}_1 \rangle \mathbf{u}_1$, *and* $\mathbf{u}_2 = \mathbf{y}_2 / \|\mathbf{y}_2\|$. *Here* $\mathbf{y}_2$ *is* $\mathbf{x}_2$ *minus the orthogonal projection of* $\mathbf{x}_2$ *onto the subspace generated by* $\mathbf{u}_1$ *(or* $\mathbf{y}_1$ *or* $\mathbf{x}_1$*) and so it is orthogonal to that subspace. In general, having defined* $\mathbf{y}_1, \mathbf{y}_2, \ldots, \mathbf{y}_k$, *and the corresponding unit vectors* $\mathbf{u}_1, \mathbf{u}_2, \ldots, \mathbf{u}_k$, *put*

$$\mathbf{y}_{k+1} = \mathbf{x}_{k+1} - (\langle \mathbf{x}_{k+1}, \mathbf{u}_1 \rangle \mathbf{u}_1 + \cdots + \langle \mathbf{x}_{k+1}, \mathbf{u}_k \rangle \mathbf{u}_k)$$

and

$$\mathbf{u}_{k+1} = \mathbf{y}_{k+1}/\|\mathbf{y}_{k+1}\|.$$

Again, since this is $\mathbf{x}_{k+1}$ *minus its orthogonal projection onto the subspace spanned by the first* k $\mathbf{y}$'s, *it is orthogonal to that subspace.*

In this way an orthogonal sequence $\{\mathbf{y}_k\}$ is constructed (along with an orthonormal sequence $\{\mathbf{u}_k\}$), with the property that the subspace spanned by the first k $\mathbf{y}$'s is the same as that spanned by the first k $\mathbf{x}$'s.

Exercises

1. (4) This problem shows that positive definiteness is not sufficient for the convergence of Jacobi iteration. Let

$$A = \begin{bmatrix} 1 & a & a \\ a & 1 & a \\ a & a & 1 \end{bmatrix}.$$

   (a) Show that A is positive definite when $-1 < 2a < 2$. (Hint: An equivalent condition to positive definiteness is that the determinants of all principal minors are positive, the principal kth minor being $[a_{ij}], 1 \le i, j \le k$.) (b) Show that Jacobi iteration to solve $A\mathbf{x} = \mathbf{b}$ will converge for $-1 < 2a < 1$. (c) Show that Jacobi iteration fails for $2a = \pm 1$.

2. (4) Using the Vector Timing Data Table (p. 11), estimate the time required for one Jacobi iteration as a function of matrix size N.

3. (5) (a) Find an optimal ordering (from a parallelization point of view) for solving the following system by Gauss–Seidel. (b) Which ordering also uses the least number of processors?

$$
\begin{array}{llllll}
a_{11}x_1 & +a_{12}x_2 & & & +a_{16}x_6 & & = b_1 \\
a_{21}x_1 & +a_{22}x_2 & & +a_{24}x_4 & & +a_{27}x_7 & = b_2 \\
& a_{32}x_2 & +a_{33}x_3 & & +a_{35}x_5 & +a_{36}x_6 & = b_3 \\
a_{41}x_1 & & +a_{43}x_3 & +a_{44}x_4 & & & = b_4 \ . \\
& a_{52}x_2 & & & +a_{55}x_5 & +a_{57}x_7 & = b_5 \\
& a_{62}x_2 & & +a_{64}x_4 & & +a_{66}x_6 & +a_{67}x_7 & = b_6 \\
a_{71}x_1 & & +a_{73}x_3 & +a_{74}x_4 & & +a_{77}x_7 & = b_7
\end{array}
$$

4. (2) How does Gauss–Seidel iteration specialize when A is upper triangular?

5. (3) The idea of this problem is to see the pattern of sparsity of the linear system matrix A for a Poisson problem. Discretize the unit square as in the text and choose some ordering of the unknowns f_{ij} different than by rows.

Write the discrete Poisson equation in the form $A\mathbf{x} = \mathbf{b}$ for this choice and compare with the ordering by rows.

6. (5) Derive the iteration equations for the Jacobi solution of the Poisson equation if the horizontal grid spacing is Δx and the vertical grid spacing is Δy.

Programming Exercises

7. (6) For the Poisson equation $u_{xx} + u_{yy} = 4$ on the unit square I with boundary condition: $u(x, y) = x^2 + y^2$, show that $u(x, y) = x^2 + y^2$ is the exact solution (throughout the square). Choose a subdivision of I and implement a Jacobi iteration solution (use the language of your choice). On each iteration of your numerical solution, compute the quadratic cost functional $F(\mathbf{x}) = \frac{1}{2}\mathbf{x}^T A \mathbf{x} - \mathbf{x}^T \mathbf{b}$.

8. (6) Solve the Poisson equation $u_{xx} + u_{yy} = 2x^2 + 2y^2$ on the unit square I with boundary condition: $u(x, y) = x^2 y^2$ by JOR with various values of γ. What is the optimal value of γ for fastest convergence?

9

Finding Eigenvalues and Eigenvectors

Eigenvalues and eigenvectors are of central importance in almost every problem that can be cast as a matrix. This includes problems in vibrations, structures, rotating bodies, population dynamics, ecology, economics, network connectivity, Markov chains, ordinary and partial differential equations among others.

Sometimes, the eigenvalues themselves are the primary object of interest. This is the case, for example, in classical mechancial problems where the eigenvalues give the frequency of the natural modes of vibration in a body. In dynamics, the eigenvalues of matrices are important for determining the stability of equilibria of the underlying system. We have also seen that the condition number of a matrix, an important quantity to know when doing large-scale computations, is determined from eigenvalues. In quantum mechanics, linear operators correspond to observables, and the eigenvalues of an operator represent those values of the corresponding variable that have nonzero probability of being measured.

It should come as no surprise that a significant fraction of scientific computation is devoted to solving for eigenvalues and eigenvectors.

9.1 Eigenvalues and Eigenvectors

Let A be an $n \times n$ matrix of real or complex numbers. We may think of A as defining a linear transformation T on n-dimensional complex space $\mathbf{C}^n$. More about this below. A complex number λ is an *eigenvalue* for A if there is a vector $\mathbf{x}$ such that $\mathbf{x} \neq 0$ and

$$A\mathbf{x} = \lambda\mathbf{x}. \tag{43}$$

This says that A maps $\mathbf{x}$ into a scalar multiple of itself. The vector $\mathbf{x}$ can

206

have complex components and is called an *eigenvector* associated with λ.[1] By multiplying both sides of (43) by a scalar, we see that a nonzero scalar multiple of an eigenvector is also an eigenvector for the same eigenvalue (so we may normalize eigenvectors if we want). More generally, the set of eigenvectors for a given eigenvalue is a linear subspace called its *eigenmanifold* or *eigenspace*.

Theorem 1. *The set of eigenvectors for the eigenvalue λ is a linear subspace.*

Proof. Let $\mathbf{x}$ and $\mathbf{y}$ be eigenvectors of A corresponding to the eigenvalue λ, then

$$A(\alpha\mathbf{x} + \beta\mathbf{y}) = \alpha A\mathbf{x} + \beta A\mathbf{y} = \lambda(\alpha\mathbf{x} + \beta\mathbf{y}).$$

So $\alpha\mathbf{x} + \beta\mathbf{y}$ is also an eigenvector for λ. ∎

By subtracting $\lambda\mathbf{x}$ from both sides of (43) and factoring $\mathbf{x}$, we obtain an equivalent form of the equation as a homogeneous linear system,

$$(A - \lambda I)\mathbf{x} = 0. \tag{44}$$

Such a system will have a nontrivial solution $\mathbf{x}$ if and only if the matrix of coefficients is singular, that is, if and only if

$$\det(A - \lambda I) = 0.$$

Expanding the determinant results in a polynomial in λ of degree n (the product of the diagonal contains the term of highest degree) called the *characteristic polynomial* of A. The roots of the characteristic polynomial are the eigenvalues of A. In this way we see that A has n eigenvalues in the complex plane counting multiple roots according to their multiplicities. The multiplicity of an eigenvalue, that is, the number of times it is repeated as a root of the characteristic polynomial, is called its *algebraic multiplicity*. We will shortly learn that an eigenvalue also has a geometric multiplicity.

Theoretically, with an eigenvalue in hand, substitution into (44) leads to an underdetermined linear system which can be solved for the eigenvectors associated to that eigenvalue. But numerically this approach is inferior to direct methods such the power method or QR, which we study below. In fact, eigenvalue solvers are so good that a competitive method for solving all the roots of a monic polynomial such as

$$x^n + a_1 x^{n-1} + \cdots + a_{n-1}x + a_n \tag{45}$$

---

[1] Recall when vectors are complex, dot product is defined by $\mathbf{x} \cdot \mathbf{y} = \sum_1^n x_i \bar{y}_i$, where $\bar{y}_i$ is the complex conjugate of y_i.

is to calculate the eigenvalues of its *companion matrix* defined to be

$$A = \begin{bmatrix} 0 & 0 & \cdots & 0 & -a_n \\ 1 & 0 & \cdots & 0 & -a_{n-1} \\ 0 & 1 & \cdots & 0 & -a_{n-2} \\ \vdots & \vdots & \ddots & \ddots & \vdots \\ 0 & 0 & \cdots & 1 & -a_1 \end{bmatrix}. \tag{46}$$

It can be verified that the characteristic polynomial of this matrix is (45) (see the Exercises).

Shifting attention to the number of linearly independent eigenvectors, we have the following.

Theorem 2. *If x_1 and x_2 are eigenvectors associated with distinct eigenvalues, $\lambda_1 \neq \lambda_2$, then they are linearly independent.*

Proof. If $x_1 = \alpha x_2$, $\alpha \neq 0$, then x_1 is an eigenvector for both λ_1 and λ_2. We have

$$\lambda_1 \alpha x_2 = \lambda_1 x_1 = A x_1 = \alpha A x_2 = \lambda_2 \alpha x_2.$$

Subtracting leads to $(\lambda_1 - \lambda_2)\alpha x_2 = 0$, which is impossible since no factor is zero. ∎

It follows that if all n eigenvalues of A are distinct, then there is a basis of eigenvectors of the space. This is a desirable situation. However, even if the eigenvalues are not distinct, it may still be possible that there is a basis of eigenvectors. The *geometric multiplicity* of an eigenvalue is the number of linearly independent eigenvectors associated with it, that is, the dimension of its eigenmanifold. Since an eigenvalue always has at least one eigenvector, the geometric multiplicity is at least 1. On the other hand, the geometric multiplicity cannot exceed the algebraic multiplicity. This is so because, as we will see shortly, the characteristic polynomial is preserved under similarity transform, that is, a change of basis. When the geometric multiplicity equals the algebraic multiplicity for every eigenvalue, then there is a basis of C^n consisting of eigenvectors of A.

Simple examples suffice to demonstrate these principles. In the following three examples, 5 is an eigenvalue of algebraic multiplicity 3 (check this) but, respectively, of geometric multiplicity 3, 2, and 1 as can be easily verified,

$$A = \begin{bmatrix} 5 & 0 & 0 \\ 0 & 5 & 0 \\ 0 & 0 & 5 \end{bmatrix}, \quad A = \begin{bmatrix} 5 & 1 & 0 \\ 0 & 5 & 0 \\ 0 & 0 & 5 \end{bmatrix}, \quad A = \begin{bmatrix} 5 & 1 & 0 \\ 0 & 5 & 1 \\ 0 & 0 & 5 \end{bmatrix}.$$

9.2 The Power Method

To see the main idea underlying the *power method* assume A is real; that is, all its elements are real, and assume the eigenvalues of A are distinct. Therefore, the space has a basis of eigenvectors. Arrange the eigenvalues in decreasing order,

$$|\lambda_1| > |\lambda_2| > \ldots > |\lambda_n|$$

and let $\mathbf{e}_i$ be an eigenvector for λ_i. All the eigenvalues of A must be real because the characteristic polynomial will have real coefficients here and any complex root would have to occur as part of a conjugate pair.

Now let $\mathbf{x}$ be a fixed but randomly selected vector in the space. Then a normalized sequence of the vectors $\mathbf{x}, A\mathbf{x}, A^2\mathbf{x}, \ldots$ converges to an eigenvector for λ_1. Furthermore, λ_1 is given as the ratio of successive normalizations. In addition, convergence is geometric with convergence rate given by $|\lambda_2/\lambda_1|$.

To see why it works, note that $\mathbf{x}$ has the representation

$$\mathbf{x} = \alpha_1 \mathbf{e}_1 + \cdots + \alpha_n \mathbf{e}_n$$

with $\alpha_i \neq 0$, $1 \leq i \leq n$, because the eigenvectors form a basis and $\mathbf{x}$ was randomly chosen (the probability that an $\alpha_i = 0$ for some i is zero). Since scalar multiples of eigenvectors are also eigenvectors, we may assume without loss of generality that $\alpha_i = 1$ for all i.

The powers $A^m\mathbf{x}$ are given by

$$A^2\mathbf{x} = \lambda_1 A\mathbf{e}_1 + \lambda_2 A\mathbf{e}_2 + \cdots + \lambda_n A\mathbf{e}_n = \lambda_1^2 \mathbf{e}_1 + \lambda_2^2 \mathbf{e}_2 + \cdots + \lambda_n^2 \mathbf{e}_n$$

$$A^3\mathbf{x} = \lambda_1^2 A\mathbf{e}_1 + \lambda_2^2 A\mathbf{e}_2 + \cdots + \lambda_n^2 A\mathbf{e}_n = \lambda_1^3 \mathbf{e}_1 + \lambda_2^3 \mathbf{e}_2 + \cdots + \lambda_n^3 \mathbf{e}_n$$

$$\vdots = \vdots$$

and in general

$$A^m\mathbf{x} = \lambda_1^m \mathbf{e}_1 + \lambda_2^m \mathbf{e}_2 + \cdots + \lambda_n^m \mathbf{e}_n$$

$$= \lambda_1^m \left(\mathbf{e}_1 + \left(\frac{\lambda_2}{\lambda_1} \right)^m \mathbf{e}_2 + \cdots + \left(\frac{\lambda_n}{\lambda_1} \right)^m \mathbf{e}_n \right). \tag{47}$$

But as $m \to \infty$, $(\lambda_i/\lambda_1)^m \to 0$, $i \neq 1$. Therefore, for m large, $A^m\mathbf{x}$ has approximately the same direction as $\mathbf{e}_1$. Putting $\mathbf{y} = A^m\mathbf{x}$, we have that $A\mathbf{y} \approx \lambda_1\mathbf{y}$. This equation shows that the components of $A^m\mathbf{x}$ will change sign if $\lambda_1 < 0$. Equation (47) also shows that $\frac{1}{\lambda_1^m} A^m\mathbf{x}$ equals $\mathbf{e}_1$ with an error on the order of $|\lambda_2/\lambda_1|^m$. It also shows why we normalize the powers; otherwise, the components of $A^m\mathbf{x}$ will become very large in magnitude (if $|\lambda_1| > 1$) or very small (if $|\lambda_1| < 1$) for higher and higher powers.

The Power Method Algorithm

> choose x at random
> loop
>   y=Ax
>   lambda = dot(y,x)
>   x = normalize(y)
>   check convergence
> end loop

It remains to see how to normalize the calculation. As seen in (47) the best normalization is to divide each iteration by λ_1 were it to be known. Otherwise, as noted above, for large m, $A^m \mathbf{x}$ becomes increasing oriented along $\mathbf{e}_1$ and so one possibility is to normalize as usual, by dividing each iterate by its norm, for example, the maximum norm $\| \cdot \|_\infty$. If λ_1 is positive, this will converge to a fixed vector, $\mathbf{e}_1$, which is an eigenvector of A for λ_1. But if λ_1 is negative, then since the norm is a positive number, the components of the iterates will flip sign.

Another possibility is to divide each iterate $\mathbf{y}^{(m)} = A^m \mathbf{x}$ by the value of some fixed component, such as the first, provided it is not zero. Thus, this component is 1 at the beginning of each iteration and is appoximately λ_1 after the application of A. For large m, the component largest in magnitude of $\mathbf{y}^{(m)}$, the kth say, will also be the largest component of $\mathbf{y}^{(m+1)} = A\mathbf{y}^{(m)}$. Choosing this component makes this method something like the one above except now the components of $\mathbf{y}^{(m)}$ maintain sign.

Another possibility implements (47) somewhat directly. Let $\mathbf{u}$ be a given vector. Put $\mathbf{y}^{(m)} = A^m \mathbf{x}$ as before and $\alpha_m = \mathbf{u}^T \mathbf{y}^{(m)}$, the dot product of an iterate with $\mathbf{u}$. Then α_{m+1}/α_m converges to λ_1 and $\mathbf{y}^{(m)}/\lambda_1^m$ converges to $\mathbf{e}_1$. The vector $\mathbf{u}$ can be optimally chosen, for example, if A is symmetric, then $\mathbf{u} = A^m \mathbf{x}$ leads to convergence on the order of $|\lambda_2/\lambda_1|^{2m}$, a rate twice the nominal (see [13]).

9.3 Jordan Cannonical Form

In order to investigate the convergence properties of the power method for more general cases, we introduce Jordan Cannonical Form. The $n \times n$ matrix B is *similar* to A if there is an invertible matrix P so that

$$B = P^{-1}AP \quad \text{or} \quad A = PBP^{-1}. \tag{48}$$

If B is similar to A, then A is also similar to B since $A = Q^{-1}BQ$, where $Q = P^{-1}$. Similar matrices have the same characteristic polynomial since (see problem 13, Chapter 5)

$$\det(B - \lambda I) = \det(P^{-1}(A - \lambda I)P) = \det(P^{-1})\det(A - \lambda I)\det(P)$$
$$= \det(P^{-1}P)\det(A - \lambda I) = \det(A - \lambda I).$$

Therefore similar matrices also have the same eigenvalues. If $\mathbf{x}$ is an eigenvector for A with eigenvalue λ, then $\mathbf{y} = P^{-1}\mathbf{x}$ is an eigenvector for B belonging to the same eigenvalue as the following shows,

$$B(P^{-1}\mathbf{x}) = P^{-1}APP^{-1}\mathbf{x} = P^{-1}A\mathbf{x} = P^{-1}(\lambda\mathbf{x}) = \lambda P^{-1}\mathbf{x}. \qquad (49)$$

Similar matrices can be viewed as matrices for the same linear transformation T but with respect to different bases. Let A be the matrix of T with respect to the basis $\{\mathbf{e}_1, \mathbf{e}_2, \dots, \mathbf{e}_n\}$. This means that $T\mathbf{e}_j$ is the jth column of A as represented in the $\mathbf{e}_i$ basis,

$$T\mathbf{e}_j = \sum_{i=1}^{n} a_{ij}\mathbf{e}_i.$$

And let B be the matrix of T with respect to the basis $\{\mathbf{f}_1, \mathbf{f}_2, \dots, \mathbf{f}_n\}$, then similarly

$$T\mathbf{f}_j = \sum_{i=1}^{n} b_{ij}\mathbf{f}_i.$$

Now let P be the matrix of the identity I with respect to $\{\mathbf{f}_1, \dots, \mathbf{f}_n\}$ in the domain and $\{\mathbf{e}_1, \dots, \mathbf{e}_n\}$ in the range. Therefore the jth column of P is I acting on $\mathbf{f}_j$ written in terms of the $\mathbf{e}_i$,

$$I\mathbf{f}_j = \sum_{i=1}^{n} p_{ij}\mathbf{e}_i.$$

The relationships can be illustrated in the commutative diagram

$$
\begin{array}{ccc}
\mathbf{C}^n & \xrightarrow{\;A\;} & \mathbf{C}^n \\
\mathbf{e}_1, \dots, \mathbf{e}_n & & \mathbf{e}_1, \dots, \mathbf{e}_n \\
\downarrow{\scriptstyle P^{-1}} & & \uparrow{\scriptstyle P} \\
\mathbf{C}^n & \xrightarrow{\;B\;} & \mathbf{C}^n \\
\mathbf{f}_1, \dots, \mathbf{f}_n & & \mathbf{f}_1, \dots, \mathbf{f}_n
\end{array}
$$

from which (48) follows.

The Jordan Canonical Form Theorem describes the simplest form that a general matrix can have under similarity. A *Jordan block* of order k is the $k \times k$ matrix having the form

$$
J_k(\lambda) = \begin{bmatrix}
\lambda & 1 & 0 & \dots & 0 \\
0 & \lambda & 1 & \dots & 0 \\
\vdots & \vdots & \ddots & \ddots & \vdots \\
0 & 0 & 0 & \dots & 1 \\
0 & 0 & 0 & \dots & \lambda
\end{bmatrix}.
$$

If $k = 1$ then $J_k(\lambda)$ is just the 1×1 matrix

$$J_1(\lambda) = [\lambda].$$

A Jordan block illustrates the difference between algebraic and geometric multiplicity: λ is an eigenvalue of algebraic multiplicity k for $J_k(\lambda)$ but its geometric multiplicity is 1 since it has only 1 linearly independent eigenvector.

The Jordan form of a matrix A of order n is a matrix composed of Jordan blocks $J_{n_1}(\lambda_1)$, $J_{n_2}(\lambda_2)$, ..., $J_{n_r}(\lambda_r)$ where $n_1 + n_2 + \cdots + n_r = n$. Thus for some change of variable P,

$$P^{-1}AP = \begin{bmatrix} J_{n_1}(\lambda_1) & 0 & \cdots & 0 \\ 0 & J_{n_2}(\lambda_2) & \cdots & 0 \\ \vdots & \vdots & \ddots & \vdots \\ 0 & 0 & \cdots & J_{n_r}(\lambda_r) \end{bmatrix}.$$

In this representation the eigenvalues λ_i are not necessarily distinct. For example, the Jordan form could be

$$\begin{bmatrix} 3 & 1 & 0 & 0 & 0 & 0 & 0 & 0 \\ 0 & 3 & 1 & 0 & 0 & 0 & 0 & 0 \\ 0 & 0 & 3 & 0 & 0 & 0 & 0 & 0 \\ 0 & 0 & 0 & 3 & 1 & 0 & 0 & 0 \\ 0 & 0 & 0 & 0 & 3 & 0 & 0 & 0 \\ 0 & 0 & 0 & 0 & 0 & 3 & 0 & 0 \\ 0 & 0 & 0 & 0 & 0 & 0 & 2 & 1 \\ 0 & 0 & 0 & 0 & 0 & 0 & 0 & 2 \end{bmatrix}. \tag{50}$$

This matrix has three Jordan blocks for the eigenvalue 3 and one for the eigenvalue 2.

Corresponding to a Jordan block $J_k(\lambda)$, there is a system of k linearly independent vectors $\mathbf{e}, \mathbf{f}_2, \ldots, \mathbf{f}_k$ satisfying

$$T\mathbf{e} = \lambda \mathbf{e} \quad T\mathbf{f}_j = \mathbf{f}_{j-1} + \lambda \mathbf{f}_j \quad j = 2, \ldots, k$$

($\mathbf{f}_1 = \mathbf{e}$ in this equation for convenience). Only $\mathbf{e}$ is an eigenvector, instead $\mathbf{f}_2, \ldots, \mathbf{f}_k$ are *generalized* or *pseudo* eigenvectors. In example (50) above, there are three linearly independent eigenvectors for the eigenvalue 3, one for each Jordan block. There is also one for the eigenvalue 2.

It will be necessary to calculate powers of Jordan blocks. Let $a_{ij}(m)$ denote the i,jth element of J_k^m. From the matrix equation $J_k^{m+1} = J_k^m \cdot J_k$, that is,

$$
\begin{bmatrix}
a_{11}(m+1) & a_{12}(m+1) & a_{13}(m+1) & \cdots & a_{1k}(m+1) \\
0 & a_{22}(m+1) & a_{23}(m+1) & \cdots & a_{2k}(m+1) \\
0 & 0 & a_{33}(m+1) & \cdots & a_{3k}(m+1) \\
\vdots & \vdots & & \ddots & \vdots \\
0 & 0 & 0 & \cdots & a_{kk}(m+1)
\end{bmatrix}
$$

$$
=
\begin{bmatrix}
a_{11}(m) & a_{12}(m) & a_{13}(m) & \cdots & a_{1k}(m) \\
0 & a_{22}(m) & a_{23}(m) & \cdots & a_{2k}(m) \\
0 & 0 & a_{33}(m) & \cdots & a_{3k}(m) \\
\vdots & \vdots & & \ddots & \vdots \\
0 & 0 & 0 & \cdots & a_{kk}(m)
\end{bmatrix}
\begin{bmatrix}
\lambda & 1 & 0 & \cdots & 0 \\
0 & \lambda & 1 & \cdots & 0 \\
0 & 0 & \lambda & \cdots & 0 \\
\vdots & \vdots & & \ddots & \vdots \\
0 & 0 & 0 & \cdots & \lambda
\end{bmatrix},
$$

we may derive several recursion equations for elements. First, for every diagonal element we have

$$a_{ii}(m+1) = \lambda a_{ii}(m), \quad a_{ii}(1) = \lambda.$$

The solution is easily seen to be

$$a_{ii}(m) = \lambda^m, \quad i = 1, \ldots, k. \tag{51}$$

Thus all the elements on the main diagonal are the same.

Next we work out the remaining elements of the first row. The recursion equation for the jth is

$$a_{1j}(m+1) = a_{1,j-1}(m) + \lambda a_{1j}(m) \quad j = 2, \ldots, k. \tag{52}$$

For $j = 2$ we can use (51) and write

$$a_{12}(m+1) = \lambda^m + \lambda a_{12}(m), \quad a_{12}(1) = 1.$$

By induction on m the solution is seen to be

$$a_{12}(m) = \binom{m}{1} \lambda^{m-1}, \quad m = 1, 2, \ldots. \tag{53}$$

Taking a clue from this solution for $a_{12}(m)$, we conjecture the solution for the other terms. For the purposes of induction on j, assume

$$a_{1j}(m) = \binom{m}{j-1} \lambda^{m-j+1}, \quad m = j-1, j, \ldots. \tag{54}$$

This is true for $j = 2$ and we may assume it is true for indices $2, \ldots, j$, we show it holds for $j + 1$ as well. From (54) and (52) with index j

$$a_{1,j+1}(m + 1) = \binom{m}{j-1}\lambda^{m-j+1} + \lambda a_{1,j+1}(m).$$

Now for the purposes of induction on m, assume (54) holds for $a_{1,j+1}(m)$ with index m running from j up to m. (We leave it to the reader to show the base case $m = j$.) Then

$$a_{1,j+1}(m + 1) = \binom{m}{j-1}\lambda^{m-j+1} + \lambda\binom{m}{j}\lambda^{m-j}$$

$$= \binom{m+1}{j}\lambda^{m-j+1}$$

since

$$\binom{m}{j-1} + \binom{m}{j} = \binom{m+1}{j} \tag{55}$$

whose veracity we also leave to the reader. Therefore (54) holds for $j + 1$ and induction on both m and j is complete.

Finally we leave it to the reader to show that, just as the main diagonal is constant, so also are the superdiagonals because the same recursion equations are satisfied. Thus we have the following for the mth power of a Jordan block

$$J_k^m(\lambda) = \begin{bmatrix} \lambda^m & \binom{m}{1}\lambda^{m-1} & \binom{m}{2}\lambda^{m-2} & \cdots & \binom{m}{k-1}\lambda^{m-k+1} \\ 0 & \lambda^m & \binom{m}{1}\lambda^{m-1} & \cdots & \binom{m}{k-2}\lambda^{m-k+2} \\ \vdots & \vdots & & \ddots & \ddots & \vdots \\ 0 & 0 & 0 & 0 & \lambda^m \end{bmatrix}.$$

Considering the columns of this matrix, for the eigenvector $\mathbf{e}$ and psuedoeigenvectors $\mathbf{f}_2, \ldots, \mathbf{f}_k$. we have

$$
\begin{aligned}
T^m\mathbf{e} &= \lambda^m\mathbf{e} \\
T^m\mathbf{f}_2 &= \binom{m}{1}\lambda^{m-1}\mathbf{e} + \lambda^m\mathbf{f}_2 \\
\vdots \quad &\quad \vdots \\
T^m\mathbf{f}_k &= \binom{m}{k-1}\lambda^{m-k}\mathbf{e} + \binom{m}{k-2}\lambda^{m-k+1}\mathbf{f}_2 + \cdots + \lambda^m\mathbf{f}_k.
\end{aligned}
\tag{56}
$$

We may now apply this to the Power method when A has pseudoeigenvectors. Let the eigenvalues of A satisfy $|\lambda_1| > |\lambda_2| \geq \ldots \geq |\lambda_r|$. There are many possible cases, depending on the pattern of algebraic multiplicities versus geometric multiplicities. We work out an example in which the largest eigenvalue λ_1 has, say, algebraic multiplicity 6 and geometric multiplicity 3; for instance matrix (50). Let $\mathbf{e}_1$, $\mathbf{f}_2$, and $\mathbf{f}_3$ be the eigenvector and pseudoeigenvectors corresponding to its first Jordan block of (50), $\mathbf{e}_2$ and $\mathbf{f}_4$ correspond to the second, and $\mathbf{e}_3$ to the third. The eigenvalue for all these blocks is 3. We could let $\mathbf{e}_4$ and $\mathbf{f}_5$ be an eigenvector and pseudoeigenvector for the fourth block, but as in the main case considered in the previous section, the influence of these vectors will diminish at the rate $(2/3)^m$; so we will focus on the development for the largest eigenvalue.

A randomly selected starting vector is given by

$$\mathbf{x} = \alpha_1 \mathbf{e}_1 + \alpha_2 \mathbf{f}_2 + \alpha_3 \mathbf{f}_3 + \alpha_4 \mathbf{e}_2 + \alpha_5 \mathbf{f}_4 + \alpha_6 \mathbf{e}_3 + \cdots$$

plus similar terms corresponding to the smaller eigenvalues. The powers $A^m \mathbf{x}$ are

$$
\begin{aligned}
A^m \mathbf{x} &= \left(\lambda_1^m + \frac{m}{1!} \lambda_1^{m-1} + \frac{m(m-1)}{2!} \lambda_1^{m-2} \right) \mathbf{e}_1 + \left(\lambda_1^m + \frac{m}{1!} \lambda_1^{m-1} \right) \mathbf{f}_2 + \lambda_1^m \mathbf{f}_3 \\
&\quad + \left(\lambda_1^m + \frac{m}{1!} \lambda_1^{m-1} \right) \mathbf{e}_2 + \lambda_1^m \mathbf{f}_4 + \lambda_1^m \mathbf{e}_3 + \cdots \\
&= \lambda_1^m \left[\left(1 + \frac{m}{\lambda_1} + \frac{m(m-1)}{2! \lambda_1^2} \right) \mathbf{e}_1 + \left(1 + \frac{m}{\lambda_1} \right) \mathbf{f}_2 + \mathbf{f}_3 \right. \\
&\quad \left. + \left(1 + \frac{m}{\lambda_1} \right) \mathbf{e}_2 + \mathbf{f}_4 + \mathbf{e}_3 + \cdots \right].
\end{aligned}
$$

We see that for large m, the largest term will be the one corresponding to the highest power of m (m^2 here). This will always be an eigenvector (or combination of eigenvectors in more general cases – which is therefore also an eigenvector) for λ_1. However the convergence could be only linear, as it is here since the coefficient of $\mathbf{f}_2$ grows with order m.

9.4 Extensions of the Power Method

Given the matrix A, let $R_\mu = (A - \mu I)^{-1}$ denote the *resolvent* operator of A. Let $\mathbf{e}_k$ be an eigenvector of A for eigenvalue λ_k, then

$$(A - \mu I)\mathbf{e}_k = \lambda_k \mathbf{e}_k - \mu \mathbf{e}_k = (\lambda_k - \mu)\mathbf{e}_k.$$

Apply R_μ and $(\lambda_k - \mu)^{-1}$ to both sides of this equation, we have

$$(\lambda_k - \mu)^{-1}\mathbf{e}_k = (A - \mu I)^{-1}\mathbf{e}_k.$$

Therefore the eigenvalues of R_μ are the complex numbers $(\lambda_k - \mu)^{-1}$ for each eigenvalue λ_k of A for the same eigenvector. By choosing μ near enough to λ_k, the power method can be extended to compute an arbitrary eigenvalue, $(\lambda_k - \mu)^{-1}$ and corresponding eigenvector $\mathbf{e}_k$. If λ_k is complex, complex arithmetic may have to be used in the computation.

Example. The matrix

$$A = \begin{bmatrix} 0 & 2 & 1 & 0 & 0 \\ -2 & 0 & 0 & 1 & 0 \\ 0 & 0 & 0 & 2 & 0 \\ 0 & 0 & -2 & 0 & 0 \\ 0 & 0 & 0 & 0 & 1 \end{bmatrix}$$

has the complex eigenvalues $\pm 2i$ with algebraic multiplicity 2 and the real eigenvalue 1. However $2i$ has only the eigenvector $\mathbf{e}_1 = [1 \ \ i \ \ 0 \ \ 0 \ \ 0]^T$ and the generalized eigenvector $\mathbf{f}_1 = [1 \ \ i \ \ 1 \ \ i \ \ 0]^T$. Similarly $\mathbf{e}_2 = [i \ \ 1 \ \ 0 \ \ 0 \ \ 0]^T$ is an eigenvector for $-2i$ and $\mathbf{f}_2 = [i \ \ 1 \ \ i \ \ 1 \ \ 0]^T$ is the corresponding generalized eigenvector. Of course, $\mathbf{e}_3 = [0 \ \ 0 \ \ 0 \ \ 0 \ \ 1]^T$ is an eigenvector for $\lambda_3 = 1$. The power method performed on $R_i = (A - iI)^{-1}$ with the starting vector

$$\begin{bmatrix} 2 \\ 0 \\ 1 \\ 0 \\ 1 \end{bmatrix} = \frac{1}{2}\mathbf{e}_1 + \frac{1}{2}\mathbf{f}_1 + \frac{-i}{2}\mathbf{e}_2 + \frac{-i}{2}\mathbf{f}_2 + \mathbf{e}_3,$$

should converge to a multiple of $\mathbf{e}_1$ since $\lambda_1 = 2i$ is closest to i. Indeed, after 30 iterations we find the approximate eigenvector is

$$[-.705 + .046i \quad -.046 - .705i \quad .023i \quad -.023 \quad 0]^T.$$

The eigenvalue approximation is

$$(\lambda_1 - i)^{-1} = .002 - 1.033i \quad \text{giving} \quad \lambda_1 = .0012 + 1.9681i$$

gotten by dividing the first component of $R_i\mathbf{x}$ by the first component of $\mathbf{x}$.

Note that although

$$(A - \mu I)^{-1}\mathbf{e}_1 = (\lambda_1 - \mu)^{-1}\mathbf{e}_1 \tag{57}$$

for the eigenvector $\mathbf{e}_1$, the mapping of generalized eigenvectors is more complicated. Suppose $\mathbf{f}$ is a generalized eigenvector for λ_1, thus $A\mathbf{f} = \mathbf{e}_1 + \lambda_1\mathbf{f}$ and so

$$(A - \mu I)\mathbf{f} = \mathbf{e}_1 + (\lambda_1 - \mu)\mathbf{f}.$$

Apply $(A - \mu I)^{-1}$ and divide by $(\lambda_1 - \mu)$,

$$(\lambda_1 - \mu)^{-1}\mathbf{f} = (\lambda_1 - \mu)^{-1}(A - \mu I)^{-1}\mathbf{e}_1 + (A - \mu I)^{-1}\mathbf{f}.$$

Take account of (57),

$$(\lambda_1 - \mu)^{-1}\mathbf{f} = (\lambda_1 - \mu)^{-2}\mathbf{e}_1 + (A - \mu I)^{-1}\mathbf{f}.$$

Therefore

$$(A - \mu I)^{-1}\mathbf{f} = -(\lambda_1 - \mu)^{-2}\mathbf{e}_1 + (\lambda_1 - \mu)^{-1}\mathbf{f}.$$

9.5 Parallelization of the Power Method

Of course one can parallelize the matrix vector product at the heart of the power method by methods we have discussed in Chapter 4 and proceed directly as above. However, given a large number of processors, there is another possibility.

Suppose A is a full (nonsparse) $n \times n$ matrix and we aim to carry the power method through k steps. Also suppose we have $O(n^3)$ processors available. From the calculations of Section 4.3, the direct method of forming k multiplications of $\mathbf{x}$ by A, this gives $A^k\mathbf{x}$, requires $O(k \log n)$ time. (This uses only n^2 processors.) On the other hand, squaring A $\log k$ times (assume k is a power of 2) gives A^k and takes $O(\log k \log n)$ time. The final matrix–vector multiply, $A^k\mathbf{x}$, is another $\log n$ calculation, so altogether the time is $O((1 + \log k) \log n)$. If only n^2 processors are available, the time becomes $O((1 + \log k)n)$ versus $O(k \log n)$ for the direct method.

For example, if $n = 32$, $n^3 = 32{,}768$ and $2^4 = 16$ power method iterations take $16 \log 32 = 80$ units of time directly or $4 \log 32 = 20$ units of time via squaring.

As can be seen, the squaring approach is advantageous only in the very special circumstance that the matrix is not sparse (squaring destroys sparsity), that n is relatively small and k is relatively large.

9.6 The QR Method for Eigenvalues

Suppose that a sequence of Givens rotations (see Section 7.2) is carried out using the rotation matrices M_k, $k = 2, \ldots, n$, reducing the $n \times n$ matrix A to right-triangular form, R,

$$R = M_n M_{n-1} \ldots M_2 A. \tag{58}$$

Recall a rotation matrix has the form

$$M = \begin{bmatrix} 1 & 0 & \cdots & 0 & \cdots & 0 & \cdots & 0 \\ 0 & 1 & \cdots & 0 & \cdots & 0 & \cdots & 0 \\ \vdots & \vdots & \vdots & \vdots & \vdots & \vdots & \vdots & \vdots \\ 0 & 0 & \cdots & \cos\theta & \cdots & \sin\theta & \cdots & 0 \\ \vdots & \vdots & \vdots & \vdots & \vdots & \vdots & \vdots & \vdots \\ 0 & 0 & \cdots & -\sin\theta & \cdots & \cos\theta & \cdots & 0 \\ \vdots & \vdots & \vdots & \vdots & \vdots & \vdots & \vdots & \vdots \\ 0 & 0 & \cdots & 0 & \cdots & 0 & \cdots & 1 \end{bmatrix},$$

where $m_{ii} = m_{jj} = \cos\theta$ and $m_{ij} = -m_{ji} = \sin\theta$. Also recall that M is an orthogonal matrix so $M^{-1} = M^T$. Let Q transpose be the product of these rotation matrices

$$Q^T = M_n M_{n-1} \ldots M_2,$$

then

$$Q = M_2^T \ldots M_{n-1}^T M_n^T, \tag{59}$$

and we can write A as the product

$$A = QR.$$

This decomposition of A into the product of an orthogonal times an upper-triangular matrix, the *QR decomposition* of A, may be used for the computation of the eigenvalues of A.

The computation is affected by an iteration scheme aimed at diagonalizing A by performing successive QR decompositions. Put $A_1 = A$, and define the sequence of matrices A_m, Q_m, and R_m by

$$A_m = Q_m R_m \qquad A_{m+1} = R_m Q_m, \quad m = 1, 2, \ldots.$$

Since $R_m = Q_m^T A_m$, we have

$$A_{m+1} = \left(Q_m^T A_m \right) Q_m,$$

showing that A_{m+1} is similar to A_m, for all m. Therefore all A_m have the same eigenvalues, the eigenvalues of A.

In the following we let R hold the updated value of A. The QR diagonalization algorithm is

QR Algorithm

```
R=A
loop
    Q ← I
    loop k=2,...
        // calc. plane rotation Mk annihilating the next
term
        R ← MkR
        Q ← QMk^T
    end loop
    R ← RQ
    // check convergence
end loop
```

Example.

$$A = \begin{bmatrix} 2 & 1 & -1 & 1 \\ 2 & 3 & 1 & -2 \\ 0 & 0 & 4 & 2 \\ 0 & 0 & -1 & 1 \end{bmatrix}.$$

$$M_2 = \begin{bmatrix} c & -s & 0 & 0 \\ s & c & 0 & 0 \\ 0 & 0 & 1 & 0 \\ 0 & 0 & 0 & 1 \end{bmatrix},$$

and

$$M_2 A = \begin{bmatrix} 2c - 2s & c - 3s & -c - s & c + 2s \\ 2s + 2c & s + 3c & -s + c & s - 2c \\ 0 & 0 & 4 & 2 \\ 0 & 0 & -1 & 1 \end{bmatrix}.$$

Take

$$c = \frac{2}{\sqrt{2^2 + 2^2}}, \quad s = \frac{-2}{\sqrt{2^2 + 2^2}} = \frac{-1}{\sqrt{2}}.$$

Then

$$M_2 A = \begin{bmatrix} \frac{4}{\sqrt{2}} & \frac{4}{\sqrt{2}} & 0 & \frac{-1}{\sqrt{2}} \\ 0 & \frac{2}{\sqrt{2}} & \frac{2}{\sqrt{2}} & \frac{-3}{\sqrt{2}} \\ 0 & 0 & 4 & 2 \\ 0 & 0 & -1 & 1 \end{bmatrix}.$$

Next, $M_3 = I$ since the 2, 1 term is already 0, and

$$M_4 = \begin{bmatrix} 1 & 0 & 0 & 0 \\ 0 & 1 & 0 & 0 \\ 0 & 0 & c & -s \\ 0 & 0 & s & c \end{bmatrix}.$$

Then

$$M_4(M_3 M_2 A) = \begin{bmatrix} \frac{4}{\sqrt{2}} & \frac{4}{\sqrt{2}} & 0 & \frac{-1}{\sqrt{2}} \\ 0 & \frac{2}{\sqrt{2}} & \frac{2}{\sqrt{2}} & \frac{-3}{\sqrt{2}} \\ 0 & 0 & 4c + s & 2c - s \\ 0 & 0 & 4s - c & 2s + c \end{bmatrix}.$$

Take

$$c = \frac{4}{\sqrt{1^2 + 4^2}} = \frac{4}{\sqrt{17}}, \quad s = \frac{1}{\sqrt{17}}.$$

Then

$$R_1 = M_4(M_3 M_2 A) = \begin{bmatrix} \frac{4}{\sqrt{2}} & \frac{4}{\sqrt{2}} & 0 & \frac{-1}{\sqrt{2}} \\ 0 & \frac{2}{\sqrt{2}} & \frac{2}{\sqrt{2}} & \frac{-3}{\sqrt{2}} \\ 0 & 0 & \frac{17}{\sqrt{17}} & \frac{7}{\sqrt{17}} \\ 0 & 0 & 0 & \frac{6}{\sqrt{17}} \end{bmatrix}.$$

Now

$$Q_1 = M_2^T M_3^T M_4^T = \begin{bmatrix} \frac{1}{\sqrt{2}} & \frac{-1}{\sqrt{2}} & 0 & 0 \\ \frac{1}{\sqrt{2}} & \frac{1}{\sqrt{2}} & 0 & 0 \\ 0 & 0 & \frac{4}{\sqrt{17}} & \frac{1}{\sqrt{17}} \\ 0 & 0 & \frac{-1}{\sqrt{17}} & \frac{4}{\sqrt{17}} \end{bmatrix}.$$

Therefore

$$A_2 = R_1 Q_1 = \begin{bmatrix} 4 & 0 & \frac{1}{\sqrt{34}} & \frac{-4}{\sqrt{34}} \\ 1 & 1 & \frac{11}{\sqrt{34}} & \frac{-10}{\sqrt{34}} \\ 0 & 0 & \frac{61}{17} & \frac{45}{17} \\ 0 & 0 & \frac{-6}{17} & \frac{24}{17} \end{bmatrix}.$$

In the limit

$$A_\infty = \begin{bmatrix} 4 & -1 & 1 & -1 \\ 0 & 1 & 2 & -1 \\ 0 & 0 & 3 & 3 \\ 0 & 0 & 0 & 2 \end{bmatrix}$$

in this case.

Convergence Properties of the QR Method

Theorem 1. *Let A be a real matrix of order n, and let its eigenvalues λ_i satisfy*

$$|\lambda_1| > |\lambda_2| > \ldots > |\lambda_n| > 0. \tag{60}$$

Then the iterates A_m of the QR method converge to an upper-triangular matrix R, which contains the eigenvalues on the diagonal. If A is symmetric, the sequence $\{A_m\}$ converges to a diagonal matrix D. The speed of convergence is given by

$$\|R - A_m\| \leq c \max_i \left| \frac{\lambda_{i+1}}{\lambda_i} \right| \tag{61}$$

for some constant c.

For a proof, see [14]. Since A is real and the eigenvalues form a strictly decreasing sequence, the eigenvalues must all be real. When condition (60) is not satisfied, the situation is more complicated.

For example, if

$$A = \begin{bmatrix} 0 & 1 \\ 1 & 0 \end{bmatrix}$$

then (among other solutions)

$$Q_1 = \begin{bmatrix} 0 & -1 \\ 1 & 0 \end{bmatrix}, \quad R_1 = \begin{bmatrix} 1 & 0 \\ 0 & -1 \end{bmatrix}, \quad \text{and} \quad A_2 = R_1 Q_1 = -A.$$

Another iteration returns A.

But in the case that A is symmetric, the sequence A_m converges to a block diagonal matrix

$$A_m \to D = \begin{bmatrix} B_1 & 0 & \cdots & 0 \\ 0 & B_2 & \cdots & 0 \\ & & \ddots & \\ 0 & 0 & \cdots & B_r \end{bmatrix},$$

where all blocks B_i have order 1 or 2. A block upper-triangular matrix with diagonal blocks having order 1 or 2 is *quasitriangular*. It is a simple matter to obtain the eigenvalues of the B_i.

From Theorem 1 we see that convergence is only linear. There are 2 ways to improve it. The first is to precede the QR iteration by a sequence of Householder reflections which more quickly nulls entries below the subdiagonal, and the second is to use shifts. These strategies may be combined.

9.7 Householder Transformations

Let w be an n-dimensional unit vector; then $(x \cdot w)w$ is the orthogonal projection of x onto the direction of w. Therefore $x - 2(x \cdot w)w$ is the reflection of x in a hyperplane perpendicular to w. Define U by $Ux = x - 2(x \cdot w)w$. Equivalently we may write this as

$$Ux = x - 2ww^*x,$$

where w^* is the conjugate transpose of w (see the Exercises). The matrix product wv^* is an $n \times 1$ column vector times a $1 \times n$ row vector and so is an $n \times n$ matrix. This operation is called the *outer product* of the 2 vectors. Hence the linear transformation U is given by

$$U = I - 2ww^*$$

and represents a reflection in the hyperplane perpendicular to w.

A reflection U is a unitary transformation because $U^* = U^{-1}$ and

$$\begin{aligned} U^*U &= I - 2ww^* - 2ww^* + 4ww^*ww^* \\ &= I - 4ww^* + 4ww^* = I \end{aligned}$$

since w is a unit vector (so $w^*w = 1$).

Now suppose w has its first r components equal to 0 and let $\hat{w} = [\, w_{r+1} \quad \ldots \quad w_n \,]^T$ denote the vector consisting of the last $n - r$ components of w. Then in block matrix form

$$U = \begin{bmatrix} I_r & 0 \\ 0 & I_{n-r} - 2\hat{w}\hat{w}^* \end{bmatrix}. \tag{62}$$

Hence for an $n \times n$ matrix A, UA leaves the first r rows of A invariant; that is, in block matrix form (let $U_4 = I_{n-r} - 2\hat{w}\hat{w}^*$) we have

$$UA = \begin{bmatrix} I_r & 0 \\ 0 & U_4 \end{bmatrix} \begin{bmatrix} A_1 & A_2 \\ A_3 & A_4 \end{bmatrix} = \begin{bmatrix} I_r A_1 & I_r A_2 \\ U_4 A_3 & U_4 A_4 \end{bmatrix}.$$

Similarly AU leaves the first r columns invariant

$$AU = \begin{bmatrix} A_1 & A_2 \\ A_3 & A_4 \end{bmatrix} \begin{bmatrix} I_r & 0 \\ 0 & U_4 \end{bmatrix} = \begin{bmatrix} A_1 I_r & A_2 U_4 \\ A_3 I_r & A_4 U_4 \end{bmatrix}.$$

Given a vector b and $1 \le r \le n - 1$, we show how to find a reflection which zeros out components $r + 1$ through n of b. This is called a *Householder reflection*. Partition b into its first $r - 1$ components, b' and its last $n - r + 1$ components $\hat{b} = [\, b_r \quad \ldots \quad b_n \,]^T$. Likewise take the first $r - 1$ components of w to be 0 and let $\hat{w}$ denote the last $n - r + 1$ components of w. As above

$$Ub = \begin{bmatrix} I_{r-1} & 0 \\ 0 & I_{n-r+1} - 2\hat{w}\hat{w}^* \end{bmatrix} \begin{bmatrix} b' \\ \hat{b} \end{bmatrix} = \begin{bmatrix} b' \\ (I_{n-r+1} - 2\hat{w}\hat{w}^*)\hat{b} \end{bmatrix}.$$

We see that b' is left invariant; we want, for some β,

$$(I_{n-r+1} - 2\hat{w}\hat{w}^*)\hat{b} = \begin{bmatrix} \beta \\ 0 \\ \vdots \\ 0 \end{bmatrix}.$$

In components this is

$$
\begin{bmatrix} b_r \\ b_{r+1} \\ \vdots \\ b_n \end{bmatrix} - 2(\hat{\mathbf{w}} \cdot \hat{\mathbf{b}})\hat{\mathbf{w}} = \begin{bmatrix} \beta \\ 0 \\ \vdots \\ 0 \end{bmatrix}. \tag{63}
$$

Since a reflection is an isometry (in the ℓ_2 norm), we must have

$$
|\beta| = \|\hat{\mathbf{b}}\|_2 = \sqrt{b_r^2 + \cdots + b_n^2}. \tag{64}
$$

Next, dot product both sides of (63) with $\hat{\mathbf{w}}$ recalling that $\hat{\mathbf{w}} \cdot \hat{\mathbf{w}} = 1$, we get

$$
\hat{\mathbf{w}} \cdot \hat{\mathbf{b}} - 2\hat{\mathbf{w}} \cdot \hat{\mathbf{b}} = \hat{\mathbf{w}} \cdot \begin{bmatrix} \beta \\ 0 \\ \vdots \\ 0 \end{bmatrix} = \beta w_r.
$$

This gives

$$
\hat{\mathbf{w}} \cdot \hat{\mathbf{b}} = -\beta w_r. \tag{65}
$$

Substituting this into the first component of (63) gives,

$$
b_r + 2\beta w_r^2 = \beta \quad \text{or} \quad w_r^2 = \frac{1}{2}\left(1 - \frac{b_r}{\beta}\right). \tag{66}
$$

Taking the square root (choosing either sign) gives w_r. To avoid numerical error and division by zero, choose the sign of β to be the negative of that of b_r so that the parenthetical term is positive and maximal,

$$
\text{sign}(\beta) = -\text{sign}(b_r). \tag{67}
$$

Together with (64) this determines β and w_r.

Write the remaining components of (63),

$$
b_j + 2(\beta w_r)w_j = 0, \quad j = r+1, \ldots, n,
$$

and solve for w_j,

$$
w_j = \frac{-b_j}{2\beta w_r}, \quad j = r+1, \ldots, n. \tag{68}
$$

We illustrate all this with an example.

Example. Find a reflection transforming $\mathbf{b} = [3 \quad 4 \quad 12]^T$ into $[\beta \quad 0 \quad 0]^T$. For the solution, $r = 1$ here and from (64) and (67) we have

$$
\beta = -\text{sign}(3)\sqrt{3^2 + 4^2 + 12^2} = -13.
$$

Then from (66)

$$w_1^2 = \frac{1}{2}\left(1 + \frac{3}{13}\right) = \frac{8}{13},$$

$$w_1 = \sqrt{\frac{8}{13}}.$$

And from (68),

$$w_2 = \frac{-b_2}{\beta w_1} = \sqrt{\frac{1}{26}}$$

$$w_3 = \frac{-b_3}{\beta w_1} = \sqrt{\frac{9}{26}}$$

Hence

$$(I - 2ww^*)\mathbf{b} = \begin{bmatrix} \frac{-3}{13} & \frac{-4}{13} & \frac{-12}{13} \\ \frac{-4}{13} & \frac{12}{13} & \frac{-3}{13} \\ \frac{-12}{13} & \frac{-3}{13} & \frac{4}{13} \end{bmatrix} \begin{bmatrix} 3 \\ 4 \\ 12 \end{bmatrix} = \begin{bmatrix} -13 \\ 0 \\ 0 \end{bmatrix}.$$

QR Via Reflections

The construction derived above culminating in the reflection Eqs. (64), (67), and (68) allows for an alternate method for the QR decomposition of a matrix. Let U_1 be the reflection that nulls out elements 2 through n of the first column of the matrix A, then

$$A_1 = U_1 A = \begin{bmatrix} a'_{11} & a'_{12} & \cdots & a'_{1n} \\ 0 & a'_{22} & \cdots & a'_{2n} \\ \vdots & \vdots & \cdots & \vdots \\ 0 & a'_{n2} & \cdots & a'_{nn} \end{bmatrix}.$$

Next let U_2 be the reflection (perpendicular to w_2) nulling elements 3 through n of the second column of A_1. Then $U_2 A_1$ leaves the first column of A_1 invariant because, since the first component of w_2 is 0, both the first column and the first row of U_2 are 0 except for the u_{11} element, which is 1, see (62). The first column of the product $U_2 A_1$ is just U_2 applied to the first column of A_1 and this in turn just a'_{11} times the first column of U_2. Therefore

$$A_2 = U_2 A_1$$

has its lower-triangular part nulled for its first two columns.

Continue in this way nulling the lower-triangular part of the remaining columns to arrive at the upper-triangular matrix R. Hence

$$R = U_{n-1} \ldots U_1 A = Q^T A \quad \text{or} \quad A = QR,$$

where $Q^T = U_{n-1} \ldots U_1$.

Example. Let

$$A = \begin{bmatrix} 3 & 2 & 2 & 1 \\ 4 & 1 & 1 & -2 \\ 0 & 0 & 4 & 5 \\ 0 & 0 & 3 & 2 \end{bmatrix}.$$

Using Eqs. (64), (67), and (68), we find that

$$\beta = -5, \quad w_1 = \frac{2}{\sqrt{5}}, \quad w_2 = \frac{1}{\sqrt{5}}, \quad w_3 = w_4 = 0.$$

Hence

$$A_1 = \left(I - 2ww^*\right) A = \begin{bmatrix} \frac{-3}{5} & \frac{-4}{5} & 0 & 0 \\ \frac{-4}{5} & \frac{3}{5} & 0 & 0 \\ 0 & 0 & 1 & 0 \\ 0 & 0 & 0 & 1 \end{bmatrix} \begin{bmatrix} 3 & 2 & 2 & 1 \\ 4 & 1 & 1 & -2 \\ 0 & 0 & 4 & 5 \\ 0 & 0 & 3 & 2 \end{bmatrix}$$

$$= \begin{bmatrix} -5 & -2 & -2 & 1 \\ 0 & -1 & -1 & -2 \\ 0 & 0 & 4 & 5 \\ 0 & 0 & 3 & 2 \end{bmatrix}.$$

Continuing with U_2, U_3, and U_4 to null the subdiagonal terms of columns 2, 3, and 4 respectively, we arrive at

$$R = \begin{bmatrix} -5 & -2 & -2 & 1 \\ 0 & 1 & 1 & 2 \\ 0 & 0 & -5 & \frac{-26}{5} \\ 0 & 0 & 0 & \frac{-7}{5} \end{bmatrix}.$$

Note that although the 3,2 and 4,2 terms of A_1 are already 0, obviating the need for U_2, we used the reflection equations nonetheless; in this way we got

$$U_2 = \begin{bmatrix} 1 & 0 & 0 & 0 \\ 0 & -1 & 0 & 0 \\ 0 & 0 & 1 & 0 \\ 0 & 0 & 0 & 1 \end{bmatrix}.$$

9.8 Hessenberg Form

An *upper Hessenberg* matrix H is one for which $h_{ij} = 0$ if $j < i - 1$. Therefore an upper Hessenberg matrix is an triangular matrix whose first subdiagonal may also be nonzero.

Evidently we can use Householder reflections to convert a matrix A to Hessenberg form, but even more is possible. We can do this and maintain the eigenvalues of A, thus H is similar to A.

To see how, let U_2 be the Householder reflection that nulls elements 3 through n of the first column of A and put $H_2 = U_2 A U_2$ (recall $U_2^* = U_2$). Because the first row and column elements of U_2 are all zero except that the 1,1 element is 1, multiplying $U_2 A$ on the right by U_2 leaves the first column invariant (see (62)). Hence

$$H_2 = U_2 A U_2 = \begin{bmatrix} a'_{11} & a'_{12} & \cdots & a'_{1n} \\ a'_{21} & a'_{22} & \cdots & a'_{2n} \\ 0 & a'_{32} & \cdots & a'_{3n} \\ \vdots & \vdots & \cdots & \vdots \\ 0 & a'_{n2} & \cdots & a'_{nn} \end{bmatrix}.$$

Continue in this way. Given H_k, let U_{k+1} be the Householder reflection nulling its elements $k + 2$ through n in column k, and put $H_{k+1} = U_{k+1} H_k U_{k+1}$, for $k = 3, \ldots, n - 1$.

Example. Let

$$A = \begin{bmatrix} 4 & 1 & 2 & 2 \\ 1 & 3 & -1 & 2 \\ 2 & -1 & -1 & 0 \\ 2 & 2 & 0 & 6 \end{bmatrix}.$$

To zero the last two components of the first column, we calculate

$$\beta = -3, \quad w_1 = 0, \quad w_2 = \sqrt{\frac{2}{3}}, \quad w_3 = w_4 = \sqrt{\frac{1}{6}}.$$

And

$$H_2 = (I - 2\mathbf{w}\mathbf{w}^*) A (I - 2\mathbf{w}\mathbf{w}^*) = \begin{bmatrix} 4 & -3 & 0 & 0 \\ -3 & 3 & \frac{10}{3} & \frac{-7}{3} \\ 0 & \frac{10}{3} & \frac{10}{3} & 0 \\ 0 & \frac{-7}{3} & 0 & \frac{5}{3} \end{bmatrix}.$$

For the second column we calculate

$$\beta = \frac{-1}{3}\sqrt{149}, \quad w_1 = w_2 = 0, \quad w_3 = \sqrt{\frac{1}{2} + \frac{5}{\sqrt{149}}}, \quad w_4 = \frac{-7/3}{w_3\sqrt{149}}.$$

And so

$$H_3 = (I - 2ww^*)H_2(I - 2ww^*) = \begin{bmatrix} 4 & -3 & 0 & 0 \\ -3 & 3 & \frac{-1}{3}\sqrt{149} & 0 \\ 0 & \frac{-1}{3}\sqrt{149} & \frac{415}{149} & \frac{-350}{447} \\ 0 & 0 & \frac{-350}{447} & 2.2148 \end{bmatrix}.$$

Householder Reflections for Eigenvalues

Because Householder reduction to Hessenberg form nulls the elements below the subdiagonal in exactly $n - 2$ steps, it is the preferred starting point for the QR algorithm for eigenvalues (see Section 9.6). Furthermore, as seen in the last Example, if A is a symmetric matrix to start with, then the Hessenberg form will be tridiagonal.

Example. Continuing with the last example, we apply QR to the matrix

$$H_3 = \begin{bmatrix} 4 & -3 & 0 & 0 \\ -3 & 3 & -4.06885 & 0 \\ 0 & -4.06885 & 2.78523 & -.78300 \\ 0 & 0 & -.78300 & 2.21477 \end{bmatrix}.$$

After a large number of iterations, one gets

$$A \rightarrow \begin{bmatrix} 8.2282 & 0 & 0 & 0 \\ 0 & 3.7122 & 0 & -0 \\ 0 & 0 & 2.0930 & 0 \\ 0 & 0 & 0 & -2.0335 \end{bmatrix}.$$

Exercises

1. (4) Show that the characteristic polynomial of the companion matrix (46) is the monic polynomical (45).

2. (6) Suppose the Jordan matrix J for a linear transformation is

$$J = \begin{bmatrix} \mu & 1 & 0 & 0 & 0 \\ 0 & \mu & 0 & 0 & 0 \\ 0 & 0 & \lambda & 1 & 0 \\ 0 & 0 & 0 & \lambda & 1 \\ 0 & 0 & 0 & 0 & \lambda \end{bmatrix}$$

in the basis $\mathbf{e}'$, $\mathbf{f}'$ $\mathbf{e}$, $\mathbf{f}_1$, $\mathbf{f}_2$. Find a basis for which the matrix of the transformation is

$$J = \begin{bmatrix} \mu & \epsilon & 0 & 0 & 0 \\ 0 & \mu & 0 & 0 & 0 \\ 0 & 0 & \lambda & \epsilon & 0 \\ 0 & 0 & 0 & \lambda & \epsilon \\ 0 & 0 & 0 & 0 & \lambda \end{bmatrix}.$$

3. (5) For the following matrices $A(\epsilon)$, determine the eigenvalues and eigenvectors for both $\epsilon = 0$ and $\epsilon > 0$. What happens in each case as $\epsilon \to 0$?

$(a) \begin{bmatrix} 1 & 1 \\ \epsilon & 1 \end{bmatrix}$ $(b) \begin{bmatrix} 1 & 1 \\ 0 & 1+\epsilon \end{bmatrix}$ $(c) \begin{bmatrix} 1 & \epsilon \\ 0 & 1 \end{bmatrix}$ $(c) \begin{bmatrix} 1 & 1 & 0 \\ 0 & 1 & \epsilon \\ 0 & \epsilon & 1 \end{bmatrix}.$

4. (3) For (column) vectors $\mathbf{w}$ and $\mathbf{x}$ show that

$$(\mathbf{x} \cdot \mathbf{w})\mathbf{w} = \left(\mathbf{w}\mathbf{w}^*\right)\mathbf{x}.$$

(Recall that $\mathbf{w}^*$ means conjugate transpose, and for complex vectors, $\mathbf{x} \cdot \mathbf{w} = \mathbf{w}^*\mathbf{x}$.)

Programming Exercises

5. (5) Use the power method to calculate the largest eigenvalue and an associated eigenvector of the matrix

$$A = \begin{bmatrix} 1 & 2 & 5 & 3 & 6 & 1 \\ 2 & 6 & 1 & 0 & 1 & 3 \\ 5 & 2 & 3 & 1 & 1 & 0 \\ 0 & 6 & 1 & 1 & 5 & 3 \\ 3 & 0 & 6 & 5 & 1 & 2 \\ 1 & 1 & 0 & 3 & 5 & 6 \end{bmatrix}.$$

What is the rate of convergence?

6. (6) Do a repeated QR diagonalization of the 6×6 Hilbert matrix. Determine whether the procedure converges to a diagonal matrix.

7. (5) Find the roots of the polynomial

$$x^7 - 4x^6 - 14x^5 + 56x^4 + 49x^3 - 196x^2 - 36x + 144$$

via the eigenvalues of the companion matrix.

8. (6) Use Householder transformations to reduce the matrix

$$A = \begin{bmatrix} 1 & 2 & 5 & 3 & 6 & 1 \\ 2 & 6 & 1 & 0 & 1 & 3 \\ 5 & 2 & 3 & 1 & 1 & 0 \\ 0 & 6 & 1 & 1 & 5 & 3 \\ 3 & 0 & 6 & 5 & 1 & 2 \\ 1 & 1 & 0 & 3 & 5 & 6 \end{bmatrix}$$

to Hessenberg form.

PART III
Monte Carlo Methods

10

Monte Carlo Simulation

The Monte Carlo method is a means for solving problems in science, engineering, economics, finance, computer science, mathematics, and other areas by techniques using random numbers in an essential way.

The Monte Carlo method and parallel computation are an excellent match because a Monte Carlo algorithm typically requires a great deal of computational cycles but very little communication or synchronization between processes supplying the cycles.

In this chapter and the next we discuss two important applications of the Monte Carlo method: simulation and optimization. Simulation is playing out on the computer, events that take place in reality; in this case, events involving elements of stochasticity. Of course, the computer rendition is abstract and must be numerically identified with the real events. Some examples are in queuing systems such as airplane arrivals and departures at major airports, statistical physics, financial market scenarios, military strategies, engineering studies, and games of all sorts. In this chapter we derive methods for evaluating integrals, especially in high-dimensional Euclidean space, from the simple game played by Georges Buffon of tossing a needle onto a lined floor and observing whether or not it lands on a crack.

10.1 Quadrature (Numerical Integration)

Consider the problem of evaluating the integral

$$\theta = \int \int \cdots \int_D g(x_1, x_2, \ldots, x_d)\, dx_1 dx_2 \ldots dx_d$$

over a region D in d-dimensional Euclidean space. For anything but very simple regions this can be difficult to calculate because of the "curse of dimension" (see [15]). Consequently, one of the very first original applications of digital computation was solving such problems in the following random or "Monte Carlo" way. Enclose the region D in an d-dimensional parallelepiped of volume V, say, and then select points from the box randomly. Out of n such points, suppose the number that falls inside D is K, then the estimate of the integral relative to V is taken as K/n, that is,

$$\frac{\theta}{V} = \frac{K}{n}.$$

This is called the *hit-or-miss method*.

For the following analysis we confine ourselves to one dimension. Let g be a nonnegative real valued function defined over the interval $D = [a, b]$. Assume we want to estimate

$$\int_a^b g(x)\,dx, \quad \text{where} \quad g(x) \geq 0,$$

which is the area under g between a and b. Let M be an upper bound for g, $g(x) \leq M$ for all $x \in D$. Then the "volume" V mentioned above is $V = M(b-a)$.

Let X and Y be values selected uniformly at random in $[a, b]$ and $[0, M]$ respectively so that the ordered pair (X, Y) is a uniformly distributed random point over the rectangle. Its probability density function is the uniform distribution

$$U(x, y) = 1/V, \quad a \leq x \leq b \quad 0 \leq y \leq M,$$

in the rectangle and 0 elsewhere. Now let the random variable H, or *hit*, be defined as

$$H = \begin{cases} 1, & \text{if } Y \leq g(X) \\ 0, & \text{otherwise} \end{cases}.$$

Our estimate $\hat{\theta}$ for the integral θ after n trials is

$$\hat{\theta} = \frac{V}{n} \sum_{i=1}^n H = V\frac{\text{\# of hits}}{\text{\# of trials}}.$$

The expectation $E(H)$ of H is

$$E(H) = \int\int_{[a,b]\times[0,M]} HU(x, y)\,dy\,dx$$

$$= \frac{1}{M(b-a)} \int\int_{\text{area under } g} dy\,dx$$

$$= \frac{1}{V} \int_a^b g(x)\,dx.$$

Therefore

$$E(\hat{\theta}) = \frac{V}{n} \sum_{i=1}^{n} E(H) = \int_{a}^{b} g(x) \, dx.$$

The *expected squared error* of such an estimate is given by

$$E((\hat{\theta} - \theta)^2) = E((\hat{\theta} - E(\hat{\theta}))^2$$
$$= \text{var}(\hat{\theta})$$

and is known as the *variance* of $\hat{\theta}$. Owing to the fact that the variance of a sum is equal to the sum of variances, we have

$$\text{var}(\hat{\theta}) = \sum_{i=1}^{n} \text{var} \left(\frac{V}{n} H \right)$$

$$= n \int_{a}^{b} \int_{0}^{M} \left(\frac{V}{n} H - \frac{\theta}{n} \right)^2 U(x, y) \, dy \, dx$$

$$= \frac{n}{n^2} \int_{a}^{b} \int_{0}^{M} [V^2 H^2 - 2\theta V H + \theta^2] U(x, y) \, dy \, dx$$

$$= \frac{1}{n} \left[V^2 \frac{\theta}{V} - 2\theta V \frac{\theta}{V} + \theta^2 \frac{V}{V} \right].$$

So

$$\text{var}(\hat{\theta}) = \frac{\theta}{n} (V - \theta).$$

Since *standard deviation*, equal to the square root of variance, is taken as the error in probabilistic estimates, this shows that the error is $O(n^{-1/2})$. By contrast, deterministic methods are typically $O(n^{-r})$ for $r > 1$, when they are applicable.

Sample Mean Estimator

There is another method, better than hit-or-miss, for estimating $\theta = \int_D g(x) \, dx$. Choose a probability density function (pdf) f, which approximates g and let $\phi(x) = g(x)/f(x)$. The modification allows the treatment of unbounded functions and unbounded intervals (see the Exercises). Rewriting the integral as

$$\theta = \int \phi(x) f(x) \, dx$$

shows that θ is the expectation of ϕ over the density function f,

$$\theta = E(\phi(X)).$$

So let $X_1, X_2, \ldots, X_n$ be samples from f and put

$$\hat{\theta} = \frac{1}{n} \sum_1^n \phi(X_i),$$

the sample mean. Then the expectation $E(\hat{\theta})$ is given by

$$E(\hat{\theta}) = \frac{1}{n} \sum_1^n E(\phi(X_i)) = \frac{1}{n} n \int \phi(x) f(x) \, dx = \theta,$$

and the variance is

$$\mathrm{var}(\hat{\theta}) = \sum_1^n \mathrm{var}\left(\frac{\phi(X_i)}{n}\right) = n \int \left(\frac{\phi(x)}{n} - \frac{\theta}{n}\right)^2 f(x) \, dx$$

$$= \frac{1}{n} \int (\phi(x) - \theta)^2 f(x) \, dx.$$

Thus, as above, the standard deviation error is on the order of $c/\sqrt{n}$ for some constant c. This also shows that the better f approximates g, the smaller the error will be. In the next subsection we exploit this idea further.

Control Variate Modification

Next let h be some function defined on D, whose integral $I = \int_D h(x) \, dx$ is easily worked out. Then the integral of g can be written as

$$\int_D g(x) \, dx = I + \int_D (g(x) - h(x)) \, dx.$$

The idea here is to apply the sample mean estimator technique above to the integrand $g(x) - h(x)$. In this case the expected error is given by

$$E[(\mathrm{error})^2] = \frac{1}{n} \int_D (\phi(x) - \theta)^2 f(x) \, dx.$$

Here $\theta = \int_D (g(x) - h(x)) \, dx$ and $\phi(x) = (g(x) - h(x))/f(x)$. These values are much smaller than those above if $h(x)$ is reasonably close to $g(x)$.

Output Analysis

The normal probability density function is

$$f(x) = \frac{1}{\sigma\sqrt{2\pi}} e^{-\frac{1}{2}\left(\frac{x-\mu}{\sigma}\right)^2}.$$

This density has mean equal to μ and variance equal to σ^2. We denote this distribution by N_{μ,σ^2}.

If X is distributed as N_{μ,σ^2}, then $Y = (X - \mu)/\sigma$ is distributed as $N_{0,1}$.

Central Limit Theorem

Let $X_1, X_2, \ldots, X_n$ be independent random samples from a distribution with mean μ and finite variance σ^2. Then

$$Y = \frac{\sum_{i=1}^{n} X_i - n\mu}{\sqrt{n\sigma^2}}$$

has a limiting distribution as $n \to \infty$ and it is $N_{0,1}$, that is normal with mean 0 and variance 1.

Thus, the random variable Y, which is a scaled average of samples X_i, is normally distributed. We take advantage of this to calculate an error estimate for $\hat{\theta}$.

As above, let $X_1, X_2, \ldots, X_n$ be n observations of the process. Note that the X_i are independent. We divide them into *batches* of size m

$$X_1 \quad \ldots \quad X_m \quad | \quad X_{m+1} \quad \ldots \quad X_{2m} \quad | \quad \ldots \quad | \quad X_{(J-1)m+1} \quad \ldots \quad X_{Jm},$$

where there are $J = n/m$ batches. The batch mean random variables

$$B_j = \frac{1}{m} \sum_{k=(j-1)m+1}^{jm} X_k, \quad j = 1, \ldots, J$$

are assumed to be normally distributed invoking the Central Limit Theorem. Then

$$\bar{B} = \frac{1}{J} \sum_{j=1}^{J} B_j \quad (= \bar{X})$$

is an unbiased estimator $\hat{\theta}$ for θ.

If we knew the variance σ_B^2 of the batch random variables, then we could use the normal distribution itself to make the error estimates as follows. The random variable

$$Y = \frac{\sum_{j=1}^{J} B_j - J\theta}{\sqrt{J\sigma_B^2}} = \frac{\hat{\theta} - \theta}{\sqrt{\sigma_B^2/J}}$$

is $N_{0,1}$ so from the normal distribution table, for example,

$$0.954 = \Pr(-2 < Y < 2) = \Pr\left(-2 < \frac{\hat{\theta} - \theta}{\sqrt{\sigma_B^2/J}} < 2\right)$$

$$= \Pr\left(\frac{-2\sigma_B}{\sqrt{J}} < \hat{\theta} - \theta < \frac{2\sigma_B}{\sqrt{J}}\right).$$

However, since we are using this data to estimate its mean and since we do not know the variance, we must use the student t *statistic* to obtain confidence intervals. The sample variance is

$$s_B^2 = \frac{1}{J-1} \sum_{j=1}^{J} (B_j - \hat{\theta})^2.$$

Thus

$$t = \frac{\hat{\theta} - \theta}{(s_B/\sqrt{J})}$$

is approximately t-distributed with $J-1$ degrees of freedom (DOF). Confidence intervals can be derived from a student-t table.

For example, given α, t_α is defined by

$$\Pr(-t_\alpha < t < t_\alpha) = \alpha.$$

These values t_α can be looked up in a t-table such as that below for $\alpha = 0.95$. Sometimes these tables give cumulative values instead of two-sided values so a conversion is required. Since the t distribution is symmetric, $\Pr(-t_\alpha < t < t_\alpha) = \alpha$ is equivalent to

$$\Pr(t < t_\alpha) = 1 - \frac{1-\alpha}{2} = \frac{1+\alpha}{2}$$

if the table gives cumulative values.

The t distribution, table gives t_β vs DOF
where t_β is defined by $\Pr(t < t_\beta) = \beta$.

$$\beta = 0.95$$

1	2	3	4	5	6	8	10	15	20	30	40	60	120	∞
6.31	2.92	2.35	2.13	2.02	1.94	1.86	1.81	1.75	1.73	1.70	1.68	1.67	1.66	1.65

$$\beta = 0.975$$

1	2	3	4	5	6	8	10	15	20	30	40	60	120	∞
12.71	4.30	3.18	2.78	2.57	2.45	2.31	2.23	2.13	2.09	2.04	2.02	2.00	1.98	1.96

An interesting question is deciding how to divide up the n samples between the number of replication of batches, J, and the number of repetitions per batch m. We want m large enough so normality is achieved and J to be large so the error estimates are small.

Parallelizing Quadrature

From the discussion above, the Monte Carlo algorithm for quadrature, for example, hit-or-miss, consists in

(1) selecting d random numbers within a parallelpiped in d-dimensional space,
(2) evaluating whether or not the resulting point hits the region D repeating (1) and (2) for a given number of trials, then
(3) summing the number of hits, and
(4) issuing the quotient of hits to trials.

As mentioned in the introduction to this chapter, it is trivial to parallelize such an algorithm since the loop has no dependencies. However many fractions of the trials can be performed on independent processors in any architecture since the only synchronization is that each must report its own sum of hits to the "master" for use in items (3) and (4). (The master must sum the hit counts coming from each processor; this is a single node accumulation in the parlance of Chapter 2.)

Example. One of the first to use probabilistic experiment for solving a scientific problem was Georges Louis Leclerc, Comte de Buffon, who, in 1777, proposed estimating π by randomly tossing a needle onto a ruled surface such as a hardwood floor. If the distance between the lines of the surface is twice the needle length, then the experiment is essentially a hit-or-miss estimate of the area under the curve $y = \frac{1}{\pi} \int_0^{\pi/2} \sin\theta \, d\theta = \frac{1}{\pi}$. To illustrate the ideas of this section, we use the following MPI program to estimate this integral (essentially helloWorld.c with a calculation). As written the program uses the known value of π. Of course Buffon did not need to know π in performing the actual experiment. The purpose of our program is not to find π but to demostrate the principle of simulation and we will show how to analyze simulation results. A way to discover the value of π by simulation is given in the Exercises.

(In this program rndm() is a uniform [0, 1) random number generator omitted so as to focus on the main ideas.)

```
1  #include  <stdio.h>
2  #include  "mpi.h"
3  #define  Pi 3.1415926
4  main(int  argc, char ** argv)
5  {
6     int  myrank;  /* id of the process*/
7     int  p;  /* number of processes, via -np flag*/
```

```
8    int  source;  /* rank of sender*/
9    int  dest;  /* rank of receiver*/
10   int  tag = 50;  /* tag for messages*/
11   char  message[100];
12   MPI_Status status;  /* return status for receive*/
13   MPI_Init(&argc, &argv);
14   MPI_Comm_rank(MPI_COMM_WORLD, &myrank); /* get my id*/
15   MPI_Comm_size(MPI_COMM_WORLD, &p);  /* get #procs*/
16   long  n=10000;
17   int  hits,trials;
18   double  x, th;  /* needle distance from crack and
     angle */
19   double  mean=0, stddev=0;
20   int  seed;
21   long  time();
22   seed = getpid()%10000 + (int )(time((long  *) NULL
     )%100000);
23   printf ("host %d, seed= %d\n\n",myrank,seed);
24   rndm(seed);
25   hits = trials = 0;
26   for ( ;  ;  ) {
27     x = rndm(0);
28     th = Pi*rndm(0);
29     if ( x < sin(th) ) ++hits;
30     if ( ++trials >= n ) break;
31   }
32   if ( myrank != 0)
33   {
34     sprintf(
35       message, "Process %d #trials: %d #hits=
       %d",myrank,trials,hits);
36     dest = 0;
37     MPI_Send(
38       message, strlen(message)+1, MPI_char , dest, tag,
       MPI_COMM_WORLD);
39   }
40   else
41   {
42       /* add in the master's contribution */
43     double  piEst=2.0*trials/(double )hits;
44     mean = piEst;  stddev = piEst*piEst;
```

```
45      printf ("process: %d, trials %d, hits %d, pi
        estimate: %ld\n",
46        myrank,trials,hits,piEst);
47        /* get slave contributions */
48      char  tempstr1[30], tempstr2[30], tempstr3[30];
49      int  rRank, rTrials, rHits;
50      for ( source=1;  source<p;  ++source )
51      {
52        MPI_Recv(
53          message,100, MPI_char , source, tag,
            MPI_COMM_WORLD, &status);
54        sscanf (message,"%s%d%s%d%s%d",
55          tempstr1,&rRank,tempstr2,&rTrials,tempstr3,
            &rHits);
56        piEst = 2.0*rTrials/(double )rHits;
57        printf ("process: %d, trials %d, hits %d, pi
          estimate: %ld\n",
58          rRank,rTrials,rHits,piEst);
59        mean += piEst;
60        stddev += piEst*piEst;
61      }
62      mean = mean/p;
63      stddev = stddev/(p-1) - mean*mean;  /* actually
        empirical variance */
64      stddev = sqrt(stddev);
65      printf ("batchMean= %ld, batchStdDev=
        %ld\n",mean,stddev);
66      printf ("trials per batch= %d, #batches= %d, total
        trials= %d\n",
67      n,p,(n*p));
68    }
69    MPI_Finalize();
70  }
71
```

Running this program with thirty-two processors yields the histogram shown in Fig. 37. The corresponding batch mean is 3.147 and the empirical standard deviation is 0.0247. Therefore the t statistic is

$$t = \frac{3.147 - \theta}{0.0247/\sqrt{32}} = \frac{3.147 - \theta}{0.00437}.$$

Histogram of Buffon Hit Or Miss

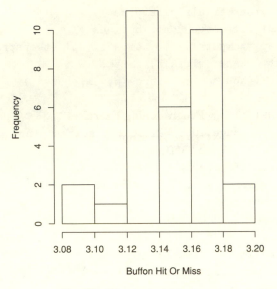

Fig. 37. Hit-or-miss histogram.

Using the t distribution table with $\beta = 0.975$, we have $t_\beta = 2.04$ for 31 degrees of freedom. Since this is a cumulative table, there is $1 - 0.975 = 0.025$ probability above 2.04; and same below -2.04; hence, we can say at the 95% confidence level that

$$-0.0089 = -2.04 * 0.00437 < 3.1467 - \theta < 2.04 * 0.00437 = 0.0089.$$

Exercises

1. (4) Use simulation to estimate the value of π by selecting random points (X, Y) in the square $[-1, 1] \times [-1, 1]$ and noting the number of hits inside the circle $X^2 + Y^2 < 1$.

2. (5) Let f be the (one-dimensional) uniform distribution on the interval $[a, b]$,

$$f(x) = 1/(b - a), \quad \text{if } a \le x \le b \text{ and } 0 \text{ otherwise}.$$

Show that the difference between the hit-or-miss variance and the sample mean variance is

$$\text{var(hit-or-miss)} - \text{var(sample mean)} = \frac{b - a}{n} \int_a^b (M - g(x))\, g(x)\, dx > 0.$$

Hence sample mean is always better.

3. (5) The exponential density is $f(x) = \lambda e^{-\lambda x}$ for $x \geq 0$ with $\lambda > 0$ a parameter. Show how this density can be used to estimate the integral

$$\int_0^\infty x^2 e^{-x}\, dx$$

by the sample mean technique.

Programming Exercises

4. (4) Use the hit-or-miss method to estimate the integral

$$\int_0^1 4\sqrt{1-x^2}\, dx.$$

Try various numbers of trials, for example, $n = 100, 1000, 10000, 100000$. What is the error as function of n?

5. (4) Repeat the problem above but this time use the sample mean method with (a) the uniform density $f(x) = 1$ on $[0, 1]$ and (b) with the density $f(x) = (5 - 4x)/3$, $0 \leq x \leq 1$.

6. (4) Write a program to estimate the integral in Problem 3 above.

11

Monte Carlo Optimization

11.1 Monte Carlo Methods for Optimization

Consider the problem of searching for the extremal values of an objective function f defined on a domain Ω, and equally important, for the points $x \in \Omega$, where these values occur. An extremal value is called an *optimum* (maximum or minimum) while a point where an optimum occurs is called an *optimizer* (maximizer or minimizer).

If the domain is a subset of Euclidean space, we will assume f is differentiable. In this case gradient descent (or ascent) methods are used to locate *local* minima (or maxima). Whether or not a *global extremum* has been found depends upon the starting point of the search. Each local minimum (maximum) has its own basin of attraction and so it becomes a matter of starting in the right basin. Thus there is an element of chance involved if globally extreme values are desired.

On the other hand, we allow the possibility that Ω is a discrete, and possibly large, finite set. In this case downhill/uphill directional information is nonexistent and the search is forced to make due with objective values only. As the search proceeds from one point to the next, selecting the next point to try is often best left to chance.

A search process in which the next point or next starting point to try is randomly determined and may depend on the current location is, mathematically, a finite Markov Chain. Although the full resources of that theory may be brought to bear on the problem, only general assertions will be possible without knowing the nature of the specific objective function. (Consider trying to guess a password as an example search problem.[1]) Although our search may proceed randomly, we assume the objective value is deterministically determined.

---

[1] See Grover's Algorithm in Section 3.7.

A Markov Chain analysis can focus attention on important factors in conducting a stochastic search, such as irreducibility, first passage times, and mixing rates, and can provide the tools for making predictions about the search such as convergence rates and expected run times.

Some strengths of stochastic search methods are that they are often unreasonably effective, they are robust, they are easy to implement (compare branch-and-bound), and they are simply and effectively parallelized. Some weaknesses are that they are computationally intensive and they engender probabilistic convergence assertions.

Of course our primary interest is in finding globally optimal values, but owing to the size of the search space, this is often unattainable in reasonable periods of time. Thus more practically we seek methods that rapidly find acceptably good values. Indeed, it is often the case that knowing whether a given objective value is the optimum or not cannot be answered with certainty.

Knowing whether or not the current point is an optimizer impacts the decision to continue the search, for if the optimum objective value could be recognized as such, the search could be stopped at that point. In general, one may wish to stop the search under a variety of circumstances such as after a fixed time has expired, or when a sufficiently good value has been found, or when the incremental cost of one more iteration becomes too great. This aspect of the problem is known as the *stopping time problem* and is beyond the scope of the present narrative.

Heuristics are used extensively in driving an optimization search and are often derived from processes in nature such as annealing or biological adaptation. In specialized applications, a heuristic can embody insight or particular information about the problem. Heuristics can often be invoked to modify a given solution into a better solution, thereby playing the role of an improvement mechanism.

We will illustrate stochastic search by presenting three different methodologies: random restart and iterated improvement (I2R2) which is based on the heuristic of gradient search mentioned above, simulated annealing (SA) which is based on the heuristic of thermal annealing and known to "find" globally minimal energy states, and genetic algorithms (GA) which is based on the heuristic of biological adaptation. We will demonstrate these methods through their application to two combinatorial optimization problems: the traveling salesman problem (TSP) and the maximum permanent problem (MPP). In addition, we will demonstrate the independent, identical processes (IIP) method of parallelization for stochastic search.

Markov Chain Considerations

Let the states $x \in \Omega$ be ordered in some fashion, $\{x_1, x_2, \ldots, x_N\}$; then subscript i can stand for x_i. The search begins in some state $X_0 \in \Omega$ and proceeds iteratively visiting one state after another. In general, let X_t denote the state of the search on the tth iteration, $t = 0, 1, \ldots$; the X_t are random variables. Furthermore, let

$$\alpha_t = [\, \alpha_1^t \quad \alpha_2^t \quad \ldots \quad \alpha_N^t \,]$$

denote the probability density vector of X_t; that is, α_i^t is the probability the chain is in state x_i on iteration t.

Given that on the present iteration t the chain is currently in state x_i, let $p_{ij}(t)$ denote the probability the next state will be x_j. These probabilities are referred to as the *transition probabilities* of the chain and the matrix they define,

$$P(t) = (p_{ij}(t)), \qquad i = 1, \ldots, N, \quad j = 1, \ldots, N,$$

is the *transition probability matrix*. In general, the transition probabilities could depend on t and if so, the chain is called *inhomogeneous*. If the transition probabilities are constant, the chain is said to be *homogeneous*. In the following we assume the chain is homogeneous.

Retention and Acceleration

If the starting solution is chosen equally likely, then α_0 will be the row vector all of whose components are $1/N$. The successive states of the algorithm are given by the matrix product

$$\alpha_t = \alpha_{t-1} P$$

and hence

$$\alpha_t = \alpha_0 P^t.$$

Suppose that a *goal* for the search is identified. This could be as strict as finding a global optimizer itself or as lenient as finding any x, whose objective value betters some preset value. The goal should translate into some subset $\Gamma \subset \Omega$. In ordering the states of Ω, we agree to list those of the goal first.

The expected hitting time E to Γ can be calculated as follows. Let $\hat{P}$ denote the matrix which results from P when the rows and columns corresponding to the goal are deleted, and let $\hat{\alpha}_t$ denote the vector that remains after deleting the same components from α_t. Then the expected hitting time is given by

$$E = \hat{\alpha}_0 (I - \hat{P})^{-1} \mathbb{1},$$

where $\mathbb{1}$ is the column vector of 1's (of the appropriate size).

This equation may be rewritten as the *Neumann series*

$$E = \hat{\alpha}_0(I + \hat{P} + \hat{P}^2 + \hat{P}^3 + \cdots)\mathbb{1},$$

the terms of which have an important interpretation. The sum $\hat{\alpha}_t \mathbb{1}$ is exactly the probability that the process will still be "retained" in the nongoal states on the tth iteration. Since $\hat{\alpha}_0 \hat{P}^t = \hat{\alpha}_t$, the term

$$chd(t) = \hat{\alpha}_0 \hat{P}^t \mathbb{1}$$

calculates this retention probability. We call the probabilities $chd(\cdot)$ of not yet seeing the goal by the tth iteration the *tail probabilities* or the *complementary hitting distribution*,

$$chd(t) = \Pr(\text{hitting time} > t), \quad t = 0, 1, \ldots. \tag{69}$$

In terms of $chd(\cdot)$,

$$E = \sum_{t=0}^{\infty} chd(t).$$

If now the subchain consisting of the nongoal states is irreducible and aperiodic, virtually always satisfied by these search algorithms, then by the Perron-Frobenius theorem,

$$\hat{P}^t \to \lambda^t \chi \omega \quad \text{as} \quad t \to \infty,$$

where χ is the right and ω the left eigenvectors for the principal eigenvalue λ of $\hat{P}$. The eigenvectors may be normalized so that $\omega \mathbb{1} = 1$ and $\omega \chi = 1$. Therefore asymptotically,

$$chd(t) \to \frac{1}{s}\lambda^t \quad t \to \infty, \tag{70}$$

where $1/s = \hat{\alpha}_0 \chi$.

The left eigenvector ω has the following interpretation. Over the course of many iterations, the part of the process which remains in the nongoal subchain asymptotically tends to the distribution ω. The equation $\omega \hat{P} = \lambda \omega$ shows that λ is the probability that on one iteration, the process remains in the nongoal states.

The right eigenvector χ likewise has an interpretation. Since the limiting matrix is the outer product $\chi \omega$, χ is the vector of row sums of this limiting matrix. Now given any distribution vector $\hat{\alpha}$, its retention under one iteration is $\hat{\alpha} \chi \omega \mathbb{1} = \hat{\alpha} \chi$. Thus χ is the vector of relative retention values. To quickly pass from nongoal to goal states, $\hat{\alpha}$ should favor the components of χ, which are smallest. Moreover, the dot product $\hat{\alpha}\chi$ is the expected retention under the distribution $\hat{\alpha}$ relative to retention, λ, under the limiting distribution.

If it is assumed that the goal can be recognized and the search stopped when attained, then we have the following theorem.

Theorem 1. *The convergence rate of a homogeneous Markov Chain search is geometric, that is,*

$$\lambda^{-t}\Pr(X_t \notin \Gamma) \to \frac{1}{s} \quad as\ t \to \infty, \tag{71}$$

provided that the subchain of nongoal states is irreducible and aperiodic.

On the other hand, if goal states are not always recognized, then we may save the *best* state observed over the course of a run. We define this to be the random variable over the chain which is the first to attain the current extreme value,

$$B_t = X_r, \quad f(X_r) \le f(X_k)\ 1 \le k \le t, \quad r \le k \text{ if } f(X_r) = f(X_k).$$

Then (71) holds for B_t.

Making the asymptotic substitutions for $chd(\cdot)$ in the expression for the expected hitting time, E becomes

$$E \approx \frac{1}{s}(1 + \lambda + \lambda^2 + \cdots)$$

$$= \frac{1}{s}\frac{1}{1 - \lambda},$$

where the infinite series has been summed. We therefore arrive at the result that two scalar parameters govern the convergence of the process, *retention* λ and *acceleration* s. In most applications, λ is just slightly less than 1 and s is just slightly more than 1.

In cases where repeated runs are possible, retention and acceleration can be estimated from an empirical graph of the complementary hitting distribution. Plotting $\log(chd)$ versus t gives, asymptotically, a straight line whose slope is λ and whose intercept is $-\log s$.

It is also possible to estimate retention and acceleration during a single run dynamically for the restarted iterative improvement algorithm (I2R2). We discuss this further below.

The tail probabilities may also be used to calculate the *median* hitting time M. Since M is the time t such that it is just as likely to take more than t iterations as less than t, we solve for M such that $chd(M) = 0.5$. Under the asymptotic approximation for $chd(\cdot)$, this becomes

$$\frac{1}{s}\lambda^{M-1} = chd(M) = 0.5$$

from which

$$M = 1 + \frac{\log(s/2)}{\log(\lambda)}.$$

11.2 IIP Parallel Search

A major virtue of Monte Carlo methods is the ease of implementation and efficacy of parallel processing. The simplest and most universally applicable technique is parallelization by identical, independent processes (IIP) parallel. When used for global optimization, this technique is also highly effective.

One measure of the power of (IIP) parallel is seen in its likelihood of finding the goal. Suppose that a given method has probability q of success. Then running m instances of the algorithm increases the probability of success to

$$1 - (1 - q)^m.$$

This function is shown in Fig. 38. For example, if the probability of finding a suitable objective value is only $q = 0.001$, then running it 400 times increases the likelihood of success to over 20%, and if 2,000 runs are done, the chances exceed 80%.

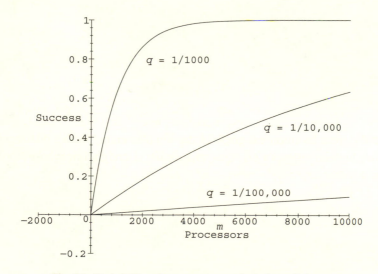

Fig. 38. Probability of success vs. number of parallel runs.

By independence, the joint expected hitting time $E(m)$, meaning the expected hitting time of the first to hit, of the parallel processes is given by

$$E(m) = \hat{\alpha}_0(I - \hat{P}^m)^{-1}\mathbb{1}$$
$$= \hat{\alpha}_0(I + \hat{P}^m + (\hat{P}^m)^2 + (\hat{P}^m)^3 + \cdots)\mathbb{1}$$
$$\approx \frac{1}{s^m}\frac{1}{1 - \lambda^m}.$$

If we define the *search acceleration* $SA(m)$ to be the expected time for the parallel search relative to that of the single-process search, we have

$$SA(m) = \frac{E(1)}{E(m)}$$
$$\approx s^{m-1}\frac{1 - \lambda^m}{1 - \lambda}$$
$$\approx s^{m-1}m,$$

where the last member follows for λ near 1.

For s and λ near one, the search acceleration curve will drop off with increasing m. But if s is on the order of 1.01 or bigger, then search acceleration will be superlinear for up to several processors (see Fig. 39).

These results show that IIP parallel is an effective technique when $s > 1$, accelerating convergence superlinearly.

The convergence rate for (IIP) is worked out for simulated annealing in [16]. Suppose for a given problem, N iterations in total are available and assume m

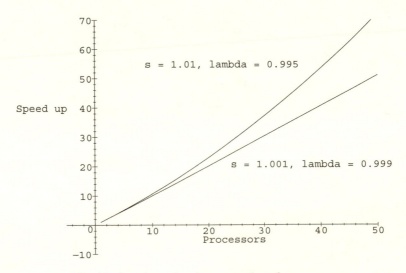

Fig. 39. Search acceleration vs. number of processors.

parallel processes will each conduct n iterations, $mn < N$. The m processes are assumed to use the same search algorithm but otherwise are independent. Let Y_N denote the best overall ending configuration among the parallel runs, $B_{i,n}$, $1 \leq i \leq m$, that is,

$$Y_N = B_{1,n} \wedge B_{2,n} \wedge \ldots \wedge B_{m,n}.$$

Then Y_N satisfies

$$\Pr(Y_N \notin \Gamma) \leq \left(\frac{mK}{N}\right)^{\alpha m}$$

for some $K > 0$ and $\alpha > 0$.

11.3 Simulated Annealing

Simulated annealing (SA) is a stochastic method for function optimization that attempts to mimic the process of thermal annealing. From an initial state, a chain of subsequent states in Ω are generated that, hopefully, converge to the global minimum of the objective function f, referred to here as the *energy* E. As in thermal annealing, a "temperature" T is assigned to the simulation on every iteration and, as the simulation proceeds, the temperature is lowered according to some predefined algorithm, $T = T(t)$, called the *cooling schedule*. Temperature is used to modify the transition probabilities, and hence SA is an inhomogeneous Markov Chain.

For each $x \in \Omega$, we assign to x a set of "neighbors," $N(x)$, also called the set of possible *perturbations* of x. Let $q_{x,y} > 0$ be the probability that $y \in N(x)$ results from a perturbation of x; $q_{x,y} = 0$ if y is not a neighbor of x. The matrix Q of these probabilities is referred to as the *proposal matrix*. Q must be irreducible so that it is possible to move from any state in Ω to any other state in Ω. The SA algorithm is described as follows.

(1) Initialize the iteration $t = 0$, the state X_0, and initial temperature $T(0)$.
(2) Choose an $X' \in N(X_t)$ according to the proposal scheme given by Q.
(3) If $f(X') < f(X_t)$, then set $X_{t+1} = X'$.
(4) If $f(X') \geq f(X_t)$, then put $\Delta f = f(X') - f(X_t)$ and with probability $e^{-\Delta f / T(t)}$ set $X_{t+1} = X'$ else set $X_{t+1} = X_t$.
(5) Decrease $T(t)$ to $T(t+1)$.
(6) If not finished, go to step 2.

Step 4 is called the *Metropolis acceptance rule*. In words it says that if the proposed transition is downhill, then accept it. But an uphill transition is not rejected outright, instead an uphill transition can be made with the specified probability as determined by the outcome of an independent Bernoulli trial such as spinning a wheel or selecting a random number. It was devised in order that the probability density for the state of the system, X_t, converge to the Boltzmann distribution; this means the probability the state of the system has energy E is given by

$$P(X_t = E) \approx \frac{1}{Z(T)} e^{\frac{-E}{T}}, \tag{72}$$

where $Z(T)$ is a normalizing constant (called the *partition function*). Notice that the Boltzmann distribution assigns high probability to low-energy states (small values of f) and as $t \to \infty$, the probability the system will be in the lowest energy state tends to 1.

Since the Metropolis acceptance rule uses only energy differences, an arbitrary constant can be added to the objective function with impunity. Thus we can assume that the objective function is nonnegative.

To obtain the transition probability matrix for SA, denote by $a_{ij}(t)$ the probability defined by the Metropolis acceptance rule for accepting a transition from state i to j, we have

$$a_{ij}(t) = \max \left\{ 1, e^{-(f(j)-f(i))/T} \right\},$$

where T is the temperature. (In actual thermodynamic annealing, T in the denominator is multiplied by *Boltzmann's constant* k; in simulated annealing we may take $k = 1$.) With q_{ij} the proposal probability of state j from state i as above, we have

$$p_{ij}(t) = q_{ij} a_{ij}(t) \ i \neq j \quad \text{and} \quad 1 - \sum_j q_{ij} a_{ij}(t) \ i = j$$

since to move from i to j, j must be proposed and, given that, accepted. The value given here for p_{ii} derives from the fact that the row sums of the transition probability matrix must be 1 and arises since the state does not change if the proposed new state is rejected.

Cooling Schedules

Clearly the choice of cooling schedule is critical to the performance of a simulated annealing algorithm. By decreasing the temperature, uphill steps become more unlikely thereby "urging" the chain toward local minima. However, uphill transition must remain sufficiently probable in order that local basins do not trap the chain. This will happen if the temperature is decreased too quickly. Decreasing the temperature too slowly wastes computational effort. The fundamental result due to Hajek [17] shows that an inverse logarimithic cooling schedule works,

$$T(t) = \frac{d}{a + \log t},$$

where d and a are constants used to control the acceptance probabilities. (Ideally d is the depth of the deepest local basin; however, this is generally not known and so d is often determined heuristically.)

Despite these theoretical results, other cooling schedules are often used in practice. In fact, Catoni has shown that if a fixed number of iterations are adhered to, then geometrical cooling, $T = ar^t, 0 < r < 1$, is best.

Application of SA to the Traveling Salesman Problem

Given n cities in terms of their x and y coordinates, $C_i \ i = 1, \ldots, n$, let a *tour* of the cities be a path starting at C_1 and leading from one city to the next in some order and finally back to C_1. Each city is to be visited exactly once. Evidently a tour is uniquely identified by a permutation of the set $\{2, 3, \ldots, n\}$. We take the space Ω to be the set of tours.

The *length of a tour* is the lengh of its path. We take the objective $f(x)$ (or energy $E(x)$) to be the length of $x \in \Omega$.

The TSP is to find the tour having the smallest length. Of course the reverse of a given tour has the same length and, for our purposes, counts as the same tour.

For n cities there are $(n - 1)!$ permutations of the set evoked above and half that when accounting for reverse tours; this can be a large number for even a small value of n. Hence finding the minimal tour is a hard problem.

To attempt a solution by SA, we need to define a perturbation for any given tour. Let $i_k, k = 2, \ldots, n$, be a permutation of $\{2, \ldots, n\}$ and randomly select two terms of the sequence, say i_{k_1} and i_{k_2}. Take the perturbation to be the tour obtained by reversing the order of the original perturbation between and including the chosen terms. This is called a *partial path reversal* (PPR) of the original tour.

For example, suppose that $\{3, 5, 2, 8, 4, 6, 7\}$ is a tour for an 8-city TSP and suppose that the terms 5 and 4 are selected. Then the associated PPR is $\{3, 4, 8, 2, 5, 6, 7\}$.

The Simulated Annealing algorithm for the TSP:

generate a random permutation x of $\{2, \ldots, n\}$ and calculate $E(x)$.
$T = T_0, B = \infty$
loop $t = 1, 2, \ldots$
        generate a random PPR x' of x and calculate $E(x')$.
        $\Delta E = E(x') - E(x)$, if $\Delta E \leq 0$ replace x by x'

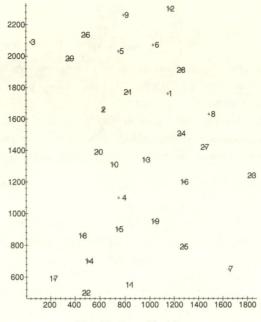

Fig. 40. Bays 29 cities.

otherwise put $r = e^{-\Delta E/T}$ and generate a uniformly distributed
random number $0 \leq R < 1$
if $R < r$ replace x by x'
put $B = \min(B, E(x))$
update the temperature $T = T(t)$
end loop

This algorithm was run on the the Bays 29 city problem. The Bays29
problem is posted on the resource `http://softlib.rice.edu/softlib/`
`catalog/tsplib.html` and consists of 29 Baverian cities (see Fig. 40). The
only remaining specification to make is in the cooling schedule.

The cooling schedule spelled out in Hajek's Theorem pertains when the
number of iterations is unbounded. But setting the schedule in an actual problem
is more of an art. It is often observed while monitoring the progress of a run that
the algorithm makes especially dramatic improvement at some point during the
run. This is known as a "phase change" in analogy to real annealing. A cooling
schedule should ensure that the phase change temperature is bracketed.

We consider a heuristic for setting the cooling schedule. Start by deciding
the number of iterations to be run, we will take that to be 10^5 for Bays29.
Next estimate the average absolute value of ΔE for the random perturbation

operation chosen, for example, PPR in the traveling saleman problem. This is easy to do by performing a small number of preliminary iterations of the algorithm and just noting the changes in energy. This came out to be about 1,000 for Bays29. Finally decide on the form of the cooling schedule; we will take inverse logarimithic cooling according to the equation

$$T = \frac{d}{a + \log t}$$

with d and a parameters to be determined.

Now arrange it so that the probability of accepting an average uphill ΔE at the beginning of the run is near 1 and at the end of the run is near 0. We chose 0.99 and 10^{-5}, respectively. Thus the ending temperature T_∞ is given by

$$10^{-5} = e^{-1000/T_\infty} \quad T_\infty = 86.86$$

and therefore d is given by

$$86.86 = \frac{d}{\log 10^5} \quad d \approx 1,000.$$

Note that a will be very small compared to $\log 10^5$ and can be neglected here. With d in hand, a can be determined. The starting temperature is given by

$$0.99 = e^{-1000/T_0} \quad T_0 \approx 99,500.$$

Since $\log(1) = 0$, we get a from

$$99,500 = \frac{1,000}{a} \quad a \approx 0.01.$$

In Fig. 41 we show the progress of the algorithm for Bays29. The envelope of best and worst of 10 runs is presented.

11.4 Genetic Algorithms

Genetic algorithms are an optimization method based on the paradigm of biological adaptation. The essential ingredients of the method are recombination, mutation, and selective reproduction working on a population of potential solutions. Fitness for a solution is directly related to the objective function being optimized and is greater for solutions closer to its global maximum (or minimum). The expectation is that by repeated application of the genetic and selection operations, the population will tend toward increased fitness.

A genetic algorithm is a Markov Chain X_t on *populations* over Ω under the action of three stochastic operators, *mutation, recombination,* and *selection*

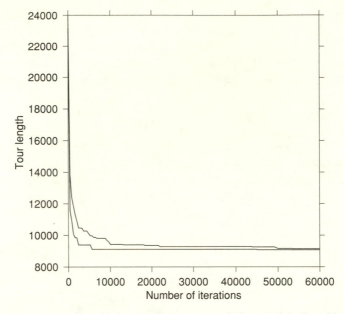

Fig. 41. Minimum and maximum convergence rates of 10 runs of the Bays29 problem.

defined on Ω. Although implementation details may vary, mutation is a unary operator, recombination or *cross-over* is a binary operator, and selection is a multiargument operator. A genetic algorithm is always irreducible and aperiodic and so converges to a stationary distribution.

The implementation of a genetic algorithm begins with the computer representation, or encoding, of the points x of the solution space Ω. Frequently this takes the form of fixed length binary strings, which are called *chromosomes*. A natural mutation of such a string is to reverse, or flip, one or more of its bits randomly selected. Likewise, a natural recombination, of two bit strings, called *parents*, is to construct a new binary string from the bits of the parents in some random way. The most widely used technique for this is *one-point cross-over* in which the initial sequence of k bits of one parent is concatenated with the bits beyond the kth position of the second parent to produce an *offspring*. Here k is randomly chosen. Of course, a fitness evaluation must be done for each new chromosome produced.

Finally, the chromosomes selected to constitute the population in the next generation might, for example, be chosen by lottery with the probability of selection weighted according to the chromosome's fitness. This widely used method is termed *roulette wheel selection*.

Initialize a population of chromosomes
Repeat
  Create new chromosomes from the present set by mutation and recombination
  Select members of the expanded population to recover its original size
Until a stop criteria is met
Report the observed best

Fig. 42. A top-level view of a genetic algorithm.

These genetic operators would be tied together in a computer program as shown, for example, in Fig. 42. However, there is no standard genetic algorithm, and many variants are found in the literature, some differing markedly from this norm.

Most genetic algorithms do not vary the probabilities of their three operators over the course of a run and are therefore homogeneous Markov Chains. One consequence is that the algorithm is unlikely to be in the globally optimal state at the end of a run since the chain is irreducible and will visit all states recurrently. Therefore it is important to save the best value discovered by the algorithm, and the corresponding structure, from iteration to iteration.

A GA for the Permanent Problem

Let M be an $n \times n$ matrix whose terms are either 0 or 1. The permanent of M is defined to be

$$\text{perm}(M) = \sum_{\sigma} \prod_{i=1}^{n} m_{i,\sigma(i)},$$

where the sum extends over all permutations σ of the first n integers. The permanent is similar to the determinant except without the alternating signs. For a given matrix size n and number d of 1's, $0 < d < n^2$, the permanent problem is to find the matrix having maximum permanent. It amounts to knowing where to put the 1's. We refer to this as the $n{:}d$ permanent problem. We illustrate genetic algorithms by solving the 14:40 permanent problem.

The points or states of the solution space are 0/1 matrices of size 14×14 having exactly 40 ones. Conceptionally, this is our chromosome.

As a unary or mutation operation we take the following: we randomly select a 1 in the 14×14 matrix, then randomly choose one of the four directions, North, East, South, or West, and exchange values with the neighbor entry in that direction. We allow wrap around; thus, the East direction from the 14th column is the 1st column and the South direction from the 14th row is the 1st row. A row-by-row storage format of the matrix makes it easy to select a 1 at random.

The actual implementation checks to see whether the value swapped is a 0 before proceeding for otherwise it will be a wasted effort.

Next we must invent a binary or recombination operation. Let A be a 14×14 solution matrix with its 196 elements written out as one long array and B a second one likewise unstacked. At random, select a position $1 \le k \le 196$ in these arrays. Starting at position k, move along the two arrays, with wrap, comparing their elements until the first time they differ, either A has a 1 where B has a 0 or vice versa. Swap these two values. Moving along from that point, with wrap, continue comparing values until the first subsequent point where the two differ in the reverse way. Swap these two values. The modified A matrix is the output of the operation. Effectively this operation interchanges a 0 and a 1 in A, using B as a template, generally over a longer distance in the matrix than adjacent elements.

We take the population size to be 16. In each generation loop, we do 8 recombination operations and 8 mutation operations adding all new chromosomes to the population. Thus, after these are performed, the population size has grown to 32 and needs to be reduced back to 16. We select out the 16 for removal, one by one, according to "a geometric distribution based on fitness rank," in other words, by Russian Roulette as follows.

The current population is maintained in fitness order: the most fit chromosome comes first, the next most fit is second, and so on. Now, starting at the bottom of the list, each chromosome must survive a random trial, such as selecting a random number and comparing it to a predesignated "survival probability" s, for example $s = 0.8$. Eventually some chromosome fails the test and is removed from the population. This selection process is geometric since the worst chromosome has probability $1 - s$ (approximately) of being selected, the second worst has probability $s(1 - s)$, and so on, the kth worst has probability $s^{k-1}(1 - s)$.

In Fig. 43, we show the results of 10 parallel runs on the 14:40 permanent problem. The globally maximum value of 2592 was achieved by 2 of the 10 processes.

11.5 Iterated Improvement Plus Random Restart

We envision a process combining a deterministic downhill operator g acting on points of the solution space and a uniform random selection operator U. The process starts with an invocation of U resulting in a randomly selected *starting*

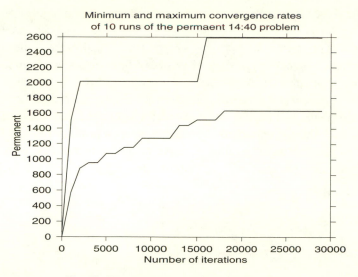

Fig. 43. Permanent vs. number of generations.

point x_0. This is followed by repeated invocations of g until a local minimizer is reached; this is the *descent sequence* starting from x_0.

The point $x \in \Omega$ is a *local minimizer* of f if for every neighbor y of x, $f(y) \geq f(x)$. Then $f(x)$ is a *local minimum*. Thus no neighbor of a local minimizer has a strictly improved objective.

Upon reaching a local minimizer, the process is restarted with another invocation of U. Thus the domain is partitioned into *basins* B_i, $i = 0, 1, \ldots,$ as determined by the equivalence relation $x \equiv y$ if and only if $g^k(x) = g^j(y)$ for some k, j. The local minimizer or *settling point* b of basin B is given as $\lim_{k \to \infty} g^k(x)$, where x is any point of B; of course, since the domain is finite, this sequence is eventually constant.

An important parameter in the I2R2 process is the probability θ of starting or restarting in the global basin B_0.

Graph theoretically, a basin is organized as a tree with the settling point being the root of the tree. Different basins are connected only by the restart process, and so, exclusive of restart, I2R2 enforces a topology on the domain whose graph is a forest of trees.

But since we are interested only in the number of iterations or steps to the root of a tree, we can simplify the transition matrix P by considering an equivalent process.

In the forest of trees model, it is clear that all states which are a given number of steps from a settling point are equivalent as far as the algorithm is concerned.

Let $r_j(i)$ be the number of vertices j steps from the local minimizer of basin $i, 0 \leq j \leq \text{depth}(B_i)$. Then put $r_j = \sum_{i=1}^{\ell} r_j(i)$ with the sum being taken over the nongoal basins, this for $0 \leq j \leq d$, where d is the depth of the deepest basin. Thus r_j denotes the total number of vertices which are j steps from a local, nongoal, minimizer. In particular, $r_0 = \ell$ is the number of local minimizers.

Therefore the forest of trees model, in which each vertex counts 1, is equivalent to a single, linear tree in which the vertex j edges from a local minimizer counts equal to r_j. Under this equivalency, the $\hat{P}$ matrix becomes

$$
P' =
\begin{bmatrix}
p_0 & p_1 & p_2 & \cdots & p_{d-1} & p_d \\
1 & 0 & 0 & \cdots & 0 & 0 \\
0 & 1 & 0 & \cdots & 0 & 0 \\
0 & 0 & 1 & \cdots & 0 & 0 \\
\vdots & \vdots & \vdots & \ddots & \vdots & \vdots \\
0 & 0 & 0 & \cdots & 1 & 0
\end{bmatrix}
\qquad p_j = r_j/|\Omega|, \quad \text{for } 0 \leq j \leq d.
$$

(73)

Note that the 1's are on the subdiagonal and consequently P' has the form of a companion matrix. Its characteristic polynomial therefore is $-\lambda^{d+1} + p_0\lambda^d + p_1\lambda^{d-1} + \cdots + p_{d-1}\lambda + p_d$. Upon setting $x = 1/\lambda$ in this, the resulting polynomial is refered to as the *fundamental polynomial* (or FP)

$$
f(x) = p_0 x + p_1 x^2 + \cdots + p_{d-1}x^d + p_d x^{d+1} - 1.
$$

(74)

Notice that the degree of the FP is the depth of the deepest basin plus 1 or, equivalently, equal to the number of vertices on the longest path to a local minimizer.

Two important observations about the fundamental polynomial are as follows. All coefficients $p_j, 0 \leq j \leq d$ of the FP are strictly positive. This is because, if there is a point j steps from a local minimum, there must also be a point $j - 1$ steps away as well.

Since restart must select some point in Ω,

$$
\theta + p_0 + p_1 + \cdots + p_d = 1.
$$

(75)

Therefore evaluating the FP at $x = 1$ yields the following.

Corollary 1. $f(1) = -\theta.$

Since combining the states as above leads to an equivalent process, the smallest root of (74) is the reciprocal of the principal eigenvalue of the deleted transition probability matrix. This is the subject of the following theorems.

Proposition 1. *The FP f has a unique root greater than 1.*

Proof. The derivative $f'(x)$ has all positive coefficients and $f(1) = -\theta$.   ∎

Let η be the root asserted in the proposition, then $1/\eta$ is the unique maximal root of the characteristic polynomial of $\hat{P}$ and hence η is the reciprocal of the retention λ.

To calculate the acceleration s, we first find the left and right eigenvectors of $\lambda = 1/\eta$. For the right, χ, use (73) to get recursion equations which may solved for χ_0,

$$\chi_k = \eta^k \chi_0, \ k = 1, \ldots, d.$$

Similarly, we get recursion equations for the components of the left eigenvector ω in terms of ω_0,

$$\omega_k = \omega_0(\eta p_k + \eta^2 p_{k+1} + \cdots + \eta^{d+1-k} p_d).$$

We may normalize ω to be a probability vector, $\sum \omega_i = 1$; it follows that

$$\omega_0 = \frac{\eta - 1}{\eta \theta}.$$

Similarly normalize χ to have unit inner product with ω, $\sum \omega_i \chi_i = 1$; it follows that

$$\chi_0 = \frac{1}{\omega_0 \eta f'(\eta)} = \frac{\theta}{(\eta - 1) f'(\eta)}.$$

But $s = 1/(\chi \cdot \hat{\alpha}_0)$, where $\hat{\alpha}_0$ is the nongoal partition vector of the starting distribution,

$$\hat{\alpha}_0 = (\, p_0 \quad p_1 \quad \cdots \quad p_d \,).$$

Substituting from above, we get

$$s = \frac{\eta(\eta - 1) f'(\eta)}{\theta}.$$

Theorem 1. *For I2R2 $s > \eta > 1$.*

Proof. The average slope of the line between $(1, -\theta)$ and $(\eta, 0)$ is less than the slope of f at η because f' is increasing; therefore, $f'(\eta) > \theta/(\eta - 1)$. Hence, since $\eta > 1$,

$$s = \eta \frac{(\eta - 1) f'(\eta)}{\theta} > \eta > 1.$$

∎

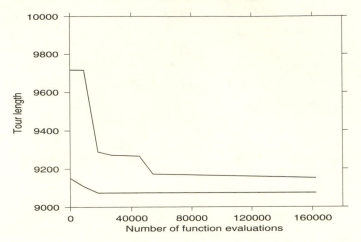

Fig. 44. Tour length vs. number of function evaluations.

Restarting in a goal basin can be regarded as a Bernoulli trial with success probability θ. Accordingly, the expected number of starts or restarts to find such a basin is $1/\theta$ and the probability of not finding a goal basin after k starts or restarts is $(1 - \theta)^k$. Taking k to be a fraction m of the expectation we have

$$\text{Pr(goal basin not found after } \tfrac{m}{\theta} \text{ restarts)} = (1 - \theta)^{\frac{m}{\theta}} \approx e^{-m} \quad \text{as } \theta \to 0.$$

Therefore the probability of not having found a goal basin within the expected number of starts or restarts, $1/\theta$, is $e^{-1} = 37\%$. Alternatively, to find the goal basin with 50% chance requires $m = 69\%$ of the expected restarts.

To illustrate the method, I2R2 may be applied to the Bays29 TSP. Partial path reversal (PPR) may be used as the downhill improvement if applied to every neighbor of a given tour and the one showing the best improvement is selected. In other words, steepest descent.

In Fig. 44 the results of 10 parallel runs are shown. In assessing the progress of the algorithm the number of function evaluations is used as a measure of time (and effort) rather than the number of restarts.

Programming Exercises

1. (7) Write a fixed temperature simulated annealer to solve the Traveling Salesman Problem. A database of problems is available at softlib.rice.edu

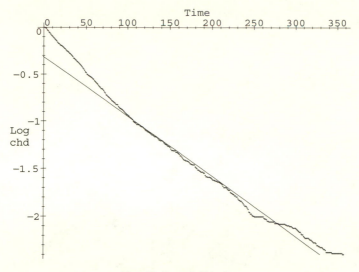

Fig. 45. Log chd( ) plot.

as on p. 254 or also at `www.iwr.uni-heidelberg.de/groups/comopt/software/TSPLIB95`. For the following you may want to make up your own city set. Establish a "goal" and run your program many times observing hitting times. Plot a histogram of hitting times and empirically estimate the expected hitting time. Also plot $\log(chd(t))$, Eq. (69). Discounting the portion of the graph for t small and t large, fit a straight line to the graph and empirically estimate λ and s (see Fig. 45); from Eq. (70), the slope is $\log(\lambda)$ and the intercept is $\log(1/s)$.

2. (7) Write a genetic algorithm to solve the perm (10:32) problem. As above, make a log(chd) plot and empirically estimate λ and s.

3. (7) As mentioned in Chapter 2, scheduling a parallel program to run on a symmetric multiprocessor can be an NP complete problem (see Fig. 12). Writing a program just to predict the time required for a given schedule is a challenge. So assume the predicted times for the 5-task problem as given in Table 2, and write a Monte Carlo optimizer to solve it (not by exhaustion). For example, use random restart with the "downhill" scheme being that from each solution, say index i, examine solution $i + 1$ (with wrap back to 0) and "step downhill" to it if better. When the next solution is no longer better, restart. Find λ and s for your algorithm.

4. (7) (Steiner Points) Cities A–H, listed below, wish to lay a cable of minimal length interconnecting them all (see Fig. 46). One or more substations, labeled "X" in the figure, called *Steiner points*, may be constructed to help.

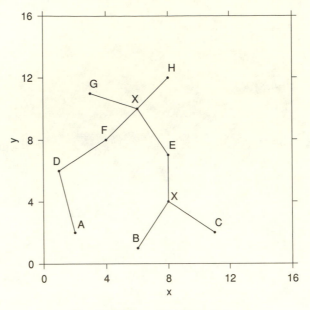

Fig. 46. Cities and Steiner points.

Find the minimum cable length, any Steiner points and the cable route. City
A:(2,2); B:(6,1); C:(11,2); D:(1,6); E:(8,7); F:(4,8); G:(3,11); H:(8,12).

5. (7) (Scheduling) A 2-day conference offers 20 different speakers each of
whom will speak 3 times. Each day there are 6 lecture time slots. In order to
accomodate the 60 talks, there will be 5 concurrent sessions. The organizers
(you play this role) have preassigned the talks, for example, Speaker 1 will
speak on day 1 in time slots 2 and 3 in session 1 and on day 2 at time
slot 4 also in session 1. A conferee registers for the conference and lists a
preference to hear 12 speakers in order of preference. Write a program to
assign an optimal schedule to the conferee (all listed talks if possible, if not,
then those with highest preference). (An alternative problem is to optimally
assign the speakers, possibly given some expected conferees preferences.)

Appendix: Programming Examples

```
mpiSendAround.c (C).
/*
from: www.tacc.utexas.edu/resources/user_guides/mpi.c/
compile with: mpicc mpiSendAround.c
execute with: mpirun -np 4 a.out
*/
#include  <mpi.h>
#include  <stdio.h>
#include  <stdlib.h>
main(int argc, char **argv)
{
    MPI_Status status;
    int npes, irank, ierr;
    int i, j, ides, isrc;
    MPI_Comm IWCOMM = MPI_COMM_WORLD;
    int one = 1;
/* Send message around ring ( 0-> 1-> 2 ... NPES-1-> 0 ) */
    ierr = MPI_Init(&argc, &argv);
    ierr = MPI_Comm_size(IWCOMM, &npes);
    ierr = MPI_Comm_rank(IWCOMM, &irank);

                    /* Determine destinations & sources */
    ides = (irank+1 )%npes;
    isrc = (irank+npes-1)%npes;
    printf(" rank: %d ides: %d isrc: %d\n",irank,ides,isrc);

    /* Start Sending from task 0, and wait (recv) for count.
    */
```

```
    if(irank = = 0){
        ierr = MPI_Send(&one,1,MPI_int, ides,9,IWCOMM);
        ierr = MPI_Recv(&j ,1,MPI_int, isrc,9,IWCOMM,
            &status);
    }
    else{
        ierr = MPI_Recv(&j ,1,MPI_int, isrc,9,IWCOMM,
            &status);
        i=j+1;
        ierr = MPI_Send(&i ,1,MPI_int, ides,9,IWCOMM);
    }

    if(irank == 0) printf("I counted %d processors\ n" ,j);
    ierr = MPI_Finalize();
}
```

mpiSendReceive.f (Fortran)

```
      program page5
CCCCCCCCCCCCC
C
C MPI_SEND
C MPI_RECV
C 2 nodes
C
CCCCCCCCCCCCC
      include 'mpif.h'
      integer myrank, numprocs, ierr
      integer status(MPI_STATUS_SIZE)
      real side, square
      side = 7.0
      square=0.0
C
      call MPI_INIT( ierr )
      call MPI_COMM_RANK( MPI_COMM_WORLD, myrank, ierr )
      call MPI_COMM_SIZE( MPI_COMM_WORLD, numprocs, ierr )
      print *,'I am node ',myrank,' out of ',numprocs,'
        nodes.'
      if(myrank.eq.1) then
        square = side * side
```

```
      call MPI_SEND(square,1,MPI_REAL,0,99,MPI_COMM_WORLD,
         ierr)
endif
if(myrank.eq.0) then
   print *,'Before receive square is ',square
   call MPI_RECV(square,1,MPI_REAL,1,99,MPI_COMM_WORLD,
         status,ierr)
   print *,'After receive square is ',square
endif
call MPI_FINALIZE(ierr)
end
```

```
   kaess.poly.c, C: polynomial evaluation.

/* Polynomial calculation, 12th degree, using fork()
operation in C */
/* CS4777 Michael Kaess, 09/28/2000 */
/* -- each barrier is one time use only (rws) -- */

#include   <stdio.h>
#include   <sys/types.h>
#include   <sys/stat.h>
#include   <sys/ipc.h>
#include   <sys/shm.h>
#include   <sys/sem.h>
#include   <errno.h>
#include   <math.h>

/* input values */
#define   DEGREE 12
double x = 2.0;
const double a[DEGREE+1] = {1.0, 2.0, 3.0, 4.0, 5.0, 6.0,
7.0, 8.0, 9.0, 10.0, 11.0, 12.0, 13.0};

#define   K 1024

int id, nprocs;
int shmid;
double *array;
double *xPow;  /* powers of x */
int bar[9];
struct   sembuf barDec = {
```

```
      0, -1, SEM_UNDO /* sem_num, sem_op(-1=try to pass),
        sem_flg */
};
struct  sembuf barInit = {
    0, DEGREE, SEM_UNDO /* sem_num, sem_op (DEGREE=nprocs),
        sem_flg;
*/
};
struct  sembuf barWait = {
    0, 0, SEM_UNDO /* sem_num, sem_op, sem_flg */
};

/* +++sss+++ */
void barrier(int id, int num) {
semop(bar[num], &barDec, 1);
semop(bar[num], &barWait, 1);
}

void work(int id, int nprocs) {
int i;
int n = 1;
int num = 0;

/* Russian Peasant */
for (i=1;  i<=4;  i++) {
   if (id<n) {
       xPow[2*n-id] = xPow[n] * xPow[n-id];
   }
   n *= 2;
   barrier(id, num++);  /* */
}

/* parallel multiplication */
array[id+1] = a[id+1] * xPow[id+1];
barrier(id, num++);  /* */

/* fan-in */
n = 8;
for (i=1;  i<=4;  i++) {
   if ((id<n) && (id+n<=DEGREE)) {
       array[id] = array[id] + array[id+n];
   }
   n = n/2;
```

```
   barrier(id, num++);  /* */
}
}

void createproc(int *pid, int nprocs) {
int j;

for (j=1;  j<nprocs;  ++j) {
if ( fork() == 0 ) {
*pid = j;  return;
}
}
*pid = 0;
}

int cleanup(void) {
int i;

for (i=0;  i<9;  i++) {
semctl(bar[i], 0, IPC_RMID);
}
shmctl(shmid,IPC_RMID,0);
return(0);
}
/* ===mmm=== */
int main(int argc, char** argv) {
int i;
int size;
double sum;

/* in case of program abort */
for ( i=0;  i<20;  ++i ) {
   signal(i,cleanup);
}
nprocs = DEGREE;
/* init barrier semaphore */
for (i=0;  i<9;  i++) {
   if ((bar[i] = semget(IPC_PRIVATE, 1, 0777|IPC_CREAT))==-1) {
      perror("barrier: semget" );
      return 0;
   }
   if ((semop(bar[i], &barInit, 1))==-1) {
      perror("barrier: semop" );
```

```
        return 0;
    }
}
/* allocate memory in multiples of K */
size = (DEGREE+1)*10*sizeof(double);
if ( size != K*(size/K) ) {
    size = K*(size/K) + K;
}
shmid = shmget(IPC_PRIVATE, size, 0777 | IPC_CREAT);
if ( (long )shmid == -1 ) {
    printf ("Couldn't allocate shared memory\ n" );
    return(0);
}
array = (double *)shmat(shmid,(char *)0,0);
xPow = array + DEGREE + 10;
if ( (long )array == -1 ) {
    printf ("Error number %d, ",errno);
    perror("Assign shared memory " );
}
/* printf ("assign succeeded, array at 0x%x\ n",array); */
/* prepare basis for Russian Peasant Alg */
xPow[0] = 1;
xPow[1] = x;
array[0] = a[0];

/* fork off processes and do the work */
createproc(&id,nprocs);
work(id,nprocs);

/* simulate a proc-join, the wait acts as a barrier */
if ( id != 0 ) {
    return(0);
}
for ( i=nprocs-1;  i>0;  --i ) {
    wait(NULL  );
}
for ( i=0;  i<=nprocs;  ++i ) {
    printf ("array[%d]: %lf\ n",i,array[i]);
}
sum = array[0];  /* get result */
printf ("sum = %lf\ n",sum);
```

```
/* free shared memory */
if ( shmdt((void *)array)== -1 ) {
    perror("shmdt " );
}

return 0;
}
```

```
  collect.c, C: Distributed execution on a LAN.
#include  <unistd.h>
#include  <stdio.h>
#include  <stdlib.h>
#include  <sys/types.h>
#include  <sys/select.h>
#include  <sys/resource.h>

#define  MAXCHILDREN 1000
#define  BUFFERSIZE 4096

static char  *helptext[]={
"",
" * collect.c - Collect and merge output from child
processes",
" 5-7-90 Mark Nailor",
" ",
" Usage: collect [ < commandlist] [ | monitor]",
" ",
" Each line of the standard input is a command to be run",
" as a child process. The standard output lines of each",
" child process are collected and written to collect's",
" standard output. This merged output may be piped to a",
" monitor program. Only text output is supported.",
"","",NULL };

printusage()
{
int  i;
```

```
        for ( i=0;  helptext[i] != NULL ;  ++i )
            printf("\ n%s" ,helptext[i]);
        exit(0);
}
/* =======mmm===== */
main( argc, argv )
int   argc;
char  **argv;
{
    int   i;  /* counter */
    int   children;  /* number of child processes */
    int   open_pipes;  /* number of children still sending */
    FILE *input_pipe[MAXCHILDREN];  /* array of input
        streams from pipes */
    int   input_fd[MAXCHILDREN];  /* corresponding file
        descriptors */
    char  buffer[BUFFERSIZE];  /* input/output buffer */
    int   length;  /* length of data in buffer */
    int   status;  /* status from system call */
    int   totalfds;  /* total file descriptors available */
    fd_set readfds;  /* descriptors to wait for read */
    fd_set writefds;  /* descriptors to wait for write */
    fd_set exceptfds;  /* descriptors to wait for exceptions
*/

    if ( argc > 1 && !strncmp(argv[1],"-h" ,2) ) {
        printusage();
        exit(0);
    }

/*
* Raise open file descriptor limit to max on Solaris. The
* first works on System V release 4, and the second works
* on any POSIX.1 system. On older systems, could use
* FD_SETSIZE for totalfds instead.
*/

#ifdef RLIMIT_NOFILE

    {
            struct  rlimit rlim;
```

```
        if  ( getrlimit( RLIMIT_NOFILE, &rlim ) < 0 )
            perror( "getrlimit" );

        rlim.rlim_cur = rlim.rlim_max;

        if  ( setrlimit( RLIMIT_NOFILE, &rlim ) < 0 )
            perror( "setrlimit" );
        if  ( getrlimit( RLIMIT_NOFILE, &rlim ) < 0 )
            perror( "getrlimit" );

        totalfds = rlim.rlim_cur;
    }

#else

    totalfds = sysconf(_SC_OPEN_MAX);

#endif

/*
 * Start up child processes specified by stdin command
 * lines.
 */
    children = 0;
    while ( gets ( buffer ) != NULL  )
    {
        if  ( children > MAXCHILDREN )
        {
            fprintf( stderr, "\ nToo many children\ n" );
            exit( 1 );
        }

        input_pipe[children] = popen( buffer, "r" );
        if  ( input_pipe[children] == NULL  )
        {
            fprintf( stderr, "\ nFailed to spawn command:
              %s\ n", buffer );
        }
        else
        {
            input_fd[children]=fileno(input_pipe[children]);
            ++children;
        }
    }
```

```
    open_pipes = children;

    /* **********
    printf( "children = %d\ n" , children );
    printf( "totalfds = %d\ n" , totalfds );
    fflush( stdout );
    ***********/

/*
* Wait for input from any child process. Each line received
* is written to stdout. This ends when all input pipes have
* reached EOF or when a signal comes in.
*/

    while ( open_pipes > 0 )
    {
        FD_ZERO( &readfds );
        FD_ZERO( &writefds );
        FD_ZERO( &exceptfds );

        for ( i = 0;  i < children;  i++ )
        {
            if ( input_fd[i] > -1 ) FD_SET( input_fd[i],
                &readfds );
        }

        status = select( totalfds, &readfds, &writefds,
            &exceptfds, NULL );
        if ( status < 1 )
        {
            perror( "select call failed" );
            exit( 1 );
        }
        for ( i = 0;  i < children;  i++ )
        {
            /* ************
            printf("testing fd[%d] = %d\ n" , i, input_fd[i] );
            fflush( stdout );
            *************/
            if ( input_fd[i] < 0 ) continue;

            if ( FD_ISSET( input_fd[i], &readfds ))
            {
```

```
            if  ( fgets ( buffer, BUFFERSIZE,
                  input_pipe[i] ) != NULL  )
            {
                fputs( buffer, stdout );
                fflush( stdout );
            }
            else
            {
                pclose( input_pipe[i] );
                input_fd[i] = -1;
                --open_pipes;
            }
        }
    }
  }
  exit( 0 );
}
```

Threads Example

```
   dynamdemoT.c, C: find primes by eliminating composites
#include  <stdio.h>
/* *****
Compile with:
   cc dynamdemoT.c -lthread
***** */
#include  <thread.h>
#include  <synch.h>
#include  <errno.h>
int nprocs = 8;
int si=2;  /* shared index, set its value before creating
threads */
mutex_t indexlock;
/*+++sss++++*/
   int
div_of(int i)
{
int k;
   for( k=2;  k <= i/2;  ++k )
      if( i == k*(i/k) ) return k;  /* k is a divisor */
   return 0;
}
/* **** */
   void *
work(int *n)
{
int i, id;
```

280

```
    id = (int)thr_self() % nprocs;   /* counting might not
start at 0 */
/*
* The next 5 lines take the place of:
* for( i=2;   i<=n;   ++i )
* Note that the shared index, si, was initialized at
* program startup.
*/
    for( ;   ;   ) { /* infinite loop */
        mutex_lock(&indexlock);
            i = si;   si++;
        mutex_unlock(&indexlock);
        if( !( i<= *n) ) break;

        if( !div_of(i) ) printf("%d is prime (%d)\n" ,i,id);
    }
}
/* ===mmm=== */
main()
{
int i, status;
thread_t tid;
int n=1500;

/*
* Args to the thr_create call are
*
* 1 stack base address
* 2 stack size
* 3 thread's work routine
* 4 pointer to args passed to work routine
* 5 flags that control the type of thread created
* 6 output arg for thr_create call, the thread id
*/
    for( i=0;   i<nprocs;   ++i ) {
        status = thr_create(NULL ,0,(void *(*)
        (void *))work,&n,0,&tid);
        if( status ) perror("thread create" );
    }
/* --- won't work without this line --- */
    while (thr_join(0,0,0) == 0);

}
```

SGI Example

The SGI *Power C compiler* (PCA) does not allow more threads than processors (cf. the document "Multiprocessing C Compiler Directives"). In this sense, programs execute like the fork() programming model.

The keyword *critical* corresponds most closely with *mutex* in that only one thread at a time can execute this code and all threads execute it. The keyword *synchronize* corresponds most closely with *barrier* in that all threads must arrive at this point before any thread can go on.

There are also additional directives. The directive *one processor* means that the first thread to reach this code executes it meanwhile other threads wait. After execution by the first thread, the code is skipped by subsequent threads. There is an *enter gate* and corresponding *exit gate* directive. Threads must wait at the exit gate until all threads have passed the matching enter gate.

Loops to run in parallel must be marked with the *pfor* directive. It takes the argument *iterate* (start index; number of times through the loop; increment/ decrement amount).

A reduction variable is local to each thread and their contributions must be added in a critical section.

```
backsub.f, backsubstitution DOACROSS by rows

c23456789
      program  backsubs
c
c— compile with f77 backsubs.f
c
      parameter(n=5000)
      real  a(n,n), b(n), x(n)
      integer  i,j
c—— obtain the data
```

```
      do  i=1,n,1
        do  j=1,n,1
          a(i,j) = (-1)**(i+j)*1.0
        end  do
        b(i) = 1.0
      end  do
c-- begin the solution
      do  i=n,1,-1
        x(i) = b(i)/a(i,i)
C$OMP PARALLEL SHARED(a,b,x,i) PRIVATE(j)
        do  j=1,i-1,1
          b(j) = b(j) - a(j,i)*x(i)
        end  do
C$OMP end  PARALLEL
      end  do
c-- print results
c do  i=1,n,1
      do  i=1,10,1
        write (*,'("x",i3,"= ",f6.2)')i,x(i)
      end  do
      end
```

References

[1] Bertsekas, D.P., and Tsitsiklis, J.N., "Parallel and Distributed Computation," Prentice-Hall, 1989

[2] Stevens, W.R., "Unix Network Programming," Prentice-Hall, 1990

[3] Northrup, C.J., "Programming with Unix Threads," Wiley, 1996

[4] Lewis, B.B., and Daniel, J., "Multithreaded Programming with P Threads," Prentice-Hall, 1998

[5] Butenhof, D.R., "Programming with POSIX Threads," Addison Wesley, 1997

[6] Allen, R., and Kennedy, K., "Optimizing Compilers for Modern Architectures: A Dependence-Based Approach," Academic Press, 2002

[7] Gershenfeld, N., and Chuang, I., "Quantum Computing With Molecules," *Scientific American*, June 1996

[8] Ekert, A., Hayden, P., and Inamori, H., "Basic concepts in quantum computation," Lecture notes from les Houches Summer School on "Coherent Matter Waves," July 1999

[9] Hanson, R., Krogh, F., and Lawson, C., A Proposal for Standard Linear Algebra Subprograms, *ACM SIGNUM Newsl.*, v. **8**, #16 (1973).

[10] Ciarlet, P.G., "Introduction to Numerical Linear Algebra and Optimisation," Cambridge University Press, 1989

[11] Atkinson, K.E., "An Introduction to Numerical Analysis," Wiley, 1989

[12] Isaacson, E., and Keller, H., "Analysis of Numerical Methods," Wiley, New York, 1966

[13] Conte, S.D., and de Boor, C., "Elementary Numerical Analysis," McGraw-Hill, New York, 1980

[14] Wilkinson, J.H., "The Algebraic Eigenvalue Problem," Clarendon Press, Oxford, 1965

[15] Traub, J.F., Werschultz, A.G., "Complexity and Information," Cambridge University Press, 1998

[16] Azencott, R., "Simulated Annealing, Parallelization Techniques," Wiley, New York, 1992

[17] Hajek, B., "Cooling Schedules for Optimal Annealing," *Math of Operations Research*, **13** (Feb. 1988).

285

Index

acceleration, 248
A-conjugate, 201
adjoint, 94
algebraic multiplicity, 207
Amdahl's Law, 21
augmented matrix, 135

banking processors, 32
banks, 83
barrier, 47
basins, 259
batches, 237
bias, 106
binary rational numbers, 106
block schedule, 39
block scheduling, 15
block tridiagonal, 170
blocking, 72
Boltzmann's constant k, 252
break-even point, 12
bus, 5
busy wait, 50

caching, 10
chain, 14, 83
characteristic polynomial, 207
child, 45
chromosomes, 256
circularly polarized, 90
clock, 5
clock time, 31
coarse-grain parallelism, 14
code segment, 5
collective communication, 72
coloring, 199
column rank, 144
column sweep, 132
communication processing time, 17
companion matrix, 208
complementary hitting distribution, 247

complexity, 31
component dependency graph, 198
concurrent, 44
concurrently, 45
condition, 111
condition number, 111, 177
condition variable, 55
context switch, 45
controlled NOT, 94
controlled U gate, 95
converges order n, 193
cooling schedule, 251
copy-on-write, 45
countably infinite, 104
CPU, 5
CPU state, 45
critical section, 52
cross-over, 256

data conversion algorithm, 130
Data or task dependencies, 15
data parallelism, 8
data segment, 5
decoherence, 97
delayed update, 152
denormalization, 107
dense, 126
descent sequence, 259
determinant, 142
diagonally dominant, 188
Diagram time, 30
diameter, 18
direct, 126
dot notation, 142
dot product, 89
dynamically schedule, 48

Efficiency, 25, 32
eigenmanifold, 207

286